The Future
100

改變未來的100件事　2024年全球百大趨勢

VML

A REPORT BY VML INTELLIGENCE

書　　名 / 改變未來的 100 件事 -2024 年全球百大趨勢

作　　者 / VML Intelligence

總編輯 / Emma Chiu, Marie Stafford

撰稿人 / Emily Safian-Demers, John O' Sullivan, Nina Jones

副編輯 / Hester Lacey, Katie Myers

設計總監 / Shazia Chaudhry

封　　面 / Peach Fuzz, Pantone Color of the Year 2024,
courtesy of The Development x Almost Studios

翻譯及協作編輯 / Evan Teng 鄧博文 , Ben Hsu 張斌淇 ,
Rita Cheng 鄭冠瑄 , Jessica Chien 簡邑儒 , Sean Hu 胡世 ,
Eric Liu 劉政泰 , Jeffery Chen 陳佳安 , Betty Kuan 關詠榕 ,
Tony Liu 劉家興 , Winnie Tung 董淑雯

出版者 / 香港商台灣智威有限公司台灣分公司

地址 / 台北市南港區市民大道 7 段 8 號 13F 之五

電話 / (02)3766-1000

傳真 / (02)2788-0260

總經銷 / 時報文化出版企業股份有限公司

電話 / (02)2306-6842

地址 / 桃園市龜山區萬壽路 2 段 351 號

書籍編碼 / Z000155

出版日期 / 2024 年 03 月

定價 / NTD 500

ISBN / 9789869899246

VML

A REPORT BY VML INTELLIGENCE

序言

**歡迎與我們一同迎接「改變未來的100件事：
2024年全球百大趨勢」十週年，今年將會是深刻而充實的一年。**

隨著 2024 年的來臨，經歷了多年來的快速變遷，世界現正刻意放緩生活與工作的步調。曾經人們認為壓力、憂鬱和污染是對於人類健康的三大挑戰，但隨著消費者用小心謹慎的態度面對即將到來的一年時，這對追求優質的生活品質會開始大幅放緩腳步。

這種慢活思想在 Pantone 2024 年度色調 Peach Fuzz（不要與氣泡飲 Peach Fizz 搞混喔）所表現出的溫暖且柔和中顯而易見。色彩預測專家認為此色彩傳遞「同情和凝聚力」的訊息（趨勢＃14 集體充電）。即便是 Z 世代族群也對社群媒體的快速發展趨勢感到厭倦，認為無法跟上腳步（趨勢＃06 緩速週期），並選擇盧德模式 (趨勢＃08) 作為應對機制。這不僅影響人們，企業在生產方面也較以往謹慎（趨勢＃53 慢美容），改以品質為優先，數量為輔，且得到正面的效果。

大型群體生活對於 2024 年是必不可少的活動。群體共享體驗正在世界每個角落上演，不論是熟識的朋友或是第一次件的陌生人，大家將有機會相聚一起（趨勢＃05 社會性的活力）。實體店面也以社區為中心，將零售帶到前端。科技也有助於與空間科技的連接，提供更流暢、更自然的沉浸感。有 67% 的人認為社區比個人更重要，並有 76% 的人相信科技有助於人們群聚在一起。

比起去年的人工智慧，OpenAI 對於今年來說，變得更加觸手可及。今年將凸顯更多關於治理、創造力和哲學思考。因為人們都在質疑，當科技技術進步帶來非常逼真的數位角色的時代，人類又意味著什麼（趨勢＃11 虛擬身分經濟以及趨勢＃91 AI 身份）。Alpha 世代是現在最年輕的群體，將深受人工智慧的巨大影響，這可能使他們成為迄今為止最有情感互動、最有目標的一代（趨勢＃93 AI 世代）。

今年更加重視情感。人們希望生活中充滿驚喜、神秘、敬畏和驚奇，從而創造新的體驗來滿足各種不同的情感需求，從空間科技到感知科技烏托邦。

這次出版的十週年「改變未來的 100 件事：2024 年全球百大趨勢」，我們也收集了於九個不同國家的原始消費者調查數據，並採訪了各個領域的專家，給出了他們對過去十年的看法以及對於 2024 年的展望。希望大家能盡情享受！

Emma Chiu and Marie Stafford
VML 智庫　全球總監
vml.com/expertise/intelligence

序言

我們發表「改變未來的 100 件事 全球百大趨勢」已經十週年，也算是一個里程碑。今年的趨勢報告透露出了一種對於慢活、品質追求和共享的生活方式的渴望。2024 年即將到來，我們將走向一個更加深思熟慮的消費觀念，不僅在個人層面體現，更在企業運營模式上有所轉變。迎來十週年之際，這份報告將引領我們探索未來，發現生活和工作的新節奏。

談到趨勢，我想不得不談到 AI，AI 人工智慧的發展，正改變了我們的工作方式，也因為 AI 的賦能，讓我們在創意的產出、影像的形成、影片的剪接、虛擬人物、甚至是短時間產出大量廣告素材都有了更高效的做法。或許你心中會有一個問題：「AI 會不會取代我們的工作？」我相信這件事情正在發生。舉個例子，在我們的實際作業中，產品 3D 影像、模特兒、電腦合成、空間設置 ...... 都可透過 AI 來完成，這代表了有些人因此失去了工作機會。不過，我還是正面看待廣告這個產業，正因為 AI 可以協助處理很多執行的工作，代表我們能有更多時間回到這個行業的本質「想法」上，去創造更有價值的產出。

這是一份涵蓋了「文化、科技、旅遊 & 觀光、品牌 & 行銷、食品 & 飲品、美容、零售、奢華、健康和創新」等十個領域的報告，這十個領域也在這場十週年的旅程中探索著自己的未來。品牌將擁抱 AI 和機器學習，提升行銷成效，使品牌更好地了解顧客，預測消費行為。奢華品牌尋找意義、匠心、緩慢和真實性，注重獨特屬性、文化和歷史。旅行不再只是對抗日常生活的解藥，更是追求寧靜的旅程等等 ......。種種跡象都在預告著我們將迎接的是一個 AI、慢活、永續、匠心、真實、友善共存的未來，且讓我們一起熱情擁抱。

鄧博文
VML 台灣 執行長

美容　　　零售　　　奢華　　　健康　　　創新

數字洞察

除非另有說明以外，這是由VML 資料庫所提供的原始全球消費者數據。
在阿根廷、巴西、中國、哥倫比亞、法國、印度、墨西哥、英國和美國進行調查，受訪者為9,000名18歲以上的成年人。
數據收集時間為2023年9月至10月。有關方法和權重請參見第261頁。

一種溫和的樂觀情緒正在顯現

儘管有焦慮，人們仍然充滿希望，尤其是在個人層面。

如何評估人們的樂觀或負面的感受

受訪者對事物的感受在他們自己的生活和世界中使用 1 到 10 做評分

● 生活   ● 世界

	生活	世界
總體	7.1	5.4
Z 世代 (18-24)	6.8	5.2
千禧世代 (25-39)	7.2	5.8
X 世代 (40-59)	7.1	5.3
嬰兒潮世代 (60-79)	7.4	5

人們對於生活現況的主要情感

選擇每種情緒百分比來捕捉現在生活中的狀況

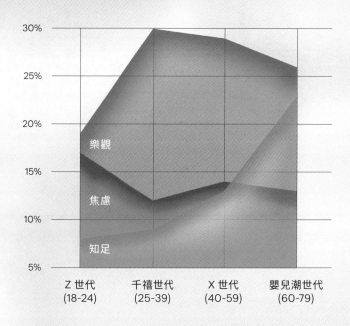

樂觀
焦慮
知足

Z 世代 (18-24)   千禧世代 (25-39)   X 世代 (40-59)   嬰兒潮世代 (60-79)

儘管挑戰仍然存在

人們對現有的複雜性和風險保有實事求是的態度。

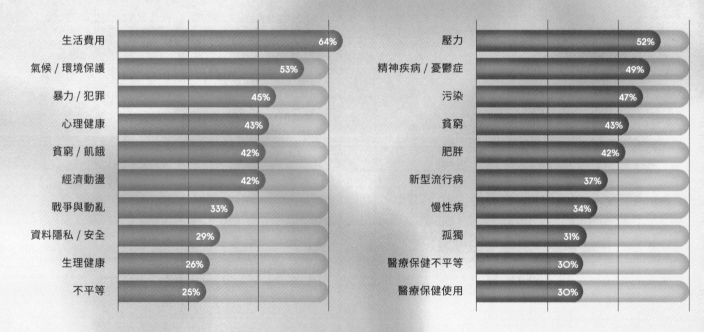

社會面臨最迫切的10個議題
前五大議題百分比

議題	百分比
生活費用	64%
氣候 / 環境保護	53%
暴力 / 犯罪	45%
心理健康	43%
貧窮 / 飢餓	42%
經濟動盪	42%
戰爭與動亂	33%
資料隱私 / 安全	29%
生理健康	26%
不平等	25%

人類健康的10大挑戰百分比

議題	百分比
壓力	52%
精神疾病 / 憂鬱症	49%
污染	47%
貧窮	43%
肥胖	42%
新型流行病	37%
慢性病	34%
孤獨	31%
醫療保健不平等	30%
醫療保健使用	30%

科技啟發人類...

大多數人都看到了它產生積極影響的潛力

認同比例

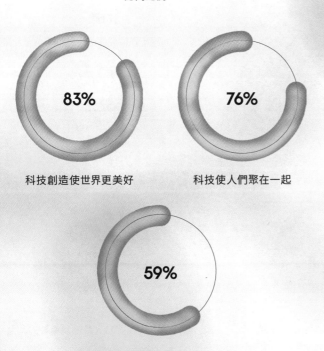

83%

科技創造使世界更美好

76%

科技使人們聚在一起

59%

我相信 AI 會按照人類的最大利益行事

...但科技不會取代人類

現在由情感定義的人性將變得至關重要

科技有超越人類的潛力

前三名項目的百分比

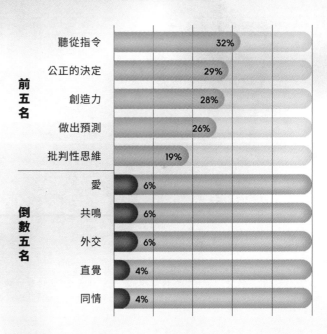

前五名	聽從指令	32%
	公正的決定	29%
	創造力	28%
	做出預測	26%
	批判性思維	19%
倒數五名	愛	6%
	共鳴	6%
	外交	6%
	直覺	4%
	同情	4%

人們希望與世界和彼此重新建立聯繫

人們普遍渴望透過以下方式來豐富生活

情感	經驗	聯繫

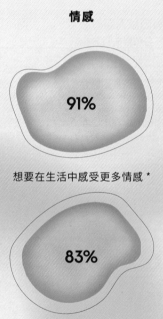

91%

想要在生活中感受更多情感 *

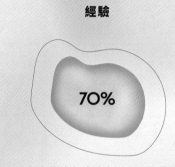

70%

更願意花錢在體驗生活而不是購物

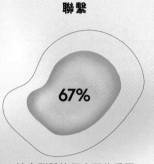

67%

社會群體比個人更為重要

83%

積極尋找帶來快樂和幸福的經驗 *

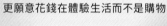

2x

花費在體驗生活而非購物的群眾
他們感到快樂的人數是原來的兩倍

73%

與他人共度美好時光是他們用餐的動力

* VML data 2023, 3,000 adults, China, United Kingdom, United States

提高人與人的相互聯繫現在是關鍵的品牌機會

人們期待品牌可以提更樂觀及精神上的鼓勵

過去五年裡，品牌角色的定義已經改變
認同比例

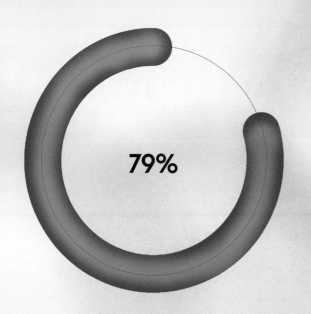

79%

品牌角色應該要是…
前三名項目的百分比

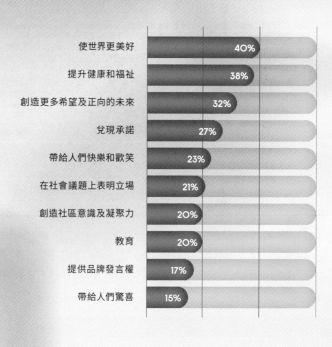

項目	百分比
使世界更美好	40%
提升健康和福祉	38%
創造更多希望及正向的未來	32%
兌現承諾	27%
帶給人們快樂和歡笑	23%
在社會議題上表明立場	21%
創造社區意識及凝聚力	20%
教育	20%
提供品牌發言權	17%
帶給人們驚喜	15%

文化

情感工程

新的品牌情感指標正在形成。

↑ The Kraken Screamfest VII: Shock Exchange

根據 VML 智庫的 2023 年研究《魔幻返潮時代》,全球三分之二的人表示,他們希望品牌能夠幫助他們感受到強烈的情感。該報告揭示了一個激發想像力的機會,通過提供再度陶醉,來讚揚令人興奮、振奮和令人驚嘆的事物。在人們感到筋疲力盡、疏離和厭倦的時候,有 77% 的人表示他們:「只是想感受一些東西,感受到活著的感覺。」品牌可以探索一個情感的光譜,並從中獲得一系列的好處。

心理學告訴我們,快樂和喜悅在我們的身心健康中扮演著至關重要的角色,同時也充當著社交潤滑劑。感受敬畏心情也是有益的,同時也幫助我們停止反芻,放眼向外看,感到更加連結。驚喜可以幫助我們建立連結,同時也重新塑造自我認知。即使是難過的情緒也有其存在的意義,幫助我們應對挑戰並增強韌性。

VML 智庫的數據顯示,打造具有情感回饋的體驗可以帶來雙贏的回報:消費者更有可能在讓他們感到愉悅、驚喜、啟發靈感等各種情感的品牌上花費。

美國蘭姆酒品牌 The Kraken 正在向其陰暗面靠攏。 2023 年萬聖節期間，它與「休閒恐懼實驗室」共同的選定了部分的英國酒吧舉辦了「第七屆尖叫節：震撼交流」的活動。 並要求飲酒者佩戴心率監測器，以此檢測身臨其境時的恐怖體驗：「心率越低，雞尾酒就越便宜。」

Daybreaker 是一個專門舉辦振奮人心的集體晨舞派對的全球健康品牌，同時也是「情感工程」的先驅。 創始人兼首席執行官 Radha Agrawal 告訴 VML 智庫：「Daybreaker 的主要關鍵績效指標之一就是喜極而泣。」

值得關注的原因：
是時候讓品牌突破理性的思維模式，探索感性的顛覆力量了。未來，一個品牌的表現可能會讓人產生肅然起敬、喜極而泣、激動不已、瞠目結舌的感覺。消費者將投資那些使其再度陶醉並為他們的生活增添情感價值的品牌。

↑ Daybreaker

VML

THE FUTURE 100   18

02
集體充電

色彩專家預測了一種能傳達溫馨和呵護的色調。

↑ Peach Fuzz, Pantone Color of the Year 2024, courtesy of The Development x Almost Studios

期望看到對社區的更多關注

Laurie Pressman, Pantone 色彩研究所副總裁

↑ Peach Fuzz, Pantone Color of the Year 2024, courtesy of The Development x Almost Studios

Peach Fuzz（柔和桃色）是一種柔和、水潤且令人安慰的色調，被 Pantone 選為其 2024 年度的代表色。與去年充滿活力的 Viva Magenta（萬歲洋紅）不同，這種色調聚焦於人性、成長和在不穩定時期的和平。Pantone 色彩研究所的執行董事 Leatrice Eiseman 表示：「Peach Fuzz 帶來歸屬感，激發重新調整的動機，提供培育的機會，營造出一種平靜的氛圍。無論是與他人共度時光還是花時間享受獨處時刻，為我們提供一個存在、感受、療癒和茁壯的空間。」

Peach Fuzz 營造出了充滿了溫柔、積極的氛圍，如夢幻般青春無邪。Pantone 公司解釋說，這傳遞出一種「溫柔」的感覺及「關懷和分享」的訊息。 人是 Pantone 在 2024 年色彩決策的核心，因為該品牌期望看到「對社區的更多關注，世界各地的人們重新定義他們想要的生活方式並評估什麼是重要的──那就是親近我們所愛的人是一種舒適感」Pantone 色彩研究所副總裁 Laurie Pressman 這樣說道。

英國塗料公司 Dulux 在其 2024 年度顏色 Sweet Embrace（甜蜜的擁抱）中也表達了類似的觀點。該品牌將這種溫暖、平靜的色調描述為「一種親切、細膩的色調，給人們的生活帶來積極的感覺」。

美國 Sherwin-Williams 選擇了一種涼爽而寧靜的藍色調，名為「Upward 向上」，作為其 2024 年度的年度色彩。這種色調喚起人們沉思和歇息的時刻，Sherwin-Williams 形容它為「當我們放慢腳步，深呼吸，並允許思緒清晰時所見到的顏色」。

值得關注的原因：

充實、感性、智慧的一年即將到來，人們被鼓勵放慢腳步，更好地與自己和他人重新建立聯繫。 2024年可能是啟迪人心的一年，為深思熟慮、以人為本的未來鋪路。

VML

氣候適應生活

極端的氣候條件正在改變我們生活的方方面面。

「全球暖化的時代已經結束，全球煮沸的時代已經到來，」聯合國秘書長 António Guterres 在 2023 年 7 月表示──那是地球有史以來最炎熱的月份。極端天氣模式的崛起，尤其是極端高溫，對日常生活產生深遠影響。《紐約時報》宣稱：「極端高溫將改變我們。」

對於勞動者而言，極端高溫可能帶來嚴重後果。據 2023 年 7 月發表在《自然》雜誌上的一項研究顯示，歐洲的熱浪在 2022 年夏季造成了超過 61,000 人死亡。在美國，職業安全與健康管理局正在加緊起草工作場所的熱標準，總統拜登宣布了 2023 年 7 月保護勞動者免受極端高溫影響的新計劃。

儘管這些新的氣候模式無疑是危險的，但它們也在各個行業中推動創新，以幫助我們適應。總部位於英國的智能服裝公司 Techniche 專注於熱調節技術，並正在為建築工人開發冷卻工作服。

總部位於美國的 Qore Performance 向 Boeing、Shake Shack、Chick-fil-A 和 FedEx 等企業提供冷卻背心，更不用說美國空軍了，自 2020 年以來，其業務增長了 300%。支持這些背心的技術是 IcePlate Curve，「世界上第一個可熱調節工具」。

熱調節和耐熱專家 James Russell 預測未來的工作服將植入可穿戴的預測技術，「我們目前正在開發印刷的生物傳感器，為藍領工人和 HSSE（健康、安全、防護和環境）團隊提供低功耗反饋。這些傳感器可以捕捉各種生物數據點，並借助人工智能，我們可以預測工人是否可能需要醫療幫助。」

VML

在農業領域，新的氣候變遷正在重塑農作物的種植地區。 一些葡萄酒商甚至在葡萄上噴灑微生物，以保護它們免受高溫影響。

鳳凰城防暑辦公室主任 David Hondula 告訴《The Daily podcast》，為了設計未來的城市，城市規劃者需要考慮「人們活動空間的熱舒適度」。 根據《紐約時報》報道，新加坡正在投入大量資源，從根本上重新思考其悶熱的城市地區。 在中國，建築師們正在復興古老的自然冷卻概念，即建築物中的天井（又高又窄的中央庭院）。 建築師 Vinu Daniel 是印度氣候響應型建築的先驅。

氣候適應性的美容產業。需要新配方來保護皮膚免受環境變化的刺激。隨著山林火災的增加，美國美容品牌 Pour Moi 於 2022 年 4 月推出了 Smoke Alarm Drops 精華液，以對抗煙霧引起的氧化壓力。2023 年 8 月，Prada 推出了護膚系列，該系列採用獨特的 Adapto.gn 智慧技術幫助肌膚即時適應環境，促進新陳代謝、再生和強化。

值得關注的原因：
Guterres說：「極端天氣正在成為新常態。」極端天氣不會消失，它將繼續重塑我們的日常生活並推動創新（請參閱第96章〈變形城市〉）。

↑ Techniche cooling garments

全球暖化的時代已經結束
全球煮沸的時代已經到來

António Guterres, 聯合國秘書長

↑ Mind your Manners, Netflix, courtesy of James Gourley

全新禮儀

文化影響者為集體體驗提供新禮儀提醒。

不良行為。突然之間，它無處不在。全球 80% 的受訪者同意，現如今人們的行為比以往任何時候都更糟糕。有關全球各地人們在公共場所搞破壞的聳人聽聞的故事登上了頭條。人們在電影院打鬥；在演唱會上向歌手投擲物品；在音樂劇中擾亂演員的歌唱，甚至在劇院裡跳上舞台與他們一同表演。

布里斯托大學文化研究專家 Kirsty Sedgman 告訴 VML 智庫：「現場表演一直是一個煤礦中的金絲雀*。」「這是一種早期警報系統，當更大規模的社會政治挫折和變革即將爆發時。」雖然一些評論家將暴亂行為歸因於後疫情時期的生疏感，Sedgman 看到了更大的細微差別和複雜性。她指出了她所稱之為「經濟脫節」和「社會契約的崩潰」的作用。

她表示：「我們所看到的是人們對彼此之間的疏離感日益增加，並進一步根深蒂固，」她補充說，由於人們觀察到當權者為所欲

↑ Mind your Manners, Netflix, courtesy of James Gourley

為，不須承擔任何後果，現在"似乎有很大一部分人抵制任何權威人士告訴他們該怎麼做。"

權威人士正在加緊提供更新的指導。 其中一個聲音是禮儀專家 Sara Jane Ho，她是中國第一所禮儀學校的創始人，她的 Netflix 節目《國際禮儀指南》於 2023 年播出。同名書籍將於 2024 年出版，講述了 Sara 關於如何在職場中的任何時候展現最好自我的見解。 在杜拜，華裔 TikTok 網紅 Zhou Ziying 正在透過研討會和私人課程向阿聯酋居民教授禮儀和社交行為。在日本，人們經歷了社交隔離和多年的戴口罩之後，對「微笑課程」的需求越來越大。《紐約時報》寫道：「經過了三年新冠疫情時期戴的口罩，一些日本人感覺自己的臉部表情有點生疏了。」微笑教練 Keiko Kawano 登場，她的輔導課程指導學生如何真誠地微笑。

各品牌也參與其中。佛羅里達州和加州的迪士尼度假區在其網站上的遊客準備指引中添加了禮貌部分，呼籲遊客們相互尊重。汽車製造商 Vauxhall 與禮儀專家 Debrett's 合作，為電動汽車駕駛編寫了一份禮儀指南，提供有關尊重排隊和通過溝通進入充電站充電的建議。 企業也重申行為準則：45% 的美國公司提供禮儀課程，強化人們對從服裝到工作場所對話等各方面的期望。

Sara 告訴 VML 智庫，禮儀不僅僅是為了禮貌：在這個極度孤獨的時代，我們比以往任何時候都更需要禮儀，它是最極致的健康方式，通過人與人的連接，是促進真實而健康的個人成長的途徑。"

值得關注的原因：
在促進團結充滿希望的時代，制定預期行為指南可以讓我們團結在一起。 Sedgman 對品牌的建議是：「仔細思考哪些規則實際上可以讓每個人都更安全，並創造更公平、更平等、更具聯繫性的體驗形式。」

*「煤礦中的金絲雀」為英文俚語，意指「不好事情即將發生的徵兆。」

VML

05

互助共鳴

大規模的集體體驗正在滿足人們對連接和歸屬的渴望。

全球 71% 的人同意孤獨是一種流行病，66% 的人表示不再有社區的感覺。對品牌來說，有一個日益增長的機會，即是設計促進與朋友和陌生人一起的大規模連接和社區的集體體驗。

集體的活力描述了由共同體驗所釋放的能量和和諧，就像是參與合唱團或節慶人群一樣。根據布里斯托大學文化專家 Kirsty Sedgman 的說法，這對我們來說是 "非常重要的，因為它確實把來自各種背景的人們聚在一起，形成牢固的社區聯繫。" 她告訴 VML 智庫：「有很多證據表明，如果你能跳出那個與你完全相似的舒適區，結識更廣泛的人群，這將帶來巨大的個人健康益處，也有助於更強大的社區和更出色的經濟表現。」

因此，Join My Wedding 是一項服務，允許國際遊客購買門票參加印度陌生人的婚禮，以便他們感受參與大型活動的喜悅。還有 The Big Quiet，一個從 25 人會議發展成擁有數千名參與者的健康活動的大規模冥想運動。

這也是為什麼瑞典零售商 IKEA 正在探索新的方法，讓人們重新聚集在其商店中，首先是在 2023 年米蘭設計週期間舉辦夜間狂歡派對。IKEA 的創意總監 Marcus Engman 告訴 VML 智庫說：「IKEA 非常重視人際關係。」該公司的理念根植於「tillsammans」──瑞典語，意為團結。「這不僅僅是 IKEA 和我們客戶之間的共同體，還包括人與人之間的連結。他說。「那麼，我們該如何創造一個共同體的空間和機會呢？這是我們從 IKEA 創立之初就一直努力著的事情。」

正如 Engman 所解釋的，零售商扮演了促成者的角色，提供

↑ The Big Quiet. Photography by Felix Kunze
→ Ikea at Milan Design Week 2023. Photography by Ozmoze

場合和場地，讓人們自行發揮。「當你像辦一場狂歡派對這樣的事情時，創造氛圍的是在場的人們。」他說。「我們只是為他們創造一個場景。」而 IKEA 不是唯一一家探索聯繫力量的零售商：百貨公司 Selfridges 將在其四樓推出一個名為「The Selfridges Lounge」的永久活動空間，遊客可以在那裡享受音樂和文化節目。

值得關注的原因：
品牌必須幫助人們相互聯繫，根據晨間大型舞蹈活動 Daybreaker 的創始人 Radha Agrawal 的說法：「品牌最大的機會是讓人們相互聯繫——這個品牌如何作為集體，而不是社區內的個體來服務一個社區。」

The Big Quiet

06

緩速週期

快速變動的趨勢週期使人感到疲憊，進而轉向較緩慢的方向。

VML

在 2023 年，由於使用者對於在 TikTok 上製造和大肆炒作新趨勢的速度感到惱火，出現了一場小規模的反叛，共同對著如「藍莓牛奶指甲」、「拿鐵妝容」和「西紅柿女孩夏天」等美容概念發出不滿。TikTok 用戶 Katie Raymond (@katiehub.org) 表示：「我們不會將淺藍變成藍莓牛奶。我拒絕。」

在接受 VML 智庫的採訪中，來自 Vogue Philippines 的記者們一致認為，被呈現為趨勢的概念並不總是像它們看起來那樣新穎。數位編輯 Andrea Ang 表示：「拿鐵妝容植根於韓國美容美學，同時也滿足了橄欖色皮膚的需求。」美容編輯 Joyce Oreña 則建議尋找潮流背後的長期變化。「我們不能忽視所有這些快速變化的趨勢，」她說。「那麼你要如何應對呢？真的是要注意更廣泛的傾向。」

對於快節奏的炒作週期，有一股同時的潮流看到了放慢速度的價值。正如我們在《Next-gen collectors》（請參閱第 63 章〈下世代收藏家〉）中報導的那樣，設計師 Phoebe Philo 拋棄了標準的季節性方法，改為推出為期限的產品，旨在保持持久性。在美容方面，愛馬仕選擇生產更少但更具創新性的美容產品，而慢美容品牌 Dieux 則將自己的使命設定為銷售更少的產品（請參閱第 53 章〈慢美容〉）。

↑ Courtesy of Katie Raymond (@katiehub.org) and Sunia Bukhari (@suniabukhari)

顯然，從可持續性的角度來看，這是有益的，而且還有跡象表明消費者可能會歡迎一些喘息的機會。根據 Ipsos 的全球研究，有 73%的人希望能夠放慢生活的節奏。

其他也有相似的現象：在 2023 年 9 月的一篇文章中，《衛報》描述消費者不再一次瘋狂追完劇的狂歡模式，將每週觀看的模式從「最近的紀錄開始看電視。」

值得關注的原因：
人們感到被敦促以極快的速度消費而感到不知所措。一些品牌選擇減速，放慢，並讓人們有時間品味體驗，然後再轉向下一件事。

品牌選擇減速，放慢，並讓人們有時間品味體驗，然後再轉向下一件事

VML

07

永恆的瞬息藝術

藝術中的無常之美象徵性地呼應了自然和人性的脆弱，
正在被讚美。

↑ Condollence. Concept, design and tailoring by Darío Simón Abelló. Photographed at HFBK Photo Studio

↑ Condollence. Concept, design and tailoring by Darío Simón Abelló. Photographed at HFBK Photo Studio

2024 年的大都會藝術博物館慈善晚宴 (Met Gala) 主題將捕捉時尚中的短暫性和保存性，名為「沉睡的美人：時尚的重生」。配套展覽將展示約 250 件珍藏服裝和配飾，這些珍藏品現在已經太嬌嫩無法穿著。

此次展覽將嘗試運用多種不同的科技，重新喚醒這些藝術品的感官能力，以展現其生命力。讓參觀者能夠在感官上與這些珍貴的歷史服飾和精緻的當代時尚「接觸」。大都會藝術博物館服裝學院的 Wendy Yu 與策展人 Andrew Bolton 表示：「自 2024 年 5 月 10 日起，參觀者可以探索這些被重新喚醒的藝術作品，博物館希望透過這次展覽再現藝術的生命力。」

西班牙服裝設計師 Darío Simón Abelló 一直研究穿在身上會改變形態的揮發性材料。2023 年 2 月，這位年輕藝術家在漢堡舉行的 HFBK 2023 年度畢業展上發表了 Condollence 系列，是一系列浸過蠟的服裝，這些服裝在穿著時會裂開和破碎，並在伸展台上留下經過的痕跡，同時也改變了穿在身上的形態。Abelló 稱這些服裝為「碎服 shattering garments」，旨在深入探討流行和人性的「易破碎 與 易受傷」。

紐約時裝設計師 Prabal Gurung 在他的 2023 年秋季成衣系列中探索了佛教概念「無常」。「這個系列是通過無常和變型的視角進行的一次靈性覺醒——這個想法是沒有什麼是固定不變的，一切都在不斷變化。」古隆表示：「變化引發了一種樂觀的情緒，即萬物一直都在持續演變。這就是無常之美，與其害怕，更應擁抱它。」

值得關注的原因：
自然和人類的脆弱在時尚流行中得到體現，被藝術家重新注入活力後，這些精美的藝術作品，有了新的欣賞角度，也有了新生命。

VML

08

盧德模式

Z 世代，無縫切換連線或退出，恣意進出數位世界。

VML

↑ Photography by Ellie Adams via Unsplash

盧德俱樂部 (Luddite Club) 是一個總部設在紐約專注青少年生活型態的團體，近年來因提倡「從社群媒體和科技中解放自我」而備受矚目。該組織的名稱源自 19 世紀英國的反工業革命運動，已成為 Z 世代領導反抗瀏覽負面訊息及社群媒體焦慮過勞的代名詞。

Voxburner 的「青年趨勢」報告證實，超過一半 (54%) 的 16-24 歲年輕人擔心在社交媒體上花費太多時間。然而，年輕的消費者並沒有完全陷入到「盧德」心態中，而是擅於在需要全面連接的時候切換，並在需要專注或冷靜的時候進入「盧德」模式。

諾基亞報告稱，近年來其『傻瓜』手機銷售持續增長，因為在 Z 世代中廣受歡迎。但，據《華爾街日報》報導，消費者買來不是為了要取代智慧手機，而是作為『便宜的第二手機』。『傻瓜』手

↑ Nokia 150, courtesy of Nokia

機可以讓使用者在夜晚約會或放鬆度假時切換到盧德模式。 在澳大利亞，音樂廠牌 This Never Happened 充分利用了這種心態，於 2023 年 7 月在墨爾本、雪梨和布里斯班舉辦了一系列不拍照、不打電話的活動，高聲倡導：體驗當下！別錄下來！（請參閱第 30 章〈類比旅行〉）

這些行為變化呼應了最近流行的「提升生產力的修行模式」，該模式鼓勵人們切斷所有干擾，以便專注於完成他們的重要工作任務。

值得關注的原因：
雖然 Z 世代的模式切換可能看起來很矛盾，但品牌需要考慮他們的產品和服務是否可以在連接和數位停機時幫助到消費者，或者，是否可以協助用戶在不同的模式之間無縫切換。

VML

09

自然權利

為自然提供法律保護正在逐漸受到重視。

在這個飽受氣候危機困擾的時代，一場為大自然爭取法律權利的全球運動正在蓄勢待發。據 Katie Surma 為《內部氣候新聞》撰寫的文章表示，我們正處於訴訟熱潮之中，大多數案件都發生在美國。

在美國，與在巴西、新西蘭和加拿大等其他國家一樣，原住民社區正在引領潮流。2023 年，西雅圖的部落領袖贏得了一場具有里程碑意義的官司，保障了鮭魚通過該市水壩洄遊的權利。在世界其他地區，各國正在考慮將自然權利寫入憲法。從菲律賓和玻利維亞到阿魯巴和愛爾蘭共和國，各國領導人正在討論效仿在 2008 年第一個這樣做的國家──厄瓜多爾。

另一種方法是將自然賦予法律上的人格。正如名字所暗示的那樣，這使得河流和森林具有與人類相同的權利。這一先例是由紐西蘭的毛利族創立的，他們在 2017 年為惠革努伊河爭取了法律人格。現在，其他地方也紛紛效仿。在 2023 年，巴西（科米·梅梅河）和西班牙（馬爾梅諾鹹水泊）取得了保護自然的成功案例，而運動者現在也在尋求波蘭的奧得河和北海的類似保護。

少數品牌也在積極響應這一倡議。在去年的「改變未來的 100 件事」中，Patagonia 和 Faith in Nature 將大自然納入其董事會，有效地賦予了大自然法律人格。2023 年 11 月，豪華室內裝潢品牌 House of Hackney 任命了兩位新董事：自然之母和 未來世代。聯合創始人 Frieda Gormley 說：「作為一家商業公司，我們認為必須要對自然的影響以及留給後代的生活品質負起高度的法律責任。」

↑ Mother Nature & Future Generations by Lukas the Illustrator for House of Hackney

值得關注的原因：
像 20 世紀爭取人權一樣，未來十年將被界定為爭取自然生態系統權利的奮鬥。

作為一家商業公司，我們認為必須要對自然的影響以及留給後代的生活品質負起高度的法律責任。

Frieda Gormley, 聯合創始人

VML

共識社區

傳統家庭結構正受到挑戰。

↑ Honeydew eco-community, Italy

VML

在全球許多地區，單人家庭正逐漸增多，同時在美國和英國，單親家庭已經佔家庭總數的五分之一以上。然而，隨著獨居人數的攀升，伴隨而來的是日益加深的孤獨感，再加上住房成本不斷飆升。共識社區應運而生：這些社區提供各種選擇，能夠互助互愛、豐富生活並享受彼此的陪伴。

「社區是良藥」是位於義大利艾米利亞 - 羅曼尼亞的非營利生態社區 Honeydew 的核心理念。該社區的創始人 Benjamin Ramm 曾是英國廣播公司 (BBC) 的記者，在離開倫敦的獨居生活後，他立志建立一個強調相互關懷、服務和療癒的多世代社區網絡。Ramm 告訴 VML 智庫：「Honeydew 正在積極打造一個全新的共識社區網絡，以團結、可持續發展和相互關懷為基石」。他進一步指出：「疫情的蔓延催生了建立在生態和社會危機後集體復原力的迫切需求」。儘管在這段時期裡，我們可能感到孤立無援，甚至絕望，但「我們仍有能力培養社會團結，共同構建身份認同，並從中獲得使命感和目標感。」

新地 (New Ground) 是英國首個為年長婦女設計的共居社區。這個由 26 位成員組成的組織由居民自行管理，每個人都擁有自己的住所，並共享康樂和社交設施。他們既可以獨立生活，又是相互支持網絡的一部分。相互支持也是「媽媽社區（Mommunes）」的理念，單親母親和她們的孩子共同分享一個家。儘管這個概念並不新穎，但在持續升高的生活成本危機中，它重新引起了人們的關心。Carmel Bos 是美國 CoAbode 配對服務公司的創始人，她在 2023 年 7 月接受《今日》節目訪問時表示，她的公司接到的電話數量簡直「一飛沖天」。

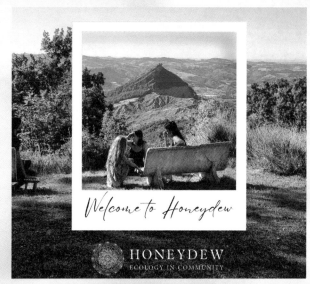

↑ Honeydew eco-community, Italy

多重世代同居是另一種解決方式。英國廣播公司 (BBC) 的一個報導顯示從加拿大到荷蘭越來越多的案例，將學生與退休人員配對在一起共同生活。

值得關注的原因：
隨著越來越多的人選擇加入提供相互支持和連結的社區，「家庭」的定義也在不斷演變。隨著共識社區的發展，品牌需要考慮如何迎合和規劃未來的家庭。

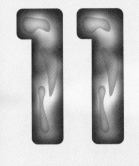

11

科技

20

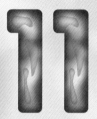

虛擬身份經濟

新經濟正在圍繞數位虛擬角色形成。

2023 年 11 月，好萊塢演員罷工經過長達 118 天的抗爭終於告一段落。美國演員工會（SAG-AFTRA）為演員爭取到了一系列新的保障措施，其中包括對電影業中人 AI 應用的新指導方針。其中一個重要的規定是，製片公司在使用演員的數位複製品或任何特徵時，必須事先獲得演員的同意並進行合理的補償。

包括阿尼爾卡普爾（Anil Kapoor）、史嘉蕾喬韓森（Scarlett Johansson）和湯姆漢克（Tom Hanks）在內的一些演員已經對未經授權使用他們的 AI 肖像採取了法律行動。雖然法律框架尚未完全確立，但這已為我們邁向以人類身份為核心的新經濟開啟了道路。其中一項新興服務是關於人物角色的創建，也就是允許任何人創造出自己的數位分身。

對於內容創作者和具有影響力的人來說，數位角色可以提供前所未有的影響力和規模。 目前，中國網紅在這方面處於領先地位，他們委託制作令人信服的 AI 克隆（AI Clon）角色，使他們能夠最大限度地提高直播輸出，全天候製作內容從而獲利。硅基智能（Silicon Intelligence）和微軟小冰（Xiaoice）等一批中國新創公司現在能僅以 1,000 美金的成本，使用一分鐘的現場原始影片製作出深偽的虛擬形象。

英國 AI 新創公司 Metaphysical，因其極為逼真的湯姆·克魯（Tom Cruise）深偽作品（@deeptomcruise）而聲名大噪，它正在幫助名人控制他們的虛擬角色。其 Metaphysical Pro 解決方案為允許用戶建立一套生物辨識資料，可用來創建面孔、聲音和表演，進而授權並達成變現。

↑ Mimio interactive personas

舊金山新創公司 Mimio.ai 正在建立 Personality Engine™ (人格引擎),將允許用戶創建自己的 AI 人物,模仿他們的聲音、語調和說話風格。 該公司預見其應用不僅限於名人和網紅,也適用於可能需要幫助處理電子郵件的一般使用者,甚至是希望為後代留下數位分身的長者。公司承諾,用戶將完全掌控其數位人物,並可按照自己的意願自由進行商業行為。

數位分身成為我們日常生活的一部分似乎已成必然。至少目前而言,在藝術表現方面,真人仍然具有優勢。在欣賞現場音樂 (75%)、有劇本的電影和電視節目 (69%)、錄製音樂 (65%) 以及品牌傳播 (52%) 時,受訪者更傾向於真人而非 AI。

受訪者更傾向於真人而非AI

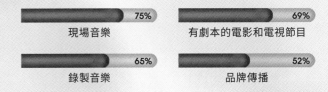

現場音樂	75%
有劇本的電影和電視節目	69%
錄製音樂	65%
品牌傳播	52%

值得關注的原因:
雖然倫理和法律標準尚待明確,但虛擬身分經濟已開始蓬勃發展。數位人物為品牌提供了高成本效益且以靈活的方式吸引人才,不過值得注意的是,真人在觀眾心目中仍然具有較高的價值。只有不到一成 (8%) 的受訪者表示,他們期待一個虛擬人物成為日常生活的一部分。

12

空間科技

隨著空間運算的進步，實體世界和數位世界繼續變得模糊。

↑ Vision Pro by Apple, courtesy of Apple

VML

ision Pro by Apple, courtesy of Apple

Apple 將於 2024 年 2 月推出 Vision Pro 混合實境頭戴裝置。購買者只需花費 3,499 美元即可獲得所謂的「首款空間電腦」。該設備承諾「將數位內容與物理世界無縫融合」，這是一項重要的大眾市場嘗試，旨在將數位介面從螢幕中解放出來。該公司在 1 月份宣布了「訪客模式」，允許親朋好友試用該設備。

在 2024 年消費性電子展 (CES) 期間，索尼公司宣布與西門子合作開發一個空間內容創建系統。包括一款擴增實境頭戴裝置和控制器，預計今年晚些時候推出。2023 年 10 月，中國增強實境公司 Xreal 推出了其 Air 2 和 Air 2 Pro 下一代輕便 AR 眼鏡，承諾「一個螢幕取代一切。」

在 CES 2024 上，Niantic 的產品 AR 平台總監 Tom Emrich 預測，智能眼鏡和頭戴裝置的情境優勢將使智能手機變成「助手」和「所有可穿戴設備的中樞」。Emrich 表示，空間科技類別「正開始成形。但這意味著它為應用開發者、網頁開發者、品牌和零售商提供了巨大的機會，尤其是讓他們有機會踏入這一領域。」他補充說：「我同意 Tim Cook 的看法—空間計算時代已經到來，而我們才剛剛開始。」

值得關注的原因：
隨著沉浸式技術的進步繼續拉近實體和數位世界的距離，空間計算將見證顯著增長。據 MarketsandMarkets 預測，該市場預計將從 2023 年的 979 億美元增長到 2,028 年的 2,805 億美元。

↑ See yourself in sound, Bang & Olufsen

13

感知科技烏托邦

創作者們正利用科技探索我們感官之間的關係。

我們感官之間引人入勝的協同作用和相互影響，成為了一波以科技驅動的共感體驗的主題。

Bang & Olufsen 的「在聲音中遇見自己」品牌活動將音樂品味轉化為色彩豐富的肖像，以動感的互動身形式呈現。這個數位體驗邀請顧客訪問一個特別設計的網站，在那裡他們回答簡短的問卷或連接他們的 Spotify 帳戶，以獲得一個獨特的定制化身，並在社交媒體上分享。

Aura 是另一項讓聲音可見的體驗，是 2023 年倫敦設計節中一個重要委託作品。由西班牙藝術家 Pablo Valbuena 與藝術組織 Artichoke 合作設計，Aura 將聖保羅大教堂的禮拜聲音視覺化。一根纖細的 20 公尺高的鋁製柱子，上面鑲嵌著定制的 LED 燈，懸掛在教堂的穹頂下。對話、音樂和歌唱的聲音被捕捉並通過演算法轉化為光束，這些光束會根據音調、音量和強度做出反應。

墨西哥裔加拿大藝術家 Rafael Lozano-Hemmer 的展覽《Atmospheric Memory》使口語變得可見。 該展覽於 2023 年 11 月在雪梨動力博物館進行了更新，提供了一個感官環境，其靈感來自 Charles Babbage 的設想，即我們周圍的空氣是一個包含了每一個字、聲音和動作的圖書館。參觀者穿越懸浮在空中的文字雲，或看到他們的聲音在水箱中激起漣漪。

除了藝術努力之外，英國藝術家團體 Universal Everything 還將其結合共感科技和經驗付諸實際應用，開發了一種原型設備，可被病患用來視覺化疼痛。在日本，NTT Docomo 和合作機構正在開發世界首個感覺共享技術，允許用戶數位化地傳送動作或觸感。Docomo 已經計劃在其 Feel Tech 技術上進一步發展，使其他感官如味覺、聽覺甚至情感的共享成為可能。

值得關注的原因：

對感官體驗的需求是巨大的。 根據 VML 智庫為「魅力再造時代」報告所做的研究，63% 的消費者希望品牌為他們提供多感官體驗，72% 的消費者表示，他們希望在體驗新事物時能夠調動盡可能多的感官感受。 共感技術為感官體驗增添了一層新的迷人層次，無論是實體還是數位。

↑ See yourself in sound, Bang & Olufsen

↑ Text Stream II, part of Atmospheric Memory by Rafael Lozano-Hemmer. Photography by Zan Wimberley @zanwimberley, courtesy of Factory International and the Powerhouse Museum Sydney

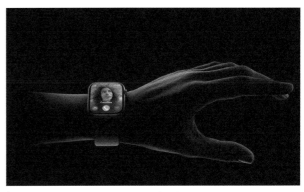

↑ Apple Watch double-tap feature, courtesy of Apple

14

空中手勢

新的非接觸式手勢讓消費者能夠與裝置更加緊密的串連。

由 Apple 推出的 Apple Watch 雙擊功能，源自於在 2024 年消費電子展 (CES) 期間，芬蘭新創公司 Doublepoint 推出了 WowMouse 應用程序，允許 Android 系統手錶使用者添加空中手勢檢測功能。 「我們不僅僅是在改變遊戲，我們還在重寫人機互動的規則，基於觸摸的手勢追蹤。這是一次躍進，為智慧手錶及其他產品提供了自然而強大的用戶體驗。」Doublepoint 執行長 Ohto Pentikäinen 表示。

同樣，Apple 於 2023 年 10 月為 Apple Watch Series 9 和 Apple Watch Ultra 2 推出了新的雙擊手勢。這使得佩戴者只需將佩戴手錶的手的食指和拇指輕按一下即可執行操作接聽電話等操作。 Apple 指出，當用戶的另一隻手被佔用時，例如當他們在「遛狗、做飯或拿著一杯咖啡」時，該手勢可以為用戶提供幫助。該手勢也將應用於該公司 2024 年發布的混合實境耳機 Vision Pro。

VML

Neural Lab 的 AirTouch 能夠僅用一個簡單的網路攝影機，將手和身體的手勢轉化為任何計算裝置的指令，為人們在不同裝置上使用空中手勢提供了選擇。

Google 於 2023 年 5 月 發 布 了 Project Gameface，「一款新型開源免持遊戲滑鼠，使用戶能夠透過頭部運動和臉部手勢控制電腦的游標。」Project Gameface 由 Google 的 MediaPipe 開源 AI 解決方案提供支援。該公司表示，其技術意味著「人們可以抬起眉毛來點擊和拖動，或者張開嘴來移動游標，讓任何人都可以玩遊戲。」 該公司與 Lance Carr 共同開發了這項技術，Lance Carr 是一位患有肌肉萎縮症、四肢癱瘓的視頻遊戲主播。 Google 指出，雖然該工具仍在開發中，但該公司「對它改變人們生活的潛力感到興奮，因為它的構建和維護成本相對較低。」

值得關注的原因：
隨著科技設備越來越融入消費者的生活，各家公司正在突破界限，讓這些設備使用起來更符合直覺和本能。 此外，這種免持手勢對於行動不便的人來說至關重要。 根據 CDC 數據，超過 12% 的美國成年人存在行動問題，此類措施使科技公司能夠使其產品和服務更具包容性。

↑ Wow Mouse App by Doublepoint

VML

15

高齡科技

科技正在解決老年人的生活方式和健康需求。

↑ Nobi smart ceiling lamp

對於日益增長的老年人群體而言,科技可以是獨立生活的關鍵。2024 年 1 月的消費電子展 (CES) 展出了大量新裝置和技術,這些產品為老年人在家中提供了增強的舒適、安全和情感支持。

一家來自比利時的高齡科技公司 Nobi,正試著解決跌倒的問題,這是老年人受傷的主要原因之一。其智能天花板燈可以檢測到跌倒位置並在需要時向醫療單位進行求助。 這款 AI 驅動工具最初提供在居家護理設施中,預計今年底將展示於大眾消費者面前,並用於居家使用。

為了提供更大的舒適度,美國初創公司 Lotus Labs 的可穿戴戒指為行動能力減弱的群眾提供無障礙便利。這款裝置預計在 2024 年秋季發貨,利用紅外線技術,僅透過指向就可以控制家中的物件,就像使用電視遙控器一樣。

VML

同樣考量到電視,因年齡而導致聽力喪失可能會使一些老年人難以與之對話。日本創業公司 SoundFun 的 Mirai 揚聲器採用專利的曲面揚聲器設計,使聲音更清晰、更容易區分,意味著每個人都可以以舒適的音量聆聽。

大型語言模型的興起帶來了一波不僅提供功能,還提供對話和陪伴的新裝置浪潮。

CES 2024 見證了 Intuition Robotics 的 ElliQ 回歸,它為老年人提供支持和豐富生活,促進社會聯繫。這款桌面機器人可以陪伴用戶,提供聊天以及日常互動和協助。

ElliQ 3.0 的升級硬件和 AI 增強功能允許自然、自由流動的對話,其中許多現在可以在「在地處理」,不需上到雲端,以提供更大的隱私性,正如 Intuition Robotics 的首席產品官 Ronen Soffer 向 VML 智庫解釋的那樣。隨著時間的推移,機器人通過記住和反思共享的對話,與用戶建立關係。

另一個重要焦點是促進與更廣泛的世界建立聯繫,無論是與 ElliQ 使用者擴展社區的接觸,還是提供當地信息和交通的協助。根據索弗 (Soffer) 的說法,ElliQ 的目標是 "理解、豐富和加強人際關係——而人際關係使你的生活更美好。我們希望能夠將您與現實世界中的更多事物聯繫起來。"

↑ ElliQ 3.0, Intuition Robotics

值得關注的原因:

根據世界衛生組織的資料,到 2030 年,全球六分之一的人口將年滿 60 歲以上。隨著全球人口老齡化,針對這一不斷增長的群體的情感和支持需求的科技發展潛力巨大。(請參閱第 92 章〈百歲未來〉)。

VML

16

氣味數位化

嗅覺數位化是未來趨勢。

↑ Osmo aims to give computers a sense of smell

視覺和聽覺已經成功數位化—但嗅覺呢？ Osmo 是一家致力於解答這個問題的公司，這家數位嗅覺新創公司希望「賦予電腦能感知嗅覺的能力」，作為 Google Research 的衍生公司，Osmo 的目標是創造一種新的數位化表現形式，能改變人類對於氣味的感知、傳導和記憶。

Osmo 聯合創始人 Josh Wolfe 將該公司定位為數位化學設計公司，Josh 接受 Wired 雜誌採訪時說道：「當人們想要一種非常特定的氣味，我們便設計調配相對應的化學成分，就像生物技術或製藥公司研發生產藥物，並且獲得藥物許可一樣」。

Osmo 執行長 Alex Wiltschko 進一步說明與生醫製藥業的其他相似之處：「AI 運用在新藥開發的領域，將是 AI 徹底改變未來人類嗅覺的先例。 而且 AI 的出現，幫助新藥開發者找到更多機會在臨床上取得成功的候選藥物一樣,我們也看到 AI 強化了合成化學家和調香師的角色。」

Osmo 的研究人員表示,除了激發新香水的靈感之外,該技術還可用於對抗蚊媒疾病。 Wiltschko 也指出,農業、食品儲存、流行病追蹤和疾病預防等領域,都將受益於數位化氣味這項新技術。

除了 Osmo 之外,日本公司 Revorn 使用 AI 和物聯網技術來再現氣味並模仿嗅覺。 在 2024 年消費性電子展 (CES) 上,它展示了氣味感測和再現設備。

頂級調香師也在探索數位化香氛。 2023 年 3 月,寶格麗在杜拜推出了 Scentsorial,這是一種將科技與嗅覺結合的沉浸式多重感官體驗。 參與者穿著穿戴式設備,測量他們的腦波和心率,以檢測對氣味的反應、想法和情緒,然後將它們即時轉化為生成可下載的收藏品。

值得關注的原因:

科技的進步正在改變我們對氣味的體驗和理解方式,隨著數位感官科技的發展,讓我們更接近真正的多感官數位體驗,就像進入感官科技烏托邦一樣。(請參閱第 13 章〈感知科技烏托邦〉)。

↑ Osmo aims to give computers a sense of smell

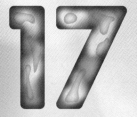

全語通科技

即時翻譯工具實現了地球村理想。

VML

↑ Multilanguage audio on YouTube, courtesy of YouTube Official Blog

科技

AI 正在打破世界上不同語言的隔閡。2023 年秋季在社群媒體上流傳的一段影片顯示，包括艾瑪·張伯倫 (Emma Chamberlain)、埃隆·馬斯克 (Elon Musk) 和馬克斯·布朗利 (Marques Brownlee) 在內的名人，使用自己的複製版聲音講著多種不同語言，這些語言不但可以即時翻譯，還能同步嘴型。總部位於洛杉磯的 HeyGen 是一家 AI 影片創作公司，提供一鍵翻譯服務。透過上傳剪輯，使用者可以立刻將影片翻譯成 14 種語言中任何一種，且該服務每個月都會新增不同語言。HeyGen 在其服務套件中添加了商業視訊翻譯，可以處理多個演講者並支援腳本編輯、長格式內容，以及特定品牌的專有名詞和語氣。

Google 也在 2023 年的 I/O 開發者大會上展示了一款通用翻譯機。就像 HeyGen 的技術一樣，可將視訊配音和口型同步成不同的語言，但目前這還只是一個概念性產品。Google 對如何推出這項實驗性技術，仍抱持謹慎態度，理由是擔心遭不當使用，或助長更多網路數位造假的可能性。

當 Google 正努力在為其翻譯軟體加上防範措施的同時，其他公司也在努力往前推進。在撰寫本文的同時，位於德拉瓦州的 Rask AI 則提供了 65 種語言的多重語音複製技術，無論使用哪種語言，都可以保留原來的聲音特徵。

這類翻譯技術等於為品牌、內容創作者、社群影響者以及教育工作者打開了全球市場，提供了增加收入的潛力。YouTube 社群創作者 Mr Beast 以其多語言策略而聞名，他聘請母語人士為他的影片配音成多種語言。2023 年，他在 11 個熱門影片上測

試了 YouTube 的內部翻譯工具，並向 YouTube 的 Creator Insider 表示，該工具"為影片帶來了極大的提升"。影音創作者現在可以只翻譯一種語言的內容即可，不再需要操作多種語言管道。另一位線上創作者 Adam Waheed 告訴《財星》雜誌，透過 AI 翻譯，他預期受眾人數將增加兩倍。

Spotify 目前也正在為 Podcast 試行 AI 翻譯，提供比配音更真實的多語言體驗。現在可到 Steven Bartlett 和 Lex Fridman 等人的精選 Podcast 內容上找到，未來會持續增加。

值得關注的原因：
對於公司和品牌來說，AI 翻譯功能將迎來全球參與的新時代，人們將能自由地與世界各地的任何人交談，而無需繁瑣的翻譯過程。未來翻譯軟體勢必會更即時運作，對客戶服務、教育、培訓，帶來更多機會。

VML

18

超級充電站

新世代EV充電站，將充電瑣事轉化成娛樂機會。

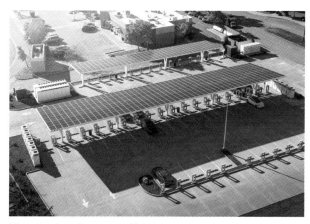

↑ Supercharging station, courtesy of Tesla, Inc

電動車 (EV) 越來越普及，美國勞工統計局引述標準普爾全球行動公司的研究顯示，2030 年美國電動車銷量，可能達到整體乘用車市場的 40-50%。

隨著電動車數量的增加，意味著大眾對電動車充電站的需求也跟著提升，一般來說充電至少需要 30 分鐘才能充滿電，許多公司正在著手計劃，將這段等待時間轉化為休閒和娛樂的商機。

特斯拉目前正在西好萊塢開發一個 24 小時超級充電站，配有 32 個充電樁和一個"20 世紀 50 年代風格的餐廳和 drive-in 汽車影院"。 在馬斯克最近發布的推文中，將其描述為「當 Grease 遇見 The Jetsons 的超級充電站」。

從娛樂的角度來看，迪士尼已經為一種全新的車內娛樂系統專利申請，根據 Blog Mickey 形容，它將是一個"身歷其境的娛樂艙"，人們可以將他們的電動車開進去，"在等待車輛充電的同時，人們將全面被沈浸式的娛樂視聽饗宴所包圍。" 根據迪士尼專利申請裡的描述，人們將身歷其境宛如置身於非洲大草原，而不僅僅是從螢幕上觀看它。

2023 年 9 月，Shell 宣佈在中國深圳開設最大的電動車充電站，擁有 258 個快速充電樁。 該空間設有「Shell 精選便利零售店、Shell 咖啡廳、自動販賣機和司機休息室。」 同時，Shell 還在武漢開設了盤龍綜合能源站。 充電站提供電動車充電以及汽油、柴油和氫氣等能源—此綜合能源站也含括便利商店、餐廳和司機休息室。

值得關注的原因：
在電動車市場將持續成長的預期下，全新的使用情境即將誕生，比如更長的充電時間，正在取代以往傳統加油站的快速加油。隨著電動車製造商、娛樂品牌和能源公司都在思考如何放大這種體驗，未來全新型態，結合娛樂和休閒的新型態充電體驗，值得你我持續關注。

結合娛樂和休閒的新型態充電體驗，
值得你我持續關注。

↑ Supercharging station, courtesy of Tesla, Inc

VML

共生科技

我們與科技的關係將更加真人化。

VML

↑ Pi chatbot from Inflection AI

Alphabet 和 Google 首席執行官 Sundar Pichai 曾表示：「我一直認為科技應該主動適應人類，而不是反過來。」 隨著 AI 的能力不斷增強，這樣想法正在逐漸轉變成現實。現在我們可以使用簡單的手勢和自然的對話跟科技溝通，而不是透過複雜的流程和命令。科技正在講我們的語言。

Pi 是 Inflection AI 公司開發的個人陪伴型聊天機器人，該公司是由曾任職於 DeepMind 的科技新創家，Mustafa Suleyman 所領導的新創公司。Pi 適用於九種不同平台，包括傳統電話在內，是一個積極參與對話的機器人，透過來回的對話並提出問題以建立深刻的理解。根據其創始人的說法，在 2023 年 5 月 2 日 Pi 上市推出後的 100 天內，Pi 聊天機器人已經交換了超過十億條消息。

個性化是新型聊天機器人 Grok 所具備的鮮明特徵，它是由伊隆 . 馬斯克 (Elon Musk) 新創公司 xAI 所開發，目前提供給社群平台 X 的用戶使用。Grok 被設計成具有「智慧中帶點叛逆」的個性。

歸功於新型態的大型語言模型，現在只要透過一個新語音指令「Alexa，讓我們聊聊吧。」Amazon Alexa 就能夠參與更自如、來回流暢的對話。 除了追蹤對話的主線外，Alexa 還可以利用電腦視覺來識別和追蹤對話者，以收集上下文。ChatGPT Plus 還具有語音的功能，最新升級的版本提供了五種聲音的選擇。它還擁有電腦視覺的功能，能夠「看到」用戶上傳的照片或圖表，並提供上下文分析。

↑ Humane AI Pin

是否有一天，AI 甚至能知道我們在想什麼嗎？儘管德州大學奧斯汀分校的一項早期實驗成功地通過使用大型語言模型，將大腦的功能性磁振造影（fMRI）掃描數據解碼，通過匹配血流模式實現，但這項研究非常費力，並且僅在個體層面上有效。就目前而言，我們的思想是安全的。

值得關注的原因：

AI 現在能夠以更自然的方式與我們交談，產生各種交流。隨著 AI 累積越來越多的數據，我們與它們的關係將變得越來越依存共生和真人化，因為它們會根據我們的需求進行適應與調整。

VML

20
人工智慧勞動力

未來由人工智慧驅動的勞動力已經存在。

VML

對於 AI 的風險和潛力的討論是 2023 年熱門討論話題,其中對全球勞動力的影響成為主要焦點。

在 2023 年 11 月在英國布萊切利公園舉行的首屆全球 AI 高峰會上,Elon Musk 將 AI 稱為「歷史上最具破壞性的力量」,並頗具爭議地補充道:「將來會有一個時刻,人們不再需要工作——你依然可能擁有一份工作,僅只為了想從中獲得個人成就感;除此之外,AI 將接手人類的一切工作。」 馬斯克的推測觀點並非所有人都認同,英國首相 Rishi Sunak 則強調:「AI 不僅僅是自動化和取代人們的工作。更好看待它的方式是作為一個輔助人類的助手。」

顯而易見的是,這項技術已經對全球勞動力產生了顯著的影響。世界經濟論壇 (WEF) 的「2023 年未來就業報告」顯示,未來五年內全球將因人工智慧而創造 6,900 萬個新工作,而這些職位已經開始被填補。

截至 2023 年 10 月,在 Indeed 職缺搜尋引擎上,有超過 3,750 個職位列表,專門招聘 AI 溝通工程師。這些 AI 溝通工程師的專業是撰寫必要的指示,以引導出人工智慧最佳的回應。發展 AI 所面臨的道德問題,也催生了對 AI 倫理學家的需求,他們的任務確保 AI 整合的設計符合全體人類的利益,而 AI 稽查人員與內容審核人員則主要防範偏見和擴散虛假信息。

儘管對 AI 了解深刻的人在技術領域也有很多工作機會,但根據蘇納克所提到的 AI 共同操作 (copilot) 的方式,現有的工作正在被精簡化,甚至高效。通信技術公司 Twilio 使用 Open AI 的

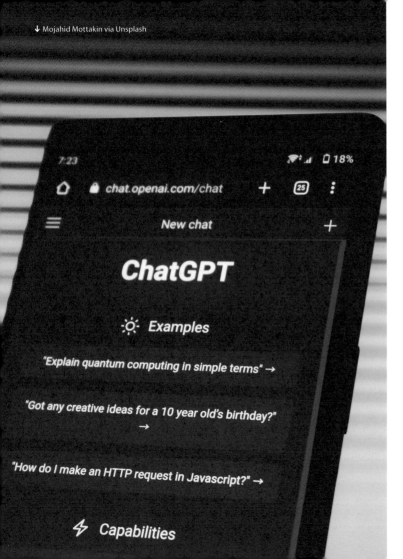

GPT-4 創建了一個工具，自動化了填寫提案請求（RFP）表格的任務。RFP Genie 在幾分鐘內完成了兩名銷售人員需要花數周才能完成的工作，使 AI 能夠轉向從事更具技能、創意或情感細膩性的任務。

為這份報告進行的研究發現，壓倒性多數（69%）表示他們對於技術淘汰工作不擔心，而 53% 的人表示他們已經在工作中使用生成式 AI 工具進行研究。根據世界經濟論壇（WEF）的預測，由機器完成的工作任務比例將從 2022 年的 34% 上升到 2027 年的 43%，現在正在出現保護人類勞動力的措施。結束美國編劇工會（WGA）編劇罷工的協議，包含確保人類工作者仍然掌握 AI 的修訂條款，而卡普吉米尼創意機構 The Works 則創建了「信任標誌」來區分由人類創意工作者完成的工作。

值得關注的原因：
隨著 AI 的不斷演進並在各個行業中應用，傳統工作正在經歷一場革命，需要新的技能並重新塑造職業生涯。未來的勞動力將與智能機器無縫協作，品牌和員工應為一個由 AI 驅動的未來做好準備（（請參閱第 93 章〈AI 世代〉）。

VML

旅遊&觀光

21

地下款待

飯店和SPA中心在尋找寧靜的過程中發現了隱藏的深處。

↑ Claridge's Spa, UK, courtesy of Andre Fu Studio

VML

↑ Subterranean spa by Studio Seilern Architects, Lithuania. Photography by Roland Halbe

2023 年夏天，Zedwell 在倫敦開設了一家地下飯店。在睡眠專家的幫助下，房間被設計成＂地下繭＂，並排除所有叼擾。「房間里沒有窗戶、電視或任何 3C 產品，取而代之的是降噪牆和依日夜變化的光源，以"打造終極庇護所"，"幫助深度休息和恢復"」Zedwell 說。

於 2023 年 4 月澳洲維多利亞州的 Sorrento 洲際飯店開設了地下 Spa 中心和療養浴場，設有鹽療室、冷水池和地熱溫泉。Woods Bagot 建築事務所的專案首席建築師 Nik Karalis 說：「健康與飯店之間的關聯是根深蒂固的。 飯店以及飯店未問世前，建立於古代貿易路線上的商隊驛站、修道院和客棧—作為避難和恢復健康的場所已有悠久的歷史。」

位於倫敦市中心的 The Londoner，延伸至地下八層，自稱是英國第一家"冰山飯店"。地下空間包含宴會廳、電影院、游泳池和 SPA 中心。

倫敦的 Claridge's hotel 在 2022 年推出了地下養身中心。 在熱門的的旅遊勝地挖掘了五層樓深的空間，為會去 Spa 中心的客人於喧囂的城市地底深處提供空間及服務。這個佔地 650 平方公尺的空間包含一間蒸氣室、游泳池、桑拿房和七間水療室。

以英國為總部的建築事務所 Studio Seilern Architects 最近在立陶宛維爾紐斯的 Boksto 6 複合式大樓中蓋了一個地下 SPA 中心。地下 SPA 中心和游泳池即建立在聯合國教科文組織 (UNESCO) 保護遺址廣闊的磚砌地窖中，為的是讓人感到幽靜。

值得關注的原因：
飯店和 Spa 中心正在地下深處為客人提供一個包羅萬象的避難所，遠離地面上的喧囂與繁忙。

22

超旅行

自我提升和肯定生命的時刻是新的旅行需求。

VML

↑ Black Tomato guests visit Poor Knights Islands, NZ. Photography by Miles Holden, courtesy of Black Tomato

旅遊公司 Black Tomato 的最新體驗 " See You in the Moment（相會的時刻）" 已於 2023 年底亮相，其宗旨是幫助你和你的旅伴 – 無論是朋友還是家人（或兩者），一起品味世界。有意義地、無縫地、難以忘懷地。不要僅僅聚集朋友在沙灘上躺著。

五種相會的時刻之一的 The Challenge，包括前往阿根廷米特雷半島的火地島探險的行程，「在那裡，旅客們將在大西洋、太平洋和南極海交匯處浪擊聲的背景下，一起挑戰極限體能。」Black Tomato 說。在旅行的行程中，遊客可以選擇乘坐符合永續發展動力的遊艇前往紐西蘭的普爾奈茨群島，「尋找一些世界上最美的潛水點。」

Black Tomato 的聯合創始人 Tom Marchant 告訴 VML 智庫：「這些體驗的想法源自於一個事實：疫情後，人們經歷過了一種「迫切渴望聯繫」的感受，同時 「很想做一些真正難忘的事情，不僅僅是與他人在一起享受當下，且要真正可以回憶真正能品味的事情，這也許會成為想再重複幾次的催化劑。」

Marchant 很清楚，這種體驗會帶來超時刻。他表示：「我認為，最重要的是能夠暫停下來，真正擁抱那一刻 – 真實地存在，並與生活中發生的其他一切斷開聯繫。 可以是三個小時，也可以是三天。但在那段時間裡，與那些人在一起，就是要讓其他一切都消失，真正地品味那一刻，然後感到滿足─充滿喜悅、啟發和感激。」

Black Tomato 的 Bring it Back 也以類似的概念規劃旅遊，即在規劃客戶的旅遊行程時，要有針對問題帶回答案的想法。這可能意味著去摩洛哥旅行啟發創造思維，或者去外蒙古旅行以發現家庭關系的新視角。 Marchant 說：「我們的想法是以旅行為載體，走出去並接觸這些社區，了解他們是如何對待家庭、事業或者愛情的。提供你另一種視角。然後把這些帶回家，融入你的日常生活。」

26% 的 Z 世代和千禧世代表示，他們選擇旅遊目的地的原因是為了深入自我發現，而 32% 表示是為了個人成長和發展。

↑ Black Tomato guests visit Poor Knights Islands, NZ. Photography by Miles Holden, courtesy of Black Tomato

值得關注的原因：

旅遊者熱衷於將自身投入到真正具有變革性的體驗中，這超越當前旅行的種種體驗將對他們的生活產生影響。正如 Black Tomato 的 Marchant 所指出：「我認為人與生俱來的天性就是好奇心。」

23

沉浸式主題樂園

主題樂園進行了升級，被重新設計為一個全方位的體驗。

VML

2024 年春季，日本行銷娛樂公司 Katana Inc. 將在東京台場開設 Immersive Fort Tokyo，稱之為「全球首座沉浸式主題樂園」。在這個佔地 3 萬平方米的樂園中共有 12 個遊樂設施、6 間商店和餐廳。

該公司表示，Immersive Fort Tokyo 將展出「電影、動畫和遊戲中出現的戲劇性場景」。

Katana 的首席執行長 Tsuyoshi Morioka 在 2023 年 10 月公司的新聞發佈會上向《日本時報》表示「沉浸式設施使每個人能夠更深入去參與體驗，因此體驗的感受是完全不同的。」 並舉例，遊客會在各個場景中成為「殺人事件的唯一目擊者」或是「深陷在槍戰中，必須立刻採取行動」，這些體驗將在各種場景中展開，有緊張刺激的大規模沉浸式劇場、駭人的沉浸式恐怖體驗以及突然在餐廳展開的劇場秀等等。

毫無疑問地，這些體驗的起源是 TeamLab 的互動式數位博物館。藝術團隊表示，其理念聚焦於「探索自我、世界以及新形式感知間的關係」，最新展覽包括 TeamLab 的 Future Park（未來園），地點位在 DFS 旗下沖繩 T Galleria 內，於 2023 年 12 月開幕。該公司將此空間描述為「一個以共同創造為概念的教育企劃，是一個能夠享受與他人一同自由地創建世界的遊樂園。」沖繩展覽館展示 8 項針對兒童和成人的互動式裝置藝術作品。

Phantom Peak（魅影峰）是倫敦的一個沉浸式主題樂園，它自稱「部分是密室逃脫，部分是沉浸式劇院，部分是電玩遊戲的現實生活版。」在這個西部風格、蒸汽龐克風格的主題樂園中，

每位賓客都扮演「探險家和偵探」的角色，解開謎團，與當地人討價還價，並捕捉鴨嘴獸。Phantom Peak 於 2022 年開業後，共同創始人 Nick Moran 告訴倫敦刊物《Wharf Life》：「當你來到 Phantom Peak 時，你基本上是來到了一款現實生活及開放世界中的角色扮演電玩遊戲。」他指出「這不像在沉浸式劇院裡，你搞不清楚自己在做什麼，在這裡你會被引導完成這些體驗。」

根據 Blooloop 報導，Phantom Peak 的共同創辦人目前正在探索將體驗擴展到美國，可能的地點有芝加哥、亞特蘭大、丹佛、達拉斯和舊金山。

值得關注的原因：

有 75% 的美國、英國和中國人表示，他們喜歡透過故事和解說深入探索異國世界，因此越來越多到主題樂園的遊客期待的是一段旅程，而不僅僅是刺激而已。無論是透過虛擬實境或是表演和故事傳遞，這些期望正在推動主題樂園體驗邁向下一個階段。

↑ Immersive Fort Tokyo visualization
↑↑ Phantom Peak, UK

24

覓食之旅

旅人們開始上山下海以尋求獨特的料理體驗。

↑ Glen Dye School of Wild Wellness & Bushcraft, Scotland

在美國太平洋西北地區經歷了異常潮濕的冬季後,《紐約時報》在 2023 年 2 月以採蘑菇的新手們為對象,出版了一份入門刊物。裡頭寫到「今年冬天的蘑菇長得非常茂盛,就跟有興趣去林地裡採蘑菇的人數大增一樣,兩種情況非常吻合,」並說「採蘑菇非常有趣,也是一個很好的理由讓人計劃旅行。」

世界各地也紛紛利用人們對覓食行程日益增長的興趣來拓展旅遊觀光。澳洲一間五星級飯店 Cappella Sydney 在 2023 年獲頒《國家地理 · 旅行者雜誌》城市之星類最佳酒店獎

(National Geographic Traveler Hotel Awards - the City Star category)，該飯店推出一項旅遊行程讓客人們可以在原住民嚮導的帶領下尋找當地特有的食物。

蘇格蘭有間新學校，專門教授野外健康與叢林生存技能。遊客們可以參加一個 3 小時的森林採集之旅，並在導遊的帶領下學習如何識別和準備可食用的植物。

豪華旅行社 Black Tomato 提供多種的覓食小旅行，包括可以在挪威羅弗敦群島搭乘 40 英尺長的傳統縱帆船去捕魚並清洗、準備鱈魚料理；以及可以在義大利參加一場由當地人帶路的松露尋覓之旅。這些行程都只需要花費一個下午的時光。

Airbnb 也有覓食體驗，其中包含了加州頗受歡迎的採海藻之旅。這個 90 分鐘的行程提供基礎的海洋藻類學和永續捕撈技術教學，並在行程尾聲，讓參加者可以享用一碗用他們新鮮採摘的海藻所製成的傳統日式拉麵。

值得關注的原因：
覓食旅遊是「教育探險」浪潮中的一個最新案例，我們可以看到旅客們希望透過豐富的行程得到更有深度的體驗和知識學習。Bellini Travel 的老闆 Emily Fitzroy 告訴《紐約時報》：「度假時也能學習料理相關技能這樣的需求明顯增加，客人們希望旅行結束回家時是有新知收穫的。」

今年冬天的蘑菇
長得非常茂盛，
就跟有興趣去林地裡
採蘑菇的人數大增一樣，
兩種情況非常吻合，
採蘑菇非常有趣，
也是一個很好的理由
讓人計劃旅行。

紐約時報

VML

↑ Glen Dye School of Wild Wellness & Bushcraft, Scotland

25

VVIP 超貴賓室

金字塔頂端旅客重振了超級專屬貴賓室需求。

溫莎套房是希斯洛機場 VIP 服務之一,是英國王室、名流和多位世界級領袖出國搭乘飛機的出發地。 使用貴賓室是希斯洛黑級服務 (Heathrow's Black service) 的一部分,三人的費用從 3,025 英鎊起。在 2023 年,希斯洛機場零售部總監 Fraser Brown 告訴英國精品官方組織 Walpole,此服務的需求正在上升,2022 年曾使用過溫莎套房的客人數量已創下歷史新高。客人可以享有往返貴賓室的私人司機服務,享用米其林級廚師 Jason Atherton 設計的餐點並由私人管家服務,如果客人有需求,還能享有私人購物專員隨時為他們提供建議。

美國公司 PS 自我期許是 "為洛杉磯國際機場和亞特蘭大機場商務航班提供服務的私人豪華候機航廈,為商務乘客提供輕鬆、私密和安全的私人飛行體驗。"這項服務在洛杉磯國際機場和亞特蘭大機場大受歡迎,德克薩斯州達拉斯機場和佛羅里達州邁阿密機場也將於 2024 年增設服務據點。如果沒有會籍,在 PS 預訂一次的私人套房的費用為 4,850 美元。而會員年費為 4,850 美元,擁有會籍預定同一間套房的費用則為 3,550 美元。

澳洲廣播公司 (ABC) 將僅提供受邀制服務的澳航總裁貴賓室 (Qantas Chairman's Lounge) 定義為 "只有政治家、法官、商界重要人物或一線明星才能使用。據 Head for Points 報導,英國航空公司的行政俱樂部貴賓卡 (也被稱為 " 黑卡 ") 只向那些 "每年在英國航空公司花費至少 200 萬英鎊旅行預算" 的人發出邀請。

VML

對於當今的
超級富豪來說，
奢華的最高境界
往往不是能見度，
而是盡可能
不受干擾地、私密地
穿梭在世界各地。

VML

以色列特拉維夫機場的 Fattal Terminal 航廈是一個私人機場服務的專用航廈，提供登機、護照檢查和安檢服務，旅客可以在這裡享受私人空間或會客室休息、茶點和免稅購物，並由私人司機專車接送至班機。這項服務共計 490 美元起。

值得關注的原因：

對於當今的超級富豪來說，奢華的最高境界往往不是能見度，而是盡可能不受干擾地、私密地穿梭在世界各地。從專屬貴賓室到私人航廈，這些高檔的機場服務體驗正迎合了這些旅客的期望，在喧鬧的民航機場中提供了專用的、低調的空間，但價格絕對不菲。

26

平流層之旅

乘坐氣球能很快將把遊客帶到太空邊緣。

↑ Céleste from Zephalto

↑ Capsule prototype from Halo Space

十年內，低碳氣球飛行將出現，將先驅的旅行者帶到平流層，並為我們的地球提供與眾不同的視野。

Céleste 是一個由巨型高空氣球提供動力的豪華加壓艙，它將提供低碳的平流層上升之旅。 這艘時尚的環保飛船由著名建築師 Joseph Dirand 為法國太空旅行新創公司 Zephalto 設計，在三個豪華的「繭」中為六名旅行者提供了空間。 從 2025 年起，每人花費 12 萬歐元，乘客將從 Zephalto 的法國太空發射基地出發，開始為期 6 小時的溫馨定制之旅。菜單上有精美的餐飲和特別精選的葡萄酒，乘客可以在 25 公里高空的太空邊緣以令人驚嘆的視角觀察地球。該公司表示，在這裡，乘客們將可以欣賞地球的曲線、藍色光暈和其他的星星。

Céleste 不會是天際中唯一的氣球。西班牙近太空新創公司

Halo Space 已在美國加州莫哈韋沙漠成功完成第二輪試飛，並希望在 2025 年開始商業飛行。該公司計劃到 2029 年，其零排放氣球每年可搭載 3000 名乘客。

總部位於佛羅里達州的 Space Perspective 聲稱將提供世界上唯一的碳中性太空船。它的海王星號太空船中的太空艙帶有在海上降落的驚喜。該公司正在與汽車品牌 Mercedes-Maybach 合作，提供真正的豪華體驗，包括太空船內的餐點和雞尾酒。總部位於亞利桑那州的 World View 建議為其公司的氣球選擇世界七大奇蹟的位置作為發射地點，這樣乘客從一開始就可以欣賞到令人驚嘆的景色，包括埃及吉薩金字塔和中國長城。其公司已經售罄了 2024 年第一年運營位在大峽谷的發射點門票。

然而，首飛的可能是日本初創企業 Iwaya Giken，該公司計劃在 2024 年 3 月推出其由氦氣球提供動力的商業飛行。最初的四小時之旅價格為 2400 萬日元，但公司希望通過"大眾化太空"的計劃降低價格。

值得關注的原因：
平流層旅行提供了真正的巔峰體驗，提供了一個機會，讓人在體驗僅存未被觸及的地方的同時，創造歷史。旅行者將有機會親身體驗著名的俯瞰效應——太空人在遠離地球時所感受到的對地球之美和脆弱時的認知轉變。

27

神經包容旅行

一項旨在讓旅行對神經多樣性 (neurodiverse) 個體
更有價值的運動。

↑ Hiking at Usery Mountain, courtesy Visit Mesa

據估計，世界上有 15% 的人口經歷了某種形式的神經多樣性（neurodiverse），因此，從航空公司到旅行社，再到整個城市，各組織都致力於為神經多樣性人群提供更多便利。

亞利桑那州梅薩 (Mesa) 於 2019 年通過美國國際資格認證和繼續教育標準 (International Board of Credentialing and Continuing Education Standards) 及自閉症旅行委員會成為世界上第一個獲得自閉症認證的城市。Autism Travel 將認證自閉症中心定義為至少 80% 的員工在自閉症領域接受過嚴格培訓、設備齊全並獲得認證的設施或組織。據英國廣播公司報道，除了梅薩，阿聯酋杜拜；加州棕櫚泉；和俄亥俄州托萊多目前正在努力獲得認證，而美國加州維塞利亞和北卡羅來納州海波因特都已成為自閉症認證目的地。

VML

旅行社還為神經多樣性的旅客客製化旅行。2023 年，美國旅遊公司 Explorateur Journeys 宣布推出 Neuro Tripping（感性之旅）服務，為神經多樣性人士提供「客製化旅遊」。該公司表示，其「新鮮而獨特的規劃」可以幫助神經多樣性的人避免常見的旅行痛點，例如人群擁擠和排隊；不確定的旅行計劃；長時間旅行；和過度刺激的地點。

航空公司也努力更加關注神經多元化旅客的體驗。2023 年 10 月，阿酋航空宣布與杜拜國際機場合作，「改善神經衰弱乘客的旅行體驗」。作為其中的一部分，該航空公司正在促進所謂的"旅行彩排"，這樣，精神衰弱者就可以在沒有實際旅行壓力的情況下練習旅行了。

在美國，微風航空 (Breeze Airways) 於 2022 年成為首家獲得美國組織 Autism Double-Checked 認證的包容自閉症的航空公司。作為認證的一部分，這家廉價航空公司為其面向客戶的員工制定了培訓計畫工作人員如何為自閉症患者提供「安全、快樂的旅行體驗」。該計劃由 Autism Double-Checked 開發，為空服員提供「識別和緩解航空旅行壓力」的培訓。

值得關注的原因：
隨著神經多樣性診斷的增加—美國疾病管制與預防中心在 2023 年報告稱，每 36 名兒童中就有 1 名患有自閉症，而 2021 年這一比例為 44 名—旅遊業正在做出改變，以確保未來能更好地為客戶服務。

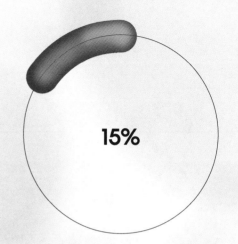

15%

據估計，世界上有 15% 的人口經歷了某種形式的神經多樣性。

VML

28

三大旅遊勝地

↑ Half-timbered houses in Bornholm, Denmark, courtesy of Destination Bornholm

1.丹麥博恩霍爾姆島（BORNHOLM, DENMARK）

由於氣溫上升和野火，南歐的夏季變得越來越不可預測，更不用說一些過度擁擠的熱門目的地的，斯堪地納維亞半島被視為理想的歐洲替代目的地。

該地區眾多迷人的目的地之一是波羅的海的丹麥島嶼博恩霍爾姆 (Bornholm)，據《孤獨星球 Lonely Planet》描述，其童話般的景觀橫跨「岩石懸崖、茂密的森林和潔白的海灘」。 其中最吸引人的地方是米其林二星的 Kadeau 餐廳，該餐廳於夏季在島上營業，其簡約的木質外牆的空間可將波羅的海的美景盡收眼底。島上風景如畫的城鎮是另一個迷人之處。 島上的主要城鎮倫訥 (Rønne) 匯集了許多以設計為主題的商店，而斯瓦內克 (Svaneke) 是一個漁村，以其色彩繽紛的半木結構房屋而聞名。

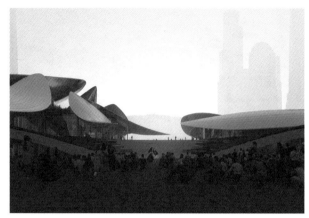

↑ → Anji Culture and Art Center, courtesy of MAD Architects

2.中國安吉(ANJI, CHINA)

位於中國東部的安吉是中國第一個生態縣,也是 2000 年電影《臥虎藏龍》的拍攝地,被 Scott Dunn 旅遊公司描述為「神奇的生態度假勝地」。

一些新的開發項目也鞏固了該地區作為旅遊目的地的地位。由北京 MAD 建築事務所設計的安吉文化藝術中心預計將於 2025 年開幕。該中心佔地 149,000 平方公尺,將包括大劇院、會議中心、休閒中心、體育中心、青少年活動中心、藝術教育中心。瑞士水療品牌 Clinique La Prairie 將與中國三竺集團合作,並在安吉開設療養度假村。Clinique La Prairie 執行長 Simone Gibertoni 告訴 Spa Business,該度假村坐落在完美的環境中,並為我們的客人提供寧靜體驗的位置"

↑ Our Habitas Atacama, Chile, courtesy of Habitas

VML

3.智利阿塔卡馬沙漠 (ATACAMA DESERT, CHILE)

為了應對不斷變化的氣候，消費者越來越多地改變他們的生活和旅行方式（請參閱第 3 章〈氣候適應生活〉）。這促使人們努力讓旅行者看到乾燥氣候更鮮明的美感。Desert Rock 開發案將於 2024 年開放，坐落在沙烏地阿拉伯的花崗岩山脈中，成為該國「引人注目的沙漠景觀」的一大特色。

智利的阿塔卡馬沙漠以其令人驚嘆的沙漠環境和無光害天空的地位吸引著遊客——它的高海拔、低濕度和極少光污染提供了理想的觀星環境。該地區是多個天文學項目的所在地。高級度假村的不斷開放，讓業餘天文學家對該地區的參觀變得更加誘人。 其中包括在聖佩德羅阿塔卡馬的度假村，於 2023 年 8 月開幕。度假村舒適奢華的大地色調客房均配有當地紡織品。 客人可以參加健行、騎自行車、登山、滑翔傘和觀星等活動，Our Habitas 將其描述為「從鹽灘到火星般的山谷，如同世外桃源的景觀」。

29

展廳留宿

時尚愛好者的睡衣派對因展廳開放供過夜而充滿想像。

↑ House of Sunny in partnership with Airbnb. Photography by Alix McIntosh

獨立時尚品牌 House of Sunny 與 Airbnb 合作，並邀請兩位賓客在其展廳過夜。2023 年 9 月，兩位客人有機會完全沉浸在在倫敦東部的 Hackney 設計師 Sunny Williams 的奇思妙想和充滿活力的世界中。

Williams 說到：「House of Sunny 的設計和精神始終受到文化、建築、室內裝飾以及我們社區對旅行、家居和美學的熱愛的交叉啟發」。 他將展廳視為自己的家，並利用 Airbnb 將時尚與熱情好客融為一體，為客人提供更親密的機會，成為 House of Sunny 的一員。過夜住宿活動包括在夢想衣櫃中試穿 House

↑ House of Sunny in partnership with Airbnb. Photography by Alix McIntosh

↑ DJ Khaled's room on Airbnb. Photography by Erick Hercules

of Sunny 最新系列的機會,以及和主持人一起參觀展廳的機會。

今年 2023 年威尼斯電影節期間,時尚顧問 Giorgia Viola 將她的陳列室安置在今年稍早開幕的五星級 Nolinski Venezia 飯店內,這是一次完美的合作;在接受《富比士》採訪時,Viola 描述了高級時裝與高端飯店服務之間的共生關係:「打造豪華飯店的體驗與製作訂製高級禮服的原則如出一轍:始終注意每一個細微差異,顏色的變化,布料的選擇,甚至是最微小的細節。」

2022 年 12 月,DJ Khaled 在 Airbnb 上提供了一次獨特的

住宿體驗,讓粉絲們可以睡在他在邁阿密舒適的運動鞋櫃中。球鞋愛好者可以在他獨特的運動鞋系列中入睡,其中還包括 Jordan 3 Grateful 和 Jordan 8 Oregon PE。

值得關注的原因:
時尚與熱情好客完美融合,為客人提供獨特時尚的展廳住宿體驗。

30

類比旅行

隨著人們在度假時放棄智能科技，旅行體驗就會加深感受。

↑ Ulko-Tammio, Finland. Photography by Annika Ruohonen

芬蘭的一個島嶼在 2023 年夏季宣稱成為第一個無手機的旅遊目的地。位於芬蘭東部芬蘭灣國家公園的烏爾科 - 塔米歐島（Ulko-Tammio）發起了一場運動，鼓勵遊客以不使用電子設備的方式，更好地擁抱大自然。Kotka-Hamina 島嶼旅遊專家 Mats Selin 表示：「我們希望敦促度假者關閉電子設備，真正停下來享受這些島嶼的生活。」

Skyscanner 在 2023 年 10 月發布《2024 年旅行趨勢》報告，發現 Z 世代已經厭倦了不斷的社交媒體發文，相反，他們選擇使用傳統的技術來記錄他們的旅行。報告顯示，在英國的 18 至 24 歲人群中，有 16% 的人在度假時攜帶拍立得相機，13% 攜帶攝影機，11% 攜帶 35mm 底片相機。這與這一世代在旅行時選擇"盧德模式"（請參閱第 8 章〈盧德模式〉）一致。

VML

↑ Ulko-Tammio, Finland. Photography by Annika Ruohonen

同樣在英國，無網（Unplugged）的自然小屋鼓勵遊客在大自然中充電。這些沒有無線網路的區域距離倫敦和曼徹斯特等主要城市僅一小時路程，客人抵達時需要將他們的電子設備鎖在一旁，整整三天。有一項有關 72 小時斷網的研究──「三天效應」的研究顯示，連續三天或更長時間沉浸在大自然中可以降低壓力並改善認知功能。

值得關注的原因：

VML 智庫的一項調查詢問了世界各地的人們旅行的個人原因，發現最重要的答案是純粹的快樂，緊隨其後的是親近大自然。這促使「類比旅行」方式的回歸，讓旅行者能夠充分融入周圍的環境。

我們希望敦促度假者關閉電子設備，真正停下來享受這些島嶼的生活。

Mats Selin,
Visit Kotka-Hamina 島嶼旅遊專家

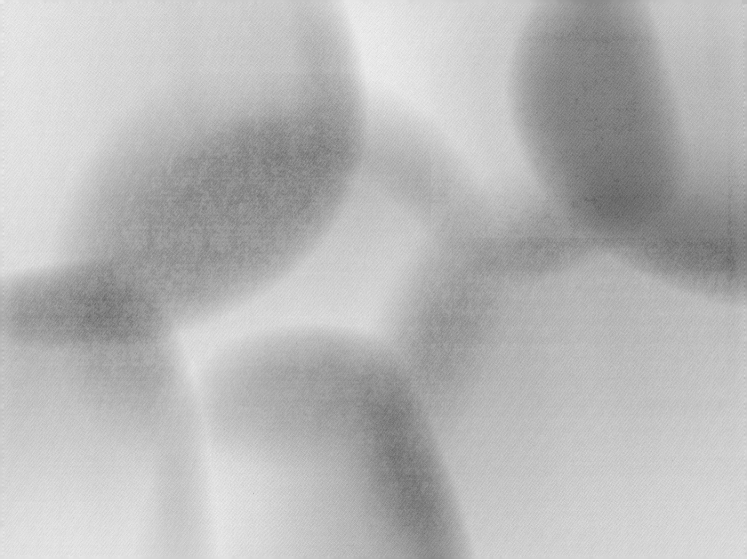

31

品牌&行銷

40

戶外廣告新貌

戶外廣告(OOH)迎來一個引人入勝、打破現實界限的轉變。

VML

↑ Burberry Lola bag (left) and BMW iX (right) by Shane Fu, courtesy of Jimmy

數位藝術家正在與現實互動,為社交媒體內容創建奇幻的動態圖形,這種新的、異想天開的流派被稱為"仿戶外"(FOOH)廣告。

在推動這種俏皮風格的藝術家中,有來自中國武漢的紐約動畫設計師 Shane Fu。 Fu 表示,他的作品融入了"數位藝術、AR/VR 設計和 3D 變幻的廣告看板"。他的作品包括為 Burberry 創作的 Lola 包的不同想像版本,其中一個巨大的、羽毛飄動的版本設在倫敦時尚街道的中央,還有一個亮片閃爍的 Lola 包似乎從寧靜的倫敦小巷中的波動金屬泡泡中浮現。在為 BMW 創作的另一件作品中,Fu 描繪了一輛 BMW iX 從一個虹彩水泡中浮現的場景。

Fu 是 Jimmy 的成員，這是一家位於紐約的街頭藝術工作室，由數位藝術家和創作者組成，旨在通過混合現實世界的影片與 3D 資產來「擴增實境」。Jimmy 的創辦人兼創意主管 Rogier Vijverberg 告訴 VML 智庫，人們正在尋求新的娛樂方式，特別是當越來越多的人不斷在手機上滑動的時候。「當你看到一些激發你想像力的東西──讓你想知道這是真實的還是虛構的，或者它具有你以前從未見過的元素──那就是停止滑動並深入探究的時刻。」

Jimmy 集體正在從品牌和觀眾中獲得越來越多的關注和正面回響。在 2023 年秋季，Jimmy 與英國珠寶品牌 Astrid & Miyu 合作，在紐約、愛丁堡和倫敦策劃了由 CGI 創建的巨大雪球。Vijverberg 表示：「人們真的喜歡這種廣告。他們喜歡它，因為它不像廣告。」他還說：「有一種驚奇的感覺。」

另一位創造出模糊現實與超現實界限的內容的藝術家Origful，這位居住在法國的美國創作者 Ian Padgham 的筆名。Padgham 是一家法國公司，也是 Jacquemus 宣傳活動的幕後推手，該活動的特色是該品牌的巨型包袋裝上輪子，在巴黎街道上疾馳而過。 Padgham 的另一項創作是為 Maybelline Lash Sensational Sky High 睫毛膏製作的社交媒體內容，其中倫敦的地鐵和巴士都戴上巨大的睫毛，被超大號的睫毛膏刷子刷過。為了推廣 Vins de Bordeaux，Padgham 創造了一個巨大的波爾多酒瓶作為穿越法國的列車，或是在塞納河上行駛的船隻。

↑ Fenty x Puma campaign by Jimmy, courtesy of Jimmy

VML

> # 人們真的喜歡這種廣告。
> # 他們喜歡它，
> # 因為它不像廣告。
>
> **Rogier Vijverberg**
> **Jimmy 創辦人兼創意主管**

VML

↑ Astrid & Miyu campaign by Jimmy, courtesy of Jimmy

雖然 Origful 的發文中，有一些評論者似乎認為這些作品是真實物品，但 Padgham 告訴《廣告周刊 Adweek》，他表示：「從來沒有試圖欺騙任何人。對我來說，CGI 是一個沙盒，它向我們展示了一切的可能性。」

值得關注的原因：

社交媒體的覆蓋力，加上數位藝術的創造力，意味著一個新的現實正在被塑造，如《改變未來的 100 件事：2023 年全球百大趨勢》中提到，這些具有創意、挑戰現實的 FOOH 創作，彰顯了這種藝術形式引起注意的潛力，能夠捕捉消費者的想像力。

32

粉絲靈感

忠實粉絲和意見領袖正激發其喜愛的品牌進行創新。

「十億人的焦點小組」：這是 Abercrombie & Fitch 的首席產品官 Corey Robinson 在接受《華爾街日報》採訪時提到 TikTok 時的說法，並補充說「每一位商人和設計師」都在使用它來指導他們的工作。這捕捉到了新的以社交媒體驅動的研發模式，品牌正在將粉絲的奇思妙想和病毒性創作者的內容轉化為寶貴的新產品開發和創新機會。

在 2023 年 1 月的一篇熱門 TikTok 貼文中，創作者 Samuel Vela (@elfisicocuenta) 抱怨哥倫比亞乳酪品牌 Alpinito 只生產 45 克的小盒裝。該品牌決定迎接挑戰，在 2023 年夏天推出了一公升裝的限量版 Alpilitro 草莓口味產品，滿足了 Z 世代消費者懷舊的渴望。該產品僅上線兩小時即銷售一空，後來更在全國上市銷售。同樣在哥倫比亞，Ramo 的巧克力蛋糕品牌 Chocoramo 響應了一場由粉絲發起的病毒性社交媒體活動，同時推出了一種新的特殊產品─Esquinas de Chocoramo，其中包含了蛋糕上那些深受喜愛的部分。

粉絲的小創意正在成為速食文化的核心，2023 年，Chipotle 響應了「凱西哥煎餅 (Keithadilla) 熱潮」，由 TikTok 美食評論家 Keith Lee 推廣的特製墨西哥煎餅為了在美國 3,200 家門店提供這道菜，培訓超過 10 萬名員工如何製作它。麥當勞也向食物黑客文化致意，推出了其 Menu Hacks 服務，該產品系列讓粉絲創作的菜單，例如哈希布朗麥鬆餅在店內出售。副總裁 Jennifer Healan 表示，美國麥當勞的行銷、品牌策略和參與度，讓「這次活動說明菜單從來都不是『我們的菜單』─是『粉絲的菜單』。」

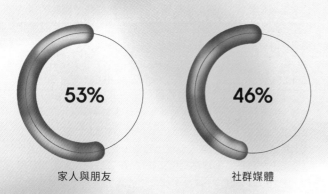

53%	46%
家人與朋友	社群媒體

社群媒體對 Z 世代的購買決策影響最大，僅次於朋友和家人。

值得關注的原因：

品牌可以利用粉絲熱情，透過基於病毒式小創意的方式在真實生活中的流行，來獎勵和取悅品牌粉絲，進而滿足消費者對自己產生創意影響力的渴望（請參閱第 39 章〈共創未來〉）。

VML

↑ TikTok creators Keith Lee and Alexis Frost are fans of Chipotle
↑↑ McDonald's Menu Hacks

33

印度品牌

印度正透過軟硬兼具的實力建設，成為新的世界強權。

↑ G20 Summit, New Delhi, September 2023, courtesy of the Government of India

2023 年對於印度無窮的成長來說是一個里程碑，因為它正式超越中國，成為世界上人口最多的國家。透過 2023 年 9 月主辦 G20 峰會，鞏固了其作為新興全球超級大國的地位，並在月球和太陽探測任務中強調其作為新太空競賽中的主要參與者的資格。

而印度才剛開始。安永（EY）預測到 2027 年，印度將成為全球第三大經濟體，同時正在著手實現在科技和創新方面的領導地位。印度政府正在從頭開始建立一個與台灣相匹敵的半導體生態系統，而 Nvidia 的首席執行官黃仁勳在宣布與印度兩大最大企業 Reliance Industries 和塔塔集團合作的會議上表示，印度將成為「全球最大的人工智慧市場之一」。諸如蘋果、三星、起亞、波音、西門子、特斯拉和東芝等眾多其他領先的全球公司正在充分利用印度的製造和技術能力。而貝恩公司預測，印度國

VML

內的精品市場將在 2030 年之前「擴大到今天的 3.5 倍大小」，Gucci、Cartier 和 Louis Vuitton 等品牌也正在加強在印度市場的投入。

印度的潛在軟實力也在增長。倫敦設計博物館的 Offbeat Sari 展覽在英國受到了熱烈歡迎，寶萊塢一線明星阿麗亞·布哈特 (Alia Bhatt)、迪皮卡·帕度柯妮 (Deepika Padukone) 和阿西婭·謝蒂 (Athiya Shetty) 最近與 Gucci、Louis Vuitton 和 Laneige 簽約。Sabyasachi Calcutta 和 Forest Essentials 等印度品牌也透過在美國和英國開設零售店而在世界各地留下了自己的印記。

VML 印度的執行長 Babita Baruah 表示，「多種因素的匯集解釋了印度品牌的崛起：“經濟增長雖然是進步的重要標誌，但人才、技術和基層創新的結合正在為印度創造一個更大的改變；這是一種積極的時代精神，使這不僅僅是一個'時刻'，而且轉化為一個構造性的「運動」。」

值得關注的原因：

2023 年 9 月，黃仁勳告訴媒體，這是「印度的時刻」。隨著其人口、國內市場和技術實力繼續快速增長，印度正在迅速成為一個全球政治、經濟和文化強權。這使得品牌、制造商和消費者無法忽視這個市場。

↑ Guler sari by Raw Mango at The Offbeat Sari exhibition, UK. Photography by Ritika Shah

↑ The Offbeat Sari exhibition, UK. ©Andy Stagg

新平台讓創作者能夠建立自己的店面,以內容、故事講述和個性的混合吸引購物者,同時為品牌和零售商提供一個新的發現渠道。

「今天的線上購物缺乏靈感,而且激勵措施未能對齊。」Bond 的共同創辦人 Maddie Raedts 說。Bond 是一個以內容優先、由創作者領導的社群商務體驗,以發現和個性化為中心。「我們正在創造明天的社群購物體驗。」Raedts 告訴 VML 智庫。

透過 Bond 的平台,創作者可以策劃數位精品店、組裝精心挑選的系列並舉辦直播。 該平台上註冊的品牌包括 Bally、Altuzarra 和 Re/Done,而其多樣化的創作者陣容擁有超過 3500 萬的聽眾。

美國新創企業 Flagship 於 2023 年 2 月推出了專為創作者打造的現成店面,提供機會讓創作者推廣並賺取來自 100 個品牌合作夥伴產品的佣金。品牌通過 Shopify 帳戶註冊,選擇他們想要合作的創作者,並根據銷售簽訂收入分潤協議。品牌負責庫存和履行物流,創作者則專注於靈感的創作。在這個方面還有更多類似的平台,如澳洲的 Pedlar,以及美國的 Canal for Creators 和 Emcee Studios。

雖然創作者已經在社交媒體上推廣品牌一段時間,但過程一直都不夠順暢。 這些新平台可望整合互利的商業模式。 Raedts 表示,品牌的好處很多,包括「建立合作夥伴關係、管理完全自動化的產品示範 / 贈品、分析以及一個新的銷售渠道」的工具。對於創作者來說,這些平台承諾更好的收入潛力和更可靠的商

34

創作者到消費者 (C2C)

品牌的新門路－創作者。

VML

↑ Bond

業模式。對於消費者來說,他們可以從人們那裡購買產品,而不是搜尋產品,它提供了故事講述和人與人之間的連接。

主要零售商也在尋找將創作者和內容放在首位的方法,儘管這與他們自己的產品有關。效仿沃爾瑪的做法,美國零售巨頭 Target 在 2023 年假期期間推出由網紅主導的快閃店,推出後的幾週內就有 300 多名創作者開設店面。而在 2023 年 5 月,電商巨頭 Amazon 向美國用戶推出了其新的創作者平台 Inspire。

現在我們看到這種趨勢已經從零售業擴展到其他類別。新創公司 Wandr 邀請旅遊意見領袖為超過 100 萬家酒店創建屬於自己的訂房介面。

值得關注的原因:

品牌可以依賴意見領袖的吸引力,以個性、故事講述和增強的探索能力吸引顧客。這一趨勢也符合年輕一代對同儕推薦的偏好:23% 的 Z 世代和千禧世代已經表示他們對直接透過網紅名人介紹而購買更感興趣。

VML

35

多巴胺包裝

品牌正在重新設計其包裝和標識，以注入多巴胺，
一種「感覺快樂」的激素。

VML

Jell-O 在十年來的首次品牌重塑中，於 2023 年 7 月更新了其包裝，採用鮮艷色彩和生動的圖樣，目的在透過想像力和遊戲引出喜悅和讚嘆。「我們要喚回那種果凍抖動的樂趣，並利用這個品牌給成人和孩子帶來的奇妙感覺。」來自負責品牌重塑的 BrandOpus 代理商的創意總監 Rebecca Williams 表示：「新的視覺標識"釋放想像力"，透過"重新想像口味如何以一種有趣的、感官的方式活躍起來，將顧客帶入 Jell-O 的果凍抖動的美好世界"」（請參閱第 36 章〈建構品牌世界〉）。

芬達在 2023 年 4 月的品牌重塑包括動態卡通圖形和充滿活力的調色板，以展現"俏皮放縱"的感覺。Lisa Smith 是 Jones Knowles Ritchie 的全球執行創意總監，該公司與可口可樂共同開發了此形象。Smith 告訴 Fast Company，這是她工作中使用過的最大範圍的顏色。設計刻意不講究精細及完美，該團隊探索了"所有正式排版所代表的相反面"。Smith 解釋說，其標誌「刻意非常非常好玩。」

「我們希望描繪一個重視即興玩樂的品牌」，可口可樂公司的全球設計副總裁 Rapha Abreu 說：「重新奪回遊戲作為所有年齡段的人都可以擁抱和受益的東西。」

7UP 於 2023 年 2 月推出了全新的形象，"一切都是為了讓人振奮"並為飲用者創造一個「愉快時刻」。「UPliftment（振奮）是一個受全世界人們熱烈迴響的概念。我們 7UP 的新視覺形象的靈感首先來自於該先前在歷史上創造的 7UP 的振奮時刻。」百事高級副總裁兼首席設計官 Mauro Porcini 說道：「我們希望創造一個新的、與我們生活的時代和品牌定位更一致的新鮮形

↑ 7UP brand identity

象，這一切都是要振奮人心。」

值得關注的原因：

倫敦科學博物館集團在 2020 年的一項研究得出結論，根據其收藏的跨越兩個世紀的日常物品分析，世界正變得不夠多彩多姿。將色彩注入到形象和包裝中，品牌可以帶來情感上的振奮。消費者會積極尋找能讓他們微笑的品牌。

VML

36

建構品牌世界

品牌不再是獨立而靜態的實體，而是一個包羅萬象的宇宙。

VML

↑ Barbie, courtesy of Warner Bros

在過去五年中 79% 的人認為品牌的角色發生了變化，88%
的人表示企業有責任照顧地球和人類。數位品牌代理公司
NickelBronx 的創辦人兼執行長 Borzou Azabdaftari 表示：
「二十年前，品牌只是一個圖標和顏色，但現在情況正在改變。」
時至今日，品牌已演變成一個有機生態系統，「打造一個更全面
的品牌世界變得更加重要。品牌被賦予生命，不僅持續改變也
在不斷進化。」

建構品牌意味著打造品牌所處的宏觀世界，並邀請消費者進
入其中。Amplify 首席創意官 Jeavon Smith 和執行創意總
監 Alex Wilson 在 SXSW 2023 專場中表示「我們將世界建構
（world building）視為品牌建造（brand building）的演進」。

根據《時尚商業》報道，Isamaya Ffrench 的化妝品牌「不
太注重美化，而是更注重『世界建構』」。 她在 2022 年 6 月推
出的同名品牌 Isamaya 中，推出了三個系列，每個系列都打造
了獨特的角色和故事。Ffrench 形容這是一個邀請，讓人「探索
更大的世界」。

為了振興芭比品牌，Mattel 與好萊塢和其他品牌合作，在
2023 年夏季引起了一場跨越玩具界限的流行文化狂潮。根據
《時代》報導，2023 年 7 月，「芭比席捲了整個世界」，在很
大程度上歸功於一系列商品推廣，讓消費者完全沉浸在芭比
的世界中。為實現這一目標，華納兄弟和 Mattel 與 Burger
King、Pinkberry、Bloomingdale's、Crocs、Gap、Xbox、
Ruggable 和 Joybird 等品牌合作，推出了以芭比為主題的
產品。Mattel 表示，芭比電影是該公司重塑品牌經營方式的第

↑ Barbie x Joybird

一步。「你即將看到的是，Mattel 正在轉變成一家流行文化公
司」Mattel 總裁兼首席運營官 Richard Dickson 告訴《Fast
Company》。

值得關注的原因：
消費者和品牌的互動正在從個別且獨立的接觸點，轉而在品牌
所建構的全方位世界中進行互動。Smith 和 Wilson 表示，展望
未來，說故事 (storytelling) 將成為品牌發展的核心。

VML

37

影響力娛樂

感性的故事表達方式能夠激勵正面的改變。

↑ Hidden Worlds Entertainment

「我們的努力目標是創造更大更有影響力的啟發,以促使世界變得更美好」。這是 Hidden Worlds Entertainment 創始人 Daniel Hettwer 的雄心,他發明了「影響力娛樂」這一概念。此概念將娛樂與積極行動相結合,以因應氣候危機或心理健康危機等存在威脅。

影響力娛樂是基於行為科學和心理學,內容是關於如何透過親身體驗,進而激發人們產生大規模的行動和改變。與教育娛樂有所不同,因為它不僅僅是傳遞知識給參與者,還包括激勵他們做出改變。「教育元素本身不一定會帶來改變。」Hettwer 告訴 VML 智庫:「有大量的科學證據強調了故事能夠刺激大腦中某些神經化學物質的力量。故事具有創造特定情感、產生同理心和激勵的巨大能力。我們希望激勵人們,幫助他們將靈感轉化為行動。」

VML

我們的努力目標是創造更大更有影響力的啟發，以促使世界變得更美好。

Daniel Hettwer,
Hidden Worlds Entertainment 創始人

一場與巴哈馬當地相關機構合作的沉浸式海洋友善用餐體驗活動，即採用了影響力娛樂概念，該活動將藝術展覽、多感官用餐和 360 度攝影相結合，突顯了這些島嶼在保護海洋方面的成功，同時向客人教育海洋的美麗和困境。在體驗結束時，客人被邀請參加淨灘活動，創造了 Hidden Worlds Entertainment 宣稱的直接影響力。

在推出時，Hidden Worlds Entertainment 的兩個重點領域是自然保育和心理健康，但 Hettwer 表示，影響力娛樂可以用於任何主題、任何消費類別的品牌。「我們的使命是打造最有趣、高品質的客戶體驗，包括休閒、娛樂、及各種款待，以促進希望、信念和創新」他說。

值得關注的原因：
Hettwer 相信，影響力娛樂將成為企業「品牌權益和長期盈利能力的最大推動力」，為企業提供了一種有趣且真實的方式來實現積極的改變，同時展示他們的目標使命。

VML

38

品牌幽默

是時候讓品牌們把歡樂帶回來了。

↑ Better Climate Store

Kantar Link+ 資料庫的數據顯示,過去二十年來,幽默廣告的數量穩定下降。 何必這麼嚴肅? 品牌一直在擺出嚴肅的表情來應對目標和疫情,但有證據表明,消費者現在想要的是笑聲,而不是說教。

在 2022 年和 2023 年期間,Kantar Link+ 報告顯示廣告中的幽默元素出現了近 20 年來的首次增加。人們想要歡笑,Oracle 的《2022 年幸福報告》發現,全球 91% 的消費者希望品牌具有幽默感,有 90% 的人表示幽默的品牌更容易記得。VML 智庫的數據還顯示,人們更有可能購買該品牌的首要原因,是它能為他們帶來一種歡樂感。

品牌正在傾向於新的喜劇子類型,為消費者帶來一些輕鬆愉快的感覺。這包括採用自嘲式幽默,就是要讓觀眾感到不自在。在 TikTok 上,引起共鳴但同樣令人感到尷尬的 #cringetok 內容,現在已經擁有超過 26 億的觀看次數。液態死亡 (Liquid Death) 這個重金屬風格的罐裝水品牌,在其最新廣告中使用大量的尷尬喜劇形式,其中包括一個盲測,比較他們的產品與從男人背上滴下的汗水的味道。

執行長 Mike Cessario 在接受 Spy.com 採訪時分享了品牌對幽默的重視,他表示:「我們知道,如果能讓人們發笑,我們就贏了。我們把創意工作看得像《周六夜現場》的編劇組,甚至我們對內容的要求更高。」

與其說幽默要取代品牌宗旨,不如說它是一種是更容易被接受的討論議題的方式。道德市場 Better Climate Store 通過一

↑ Liquid Death

則幽默的廣告推出其 Greenwash 肥皂,這則廣告指向氣候危機,同時輕描淡寫地嘲笑那些僅僅為了讓自己感覺更好而做出道德選擇的消費者。

Better 聯合創始人兼創意總監 Ben Becker 告訴 VML 智庫:「地球顯然有市場推廣的問題」,因為地球上「最有科學知識和經驗的有志之士不一定是地球最好的品牌故事講述者。但假設我們可以透過有趣的內容和產品吸引人們的注意力,讓人們離開電腦前的舒適圈,轉身投入到一些不費力氣的氣候行動,這對每個人來說都是一個巨大的勝利。」

值得關注的原因:
幽默有助於使產品與眾不同,並吸引消費者的參與,同時可以振奮仍然在艱難中努力奮鬥的消費者。

39
共創未來

品牌正在賦予消費者對產品創意的控制權。

↑ Kiki

安潔莉娜・裘莉在 2023 年夏季推出了她的創意事業 Atelier Jolie，一個將購物者變成設計師的「集體創意」。在正式公告中，裘莉反思道：「當你可以自己創造時，為什麼只要買別人設計好的？」這個品牌不是只販售預先設計好的服飾，而是讓消費者從現有產品和工藝面料中挑選，再由品牌內部的裁縫，製作個人化的定制服裝。Atelier Jolie 還提供維修服務、外帶維修套件，以及店內免費使用的「自己動手裝飾活動站」。

裘莉告訴《Vogue》：「我不想只是成為一位知名的時裝設計師，我想打造一個，人人都能成為設計師的平台。」

VML

Kiki 正在用共同創作的方式開發產品。這個創立於 2023 年 5 月的美妝品牌，將其產品開發的工作交給了社群網民。聯合創始人兼首席產品長 Brendon Garner 告訴 Glossy：「任何希望參與我們產品開發的人都可以這樣做」。該品牌首次推出的是一款指甲油，未來所有產品發布都將由網路投票決定。聯合創始人兼創意長 Ricky Chan 告訴《WWD》：「我們希望改變品牌的未來發展方式，它不僅是個美妝品牌。」

Golden Goose 讓購物者「隨時隨地共創一切」。 該品牌提供全新的共創店內體驗，於 2023 年在澳洲首次亮相，購物者可以選擇自己客製化設計基礎商品，包括運動鞋、包包、外套、丹寧牛仔和 T 恤。 然後由藝術家現場製作出來。

值得關注的原因：
購物本身就是一種自我表達，對於年輕消費者來說尤其如此──根據 VML 智庫「Z 世代：建立更好的常態」報告的數據，60% 的美國 Z 世代表示，他們透過品牌選擇來表達自我意識。未來品牌要超越個性化，進而邀請消費者參與到他們所購買的產品創作中。

VML

↑ Kiki

40
生物設計品牌

善用自然的力量，發展下一世代的織物和染料。

倫敦的 Normal Phenomena of Life 被其創始人形容為「第一個運用生物設計的生活風格品牌。」據 Dezeen 雜誌報導，這個線上平台只展示「借由細菌、藻類、真菌、酵母、動物細胞和其他生物製造的衣物和物品」。生物設計的主要概念，即利用自然生物的生長機制，來創造創新材料和染色技術。Normal Phenomena of Life 的主力產品「探索夾克」便是這種科技外套，它由 100% GOTS 認證的絲綢製成，並用野生型天藍色鏈黴菌為布料進行染色。

在 2023 年倫敦設計節上，丹麥品牌 Ganni 推出了 Bou Bag 的原型版本，這款包使用了倫敦生物科技公司 Modern Synthesis 的一種替代皮革製成，完全不含塑膠或石化成分。這種材料是透過在支撐結構上培養細菌，以農產廢棄物為餌料而產生的。這些微生物能將糖轉化為奈米纖維，所得的纖維比鋼鐵強八倍，並具有天然的結合能力。

2019 年，倫敦中央聖馬丁學院開設了生物設計的碩士課程，課程宗旨在「探索生物知識設計策略，作為永續創新的驅動力」。課程畢業生進行研究的概念包括 Mia Luong 的《未來珍珠》，此概念是要設想在產生珍珠的牡蠣已經滅絕的世界中，「使用細菌纖維和奈米纖維，來設計和重新構想珍珠母和珍珠的未來」。

值得關注的原因：
利用自然生物機制所產生的創新材料，幫助人類探索更永續的未來。儘管這些材料目前還處於初期階段，但它們的潛力令人期待，吸引各大品牌紛紛參與其中。

VML

↑ Modern Synthesis x Ganni Bou Bag

食品&飲品

Alpha世代的味蕾

Alpha世代正啟發出一系列新的風味。

VML

↑ Coca-Cola Y3000 limited edition

國際胃口

Alpha 世代正朝著超越 Z 世代成為迄今最多元的一代的方向發展：美國人口普查局的數據顯示，Alpha 世代將比美國其他人口更加多元化。這就意味著他們的味蕾也將隨之多樣。據紐約時報報導，如今兒童玩具正在演變，以"反映更多種多樣的美食和最新的飲食習慣"為特點。兒童生活品牌 Lalo 銷售玩具壽司和熟食套裝，而 Target 則銷售包含來自墨西哥、印度和日本的布偶糖果的玩具套裝。

由於接觸到更廣泛的文化和美食，Alpha 世代將繼 Z 世代之後，繼續推動用餐多樣性。

AI風味

除了多元文化餐點，數位化生活習慣也為新的風味靈感提供了新的來源。新興世代沉浸在數碼環境中，這影響了他們對食物的看法和互動方式。可口可樂在 2023 年 9 月推出了由 AI 創建

↑ Nour: Play With Your Food video game

↑ Pringles Crisps and Caviar collection

的限量版 Y3000 汽水。「我們挑戰自己去探索未來可口樂可能的味道？」可口可樂公司全球戰略高級總監 Oana Vlad 說。為此，它邀請了 AI 的幫助──這種創意合作可能在 Alpha 世代的廚房中變得司空見慣。

一款名為 "Nour：Play With Your Food" 的新視頻遊戲在 2023 年 6 月發布，邀請用戶「重新發現與食物玩耍的樂趣」。《金融時報》報導稱，《Nour》教導玩家「像第一次接觸食物一樣，並陶醉在產生的雜亂和無章」── 盡情進行一場探索、去實驗並嘗試各種不完美對待食物的方式。

數位習慣鼓勵食客更有創意和實驗性地思考食物，賦予新興世代廚房中輕鬆愉快的氛圍。

趣味搭配
全球味蕾和經數位增強的食物遊戲正在激發 Alpha 世代對零

食世界中趣味和意外搭配的胃口。在 TikTok 上，品客洋芋片與魚子醬搭配的影片引起了病毒式傳播並獲得了超過 100 億次的瀏覽量後，品客隨即於 2023 年 9 月和 The Caviar Co. 合作推出了 Crisps and Caviar 洋芋片＋魚子醬組合包裝產品。French's 和 Skittles 於 2023 年 7 月合作推出了芥末口味的彩虹糖。百事可樂在 2022 年底推出了烤棉花糖、巧克力和格蘭姆餅乾口味的汽水，消費者甚至可以自己混合製作自己的汽水。

Alpha 世代要的是享受食物時所帶來的樂趣，並挑戰各大品牌在食物和口味搭配上要超越傳統的限制。

↓ French's mustard Skittles

一家由 AI 設計的澳洲快閃餐廳將用餐者帶入了夢幻的世界。2023 年 3 月，Applejack Hospitality 發起了「創建您的夢想餐廳」競賽，邀請參賽者利用 AI 突破餐飲業的界限，打造超現實的用餐體驗。由 Stephanie Wee 設計的獲獎概念 "Luminary 發光體" 於 2023 年夏季在位於雪梨的 Applejack Hospitality 集團旗下的 Rafi 餐廳中營業一週。該概念使用朦朧的、多彩的照明以及 " 大氣效果 "，營造出「一種神秘而引人入勝的氛圍」，根據餐廳的說法，最佳的體驗時間是在黑暗中。

Underbar 被設計成一個「夢的國度」。 這家快閃酒吧是由室內建築師 Jonas Bohlin 和餐廳設計師 Christine Ingridsdotter 為 2023 年斯德哥爾摩家具展所構想設計，以毛氈燈、加上佈滿正裝襯衫的牆面，搭配透過紫色玻璃透出的微弱燈光所結合在一起，創造一個可以喚醒潛意識幻想的空間。

Hello Sunshine 也深入潛意識中尋找靈感，自稱為「迷幻倒置小屋」。加拿大的 Frank Architecture 工作室為位於阿爾伯塔省班夫的這家日式酒吧和餐廳設計了一個「替身現實」，工作室告訴 Dezeen，他們從「日式迷幻，義式西部片，以及山間小屋不太可能的組合」中獲得了靈感。就像夢境一樣：「餐廳不會立即顯露，而是隨著人們在空間中移動逐漸呈現。」

值得關注的原因：
用餐者正在尋找一種逃避現實的感覺和奇妙的體驗，讓他們擺脫平凡，滿足對重新賦予魔力的渴望（請參閱第 1 章〈情感工程〉）。

42

夢幻餐飲

最新的餐廳和酒吧要讓用餐的人沉浸在神話的夢境中。

↑ Luminary at Rafi
↑↑ Smoking cocktail at Luminary at Rafi

VML

用餐者正在尋找一種
逃避現實的感覺
和奇妙的體驗，
讓他們擺脫平凡，
滿足對重新賦予魔力的
渴望。

正餐零食化

隨著價值數十億美元的零食市場持續增長，小零食成了大生意。

↑ Moonshot climate-friendly crackers are now part of the Patagonia Provisions brand

↑ Patagonia Provisions crackers

年輕一代感覺特別愛吃零食，這可能是因為 69% 的 18-29 歲人群認為零食是一天中的重頭戲，而全球平均比例為 55%。根據蒙代爾國際公司和哈里斯民意調查公司於 2023 年 1 月發布的《零食現狀報告》，全球 71% 的消費者每天至少吃兩次零食，而這一領域的增長主要歸功於年輕一代，因為千禧一代和 Z 世代的生活方式更忙碌，他們每天的零食消費量比老一代人多 10%。

目前，家樂氏公司已於 2023 年 10 月推出以零食為導向的公司 Kellanova。 該 公 司 由 Cheez-It、Pringles、Rice Krispies Treats 和 Pop-Tarts 等流行零食品牌組成。據家樂氏公司報告，

僅這些零食品牌就占其北美零食銷售額的 70% 左右。根據市場研究公司 Circana 表示，近一半的美國消費者每天吃三種或更多的零食。Kellanova 公司對此寄予厚望，預計 2024 年該公司的淨銷售額將達到 22.5 億至 23 億美元。

隨著人們對零食的需求增加，氣候友善零食開始出現需求。在飲食方面，全球 51% 的受訪者表示他們會考慮對環境的影響，83% 的受訪者表示他們希望品牌能在解決氣候變化等挑戰方面發揮自己的作用。

Patagonia Provisions 於 2023 年 3 月收購了氣候友善餅乾公司 Moonshot。這家新創公司的創辦人 Julia Collins 表示：「我創立 Moonshot 的願景是利用食物的力量幫助應對氣候變遷。最近，巴塔哥尼亞食品公司將地球作為其唯一股東，通過加入巴塔哥尼亞食品公司，Moonshot 現在屬於地球了。」

為了提高人們對這項事業的認識，總部位於科羅拉多州的 Quinn 公司於 2023 年獲得了美國食品永續發展評級公司 HowGood 授予的「氣候友善 (Climate Friendly)」稱號，並添加到其包裝上。Quinn 的目標是：「通過重塑零食來撼動食品行業」，其產品包括爆米花和椒鹽脆餅。

值得關注的原因

零食正在佔據食品業的很大一部分。根據 Euromonitor 的數據顯示，2024 年全球零食銷售額預計將超過 6750 億美元，到 2028 年將超過 8310 億美元。品牌將需要迎合年輕一代的胃口，同時堅持對他們很重要的可持續價值觀。

44

佳餚雞尾酒

調酒師調製出融合了一絲懷舊和一抹舒適的飲用佳餚。

↑ Cold Pizza and Key Lime Pie cocktails at Double Chicken Please, New York City

冷披薩、華爾道夫沙拉和法式吐司都可以在位於紐約下東區的 Double Chicken Please 的點單上找到，只是在這裡它們都是雞尾酒。Double Chicken Please 的品牌和公關經理 Tako Chang 告訴 VML 智庫：「在店內的 Coop 廳提供的手工調製飲品，是基於駭客設計的方法，將烹飪菜餚拆解，再將其味道重新組合成獨特的雞尾酒。」該酒吧於 2020 年 11 月開業，在 2023 年北美 50 家最佳酒吧排行榜中排名第一，在 2023 年全球 50 家最佳酒吧排行榜中排名第二。 創辦人 GN Chan 和 Faye Chen 雞尾酒的靈感源泉是對美食的熱愛，每一杯都是創新與舒適的完美融合。

位於墨西哥城的 Colonia Juárez 街區的 Handshake Speakeasy，採用分子調配法來調製雞尾酒。在雞尾酒單上還可以找到美味的甜點，包括草莓煎餅和香蕉拼盤，其中香蕉拼盤

VML

↓ Banana Split at the Handshake Speakeasy, Mexico

的特色是香蕉利口酒、雪利酒和以樂高為靈感的巧克力，巧克力中裝滿了香蕉奶油作為特別裝飾。 Handshake Speakeasy 在 2023 年全球 50 家最佳酒吧排行榜中排名第三，目前在拉丁美洲雞尾酒界獨占鰲頭。

那些想品嚐帶有甜味和鹹味的南薑椰汁湯雞尾酒的人，應該前往德克薩斯州奧斯汀的 Bar Mischief 酒吧。飲料總監 Jorge Viana 為他的南薑椰汁雞尾酒調製了一種鹹味混合酒，其中包括一種加了蘑菇的伏特加，並在上面澆上甜檸檬草和椰子泡沫。

值得關注的原因：
隨著雞尾酒產業的發展，Chan 發現人們已經不再滿足以甜味、花香、泡沫和酸味為主的口味。他解釋說：「隨著時間的推移，酒吧行業將其技術擴展到美食版圖，顧客也開始探索飲用美食佳餚的美味。」

探險式用餐

精緻餐飲從大海,航向太空。

↑ Iris restaurant, Norway

VML

從 2024 年起，法國太空旅遊公司 Zephalto 將在其設計的 Céleste 豪華加壓太空艙中提供精緻的餐食和品酒之旅，太空艙由平流層氣球掛載飛向「黑暗的太空」。 每次航程僅招待六名賓客，在氣球開始升空之前，他們將先享用一份精心規劃菜單的佳餚，並在六小時的航程中品嚐美酒。

如果覺得太空太遙遠，迫不及待的饕客們可以穿越挪威西部的哈當厄爾峽灣，前往位於 Salmon Eye 漂浮藝術裝置內的餐廳。Iris 餐廳僅能容納 24 位客人，它提供的用餐體驗被描述為開啟「一個充滿挑戰、風味和可能性的故事」。 體驗過程包括從羅森達爾鎮乘船出發，接著在主廚 Anika Madsen 位於 Snilstveitøy 島的船屋停留並享用迎賓點心。 然後在藝術裝置上進行「多感官水下體驗」，客人最後在餐廳體驗品嚐佳餚同時將峽灣和山脈美景都盡收眼底。

為了體驗在波羅的海深處熟成香檳的味道，凱歌香檳 Veuve Clicquot 推出了海底酒窖的體驗活動。 這場體驗活動中的 14 位賓客，且必須都是經驗豐富的潛水員，將有機會在芬蘭離岸的奧蘭群島潛入 43 公尺深的海洋深處，取回沈入海中的香檳。據說這次潛水之旅的價格高達「數萬英鎊」。 下一次探險將於 2024 年夏季進行。

值得關注的原因：
研究指出環境會影響人們對味道的認知。中國在 2022 年進行《美麗的環境是否會讓食物變得更好》的研究中發現，「在更美

↑ Iris restaurant, Norway

觀令人愉悅的環境中，食物會嚐起來更美味、聞起來更香，在特定條件下，外觀看起來更漂亮，產生更多正面的情緒。這些令人難忘的高級餐飲體驗，能連結無數層面的感官認知，絕多數只是為了豐富美食體驗。」

46

美食文化遺產

隨著美食的多樣化，各國都在積極保護傳統美食。

VML

義大利的菜單上不會出現任何培植肉，而且這種情況可能會一直持續下去。2023 年 7 月 19 日，義大利共和國參議院通過了一項法案，禁止生產和進口合成肉類和其他合成食品，以保護國家的傳統食品。義大利政府希望透過將其列為聯合國教科文組織非物質文化遺產來進一步加強該國的飲食文化遺產。聯合國教科文組織將於 2025 年 12 月對此做出裁定。

聯合國教科文組織對傳統食品的保護並非第一次。在 2022 年 11 月，該組織將製作法式長棍麵包的傳統手工，以其四種原料和特定技術，列入非物質文化遺產名錄。消息傳出後得到了正面的迴響，法國總統馬克宏 (Emmanuel Macron) 在推特上形容法式長棍麵包為「我們日常中 250 公克的魔法與完美」。長棍麵包與其他傳統美食一起被聯合國教科文組織列入遺產名錄，包括烏克蘭羅宋湯、韓國泡菜和海地的珠穆湯。

中東正在求助於烹飪機構來保存其豐富的傳統食品。杜拜國際烹飪藝術中心主任兼首席執行長 Sunjeh Raja 告訴《Fast Company》：「每個烹飪機構都必須提供對民族美食的結構化學習，並在創新的同時促進對傳統烹飪的尊重。」

值得關注的原因：
細胞培養食品替代品的快速發展正受到一些國家的抵制，這些國家加倍努力地去保護其傳統飲食文化遺產，並重新定義每個國家及其文化的口味、工藝和技術。畢竟有 74% 的人表示食物是他們與文化相連的方式，83% 的人表示食物是他們發現新文化的方式。

74%

食物是他們與文化相連的方式

83%

食物是他們發現新文化的方式

↑ Baguette making, courtesy of Frédéric Vielcanet
↑↑ Baguette making, courtesy of Jean-Luc Valteau

VML

47

食物藥局

現在，食物對公眾健康至關重要。

隨著研究強調健康食品在預防甚至是扭轉慢性疾病方面的功效，新鮮農產品處方正逐漸開始流行。食品品牌和零售商現在是否應將自己視為醫療保健提供者？

根據 2023 年發表於美國心臟協會同行評審期刊《循環》上的一項研究，農產品處方可以帶來多種健康益處，從降血壓到減少 BMI。

在美國、英國和澳洲的醫生率先將"食物作為處方"的服務作為一種預防性健康策略。美國蒙大拿州、加州和麻州等多個州的醫生現在已可以開"農產品處方"。在倫敦，普通科醫生也為低收入患者開水果和蔬菜處方，這是一項先導計劃的一部分，最終可能在全國進行推廣。

通常處方計劃的參與者會收到兌換券、會員卡點數或簽帳卡，用於補貼或支付在雜貨店和菜市場購買健康食品的費用。其他計劃則以水果和蔬菜盒的形式發放保健用品。

Kroger 和 Giant Food 等食品雜貨零售商已經在支持這些計劃，其他零售商也正在抓住整個業界的機會，更進一步教育或引導消費者養成更健康的飲食習慣。

英國零售商 Tesco 為自己設定了目標，讓 65% 的購物籃中是由健康食品組成，並承諾到 2025 年從自有品牌的產品中減少

VML

1000 億卡路里的熱量。在美國,雜貨連鎖店 Albertsons 在其 Sincerely Health 平台上增加了一個數位營養計算器,購物者可以根據美國農業部的「我的餐盤 My Plate」指南來計算所購買食品的營養價值。

英國健康食品零售商 Holland & Barrett 最近更新了其食品標示,重新打出「愛你的食品」的旗幟。該店在包裝上推出了「植物點數 Plant Points」計劃,鼓勵購物者每周在飲食中至少攝入 30 種植物。反觀超加工食品(UPFs),正受到越來越多的關注。在英國和美國,這些食品現在占了所有飲食的一半,《英國醫學雜誌》上發表的研究報告顯示,七分之一的成年人和八分之一的兒童可能會對這些食物上癮。人們期待看到更健康的替代品或具有保健功效的新配方上架。

英國食品雜貨零售商 Marks & Spencer 最近與「超級麵包 Superloaf」的創始者 Modern Baker 簽訂了獨家經銷權。經過六年的研發,超級麵包營養豐富,有益腸道蠕動,熱量低於普通麵包。該製造商已獲得政府資助,將其研究擴展到其他品項的營養配方,包括糕點、速煮食物和早餐麥片。

值得關注的原因:
除了「對抗不良飲食」的國家策略外,食品製造商和零售商還有機會擴大這些努力,發起更多的教育和宣傳活動,促進更健康的飲食,並在提供超加工食品的同時提供健康的替代品。

↑ Superloaf by Modern Baker
↑↑ Holland & Barrett's healthy groceries

48

人際餐敘

人們正在與陌生人共進晚餐，以對抗孤獨感並培養社區聯繫。

《紐約時報》表示「與陌生人一起用餐是一種極致的行為表現」，而這股為了鼓勵社區／社群連結而興起的概念正形成餐飲新浪潮。

「與朋友共進晚餐」的概念是一種親密的晚宴派對，它讓八位陌生人聚在一起共享一頓家常晚餐。Anita Michaud 在搬到紐約並且為了找人一起吃飯所苦後，終於在 2022 年 5 月創辦了「與朋友共進晚餐」服務。推出以來，已有超過 800 人報名用餐，相當於四年的候補名單。

Soup Doula 也是透過食物連結社區／社群。它最初的服務內容是為那些新手父母們提供送湯服務，而現已發展成為鄰里社交的促進者。發起者兼主廚 Marisa Mendez Marthaller 於 2023 年 2、3 月時在紐約布魯克林的一家店裡每週舉辦「共享湯」活動，每到週日下午社區成員們就可以前來並聚在一起喝湯。雖然這項服務最初是為了新手父母所建立的，但主廚表示任何需要營養的人都可以前來共聚喝湯，像是：年長的父母、COVID-19 患者、情緒低落的人、或掙扎於心理健康的人，或大學生或研究生等等。

VML

現在，
社區/社群意識
是前所未有的強大。

Denise Lefebvre,
PepsiCo Foods 食品研發部的資深副總

根據賓州大學華頓商學院教授，也是《社會化學：解碼人類連結的元素 (Social Chemistry: Decoding the Elements of Human Connection)》一書的作者 Marissa King 的研究表示：疫情期間人們的社交規模平均縮水了 16%。為了減少疫情造成的社交匱乏，人們在外出用餐時尋求的不僅止是一頓美味的餐。

PepsiCo 食品研發部的資深副總 Denise Lefebvre 告訴《紐約時報》：「如果你回頭看會發現我們這數年來的生活都沒有與人分享，因為分享被認為是危險的。而現在，社區 / 社群意識是前所未有的強大。」

值得關注的原因：
雖然餐桌一向都是家人和朋友聚會的場所，但現在它更向下紮根；分享與共食的社群正在強化並且重新建立連結（請參閱第 10 章〈共識社區〉）。

VML

清酒熱潮

清酒的餐酒搭配愛好正於全球掀起熱潮。

↑ Dassai Blue sake from Asahi Shuzo

亞洲美食和文化的流行幫助了全球群眾認識了清酒精緻的品質。現在，有些人甚至開始著手釀製清酒。

在過去幾年，小量生產的在地清酒釀造商在美國如雨後春筍般湧現，目前已有 20 多家，其中包括阿肯色州的 Origami Sake 清酒公司，該公司於 2023 年中開始運營。這些後起之秀充分利用美國的傳統和風土，更對美國人的口味。由於他們的成功，日本釀酒商也想加入。Asahi Shuzo 在哈德遜河谷開設了一家釀酒廠和品酒室，並將推出美國品牌 Dassai Blue。此外，它還與美國烹飪學院 Culinary Institute of America 聯合開設了清酒教育課程。

→ IWA kura (sake brewery) in Shiraiwa, Japan

倫敦最熱門的餐廳之一的 Evelyn's Table 菜單上就有倫敦 Kanpai 釀酒廠生產的在地清酒。當然，清酒的鮮美特質意味著它也越來越常與食物搭配享用。在新加坡，Rasen Sake 清酒專門用於搭配新加坡菜餚。洛杉磯餐酒館 Ototo 供應牛仔牌清酒，專為搭配牛排或牛肉而設計。即使在熱愛葡萄酒的巴黎，手工起司製造商 Taka & Vermo 也會在店內舉辦起司和清酒的品嚐活動。

為了釀造出更適合搭配食物的酒，清酒釀造商現在開始與葡萄酒和香檳產業的專家合作。曾在香檳王 Dom Pérignon 擔任釀酒師的 Richard Geoffroy 現在是日本清酒新創公司 IWA 的創始人兼釀酒師。IWA 5 是第一款推出的量產商品，採用了不同大米混合品種的組合工藝。這種飲品已經受到米其林星級廚師 Thomas Keller 等人的青睞。據《羅博報告 Robb Report》報道，Thomas Keller 正計劃在 The French Laundry 用這種飲品搭配魚子醬。Geoffroy 告訴 VML 智庫：「我鼓勵 IWA 的追隨者和愛好者像我一樣可以冒一點險去嘗試不同的搭配。」

值得關注的原因：
隨著國際食客越來越了解清酒的多變性，專家預測清酒有望與最受歡迎的西方飲品葡萄酒相媲美。

50

凍原到餐桌

北極美食正在崛起。

↑ Moss at the Blue Lagoon resort, Iceland, courtesy of Blue Lagoon Iceland

↑ Hurtigruten Group's MS Kong Harald. Photography by Stian Klo

在 2023 年，挪威有六家餐廳獲得了首顆米其林星星，使北極地區的餐廳數量不斷增加，提升了該地區的美食地位。在冰島，Blue Lagoon Resort 的 Moss 餐廳於 2023 年 6 月獲得了首顆米其林星星。除了冰島羊肉、挪威帝王蟹和當地捕撈的魚等地方菜餚外，Moss 餐廳還提供應一種凸顯地方特色的奶油。這種奶油是由當地小農提供的冰島優酪乳、紫紅藻和現場制作的海鹽打發而成。Blue Lagoon 餐飲總監 Ingi Thorarinn Fridriksson 廚師告訴美國美食餐飲月刊《美食與美酒》：「我們的奶油，靈感來自於我們對冰島優格的自豪。我們添加了紫紅藻，以向藍湖所在的漁業小鎮格林達維克(Grindavik)致敬。(在撰寫本文時，此服務已經因該地區的火山活動而中斷)。

「我們的當地食材都有一個故事。要嘛是你親手捕捉、釣取或採集的，要嘛是你認識的人親手捕捉、釣取或採集的，」格陵蘭旅遊局 CEO Anne Nivika Grødem 告訴《BBC》：「我們的飲食文化與我們的身份緊密相連。」

北極旅行路線越來越凸顯該地區的美食。郵輪運營商海達路德公司 (Hurtigruten) 已於 2023 年推出了兩條新航線，展示挪威 " 從峽灣到餐桌 " 的美食，為遊客提供當地美食，如在羅爾夫索伊 (Rolvsøy) 小島上採集的雲莓蜂蜜、在家族企業特倫德索普 (Trøndersopp) 農場種植的杏鮑菇，以及從原住民—薩米人那收集來的食譜和食材。

對北極美食的食慾正在向新的海岸蔓延。2023 年 6 月，米其林三星挪威餐廳 Maaemo 在雪梨開業，提供每人 400 美元的 tasting menu，供應當地獵捕的鹿和燻製的馴鹿心。2023 年 5 月，紐約市舉辦了首屆冰島之味節，在著名的 Coarse 餐廳推出了為期一週的冰島特色菜單，並開了冰島調酒課程。

值得關注的原因：
北極圈最北端社區的廚師正在振興被忽視的飲食文化，迎合著一群不斷增長的文化愛好者和渴望冒險、追求深度融入冰冷草原的旅行者，提供具冒險精神和極具當地特色的美食。

↑ Moss at the Blue Lagoon resort, Iceland, courtesy of Blue Lagoon Iceland

51

美容

60

Alpha世代護膚

最年輕的這一代已經被美容儀式感套牢。

↑ Evereden, courtesy of Evereden

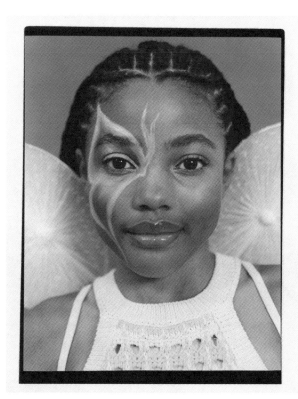

↑ Evereden, courtesy of Evereden

請讓路給社群上的少年護膚達人,他們要接管在社群媒體上提供各種清潔、爽膚、保濕等護膚技巧的教學建議。根據《People》雜誌,11 歲的 Riley Curry 的母親,女演員 Ayesha Curry,說她女兒堅持一個自己的「全面且不容妥協的」的護膚程序。10 歲的 North West 一直不斷地在 TikTok 上發布自己的美容養生影片。

「許多 Alpha 世代都有自己的護膚程序」跨世代護膚品牌 Evereden 的創始人兼首席執行長 Kimberley Ho 告訴 VML 智庫:「身為數位原住民,這一代人對社群媒體上展示的護膚功效瞭如指掌。不管父母輩是否認同,這一代人都想要屬於他們的產品。」Ho 解釋道:「他們要自己的例行程序,他們非常獨立。」

Evereden 的產品系列「適合每個年齡層和每個階段」,都經過科學檢驗。該公司有少年產品系列,其中包括孩童每日的日常保養品,產品線也擴充到護髮領域,並推出孩童用彩妝系列。在 2023 年 9 月還推出了 Evereden At Play,於遊玩時使用的保養品。Ho 說:「與上一代人相比,3 至 13 歲的孩童對護膚和美容產品有更濃厚的興趣。」Evereden 也正在進行各種研究來滿足該群體的各種特定護膚需求。

Proudly 是一個專為黑色皮膚嬰兒和兒童量身定制的保養品牌,在 2022 年 4 月首次亮相。創始人 Gabrielle Union 和 Dwyane Wade 創建該品牌是為了解決「有色人種兒童缺乏選擇」的問題。2023 年 9 月 Proudly 也上市了他們首個護髮系列產品。

VML

許多 Alpha 世代都有自己的護膚程序 跨世代護膚品牌

Kimberley Ho, Evereden 創始人兼首席執行長

英國的豪華家庭旅館也加入爭取 Alpha 世代的護膚消費市場，於 2023 年 10 月推出 Little Ishga，一個專為 3 歲至 16 歲的孩童規劃設計的護膚療程，「舒緩壓力，保養要從小做起」。希望藉此促進全家人一起享受旅館提供的 Spa 療程。

隨著 Alpha 世代走向美妝世界，他們也開始與父母交換美妝心得。菲律賓《Vogue》雜誌行銷傳播負責人 Ranice Faustino 告訴 VML 智庫，身為一位千禧世代的母親，她經常與她 12 歲的女兒分享化妝方法，「她學我，我也學她化妝。在她身上學到了很多。」這種交流也延伸到了美容保養領域，Faustino 也會與女兒一起嘗試網紅推薦的美容保養方式。

值得關注的原因:
Evereden 創辦人 Ho 說：「Alpha 世代比他們的兄姊和長輩們更早接觸美容。」這個世代從社群媒體上學習護膚並吸收大量知識，有些人在父母的全力支持下已經向全世界分享他們的護膚方法了，這使其成為美容品牌重點發展的豐富市場。

VML

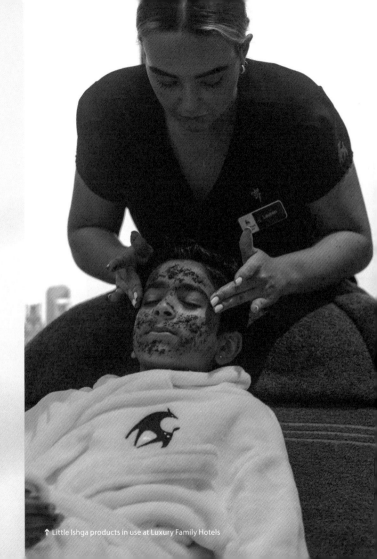

↑ Little Ishga products in use at Luxury Family Hotels

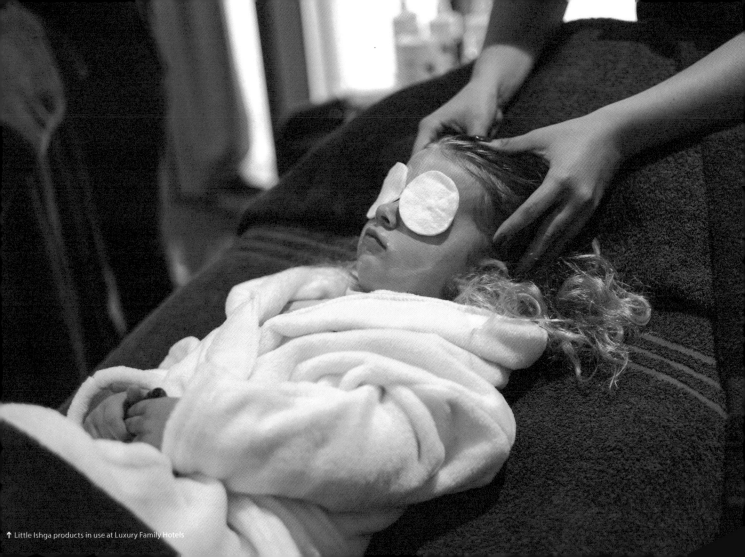

↑ Little Ishga products in use at Luxury Family Hotels

↑ Isamaya Beauty

哥德式優雅

時至今日美妝也進入了有顛覆能量的巫術世界。

VML

季節性時裝秀正相繼用溫柔的哥德式魅力作為 2024 的主題，深色唇膏和眼影，搭配極具戲劇張力的睫毛是主要的表演形式。

魔女是 Dior 一場在 2023 年 9 月巴黎時裝周上舉辦的時裝秀的靈感來源，模特們的裸唇直接被精心地染黑，以襯托會發光的皮膚。Dior 的彩妝創意暨彩妝形象總監 Peter Philips 向《Harper's Bazaar》表示，他的創意總監 Maria Grazia Chiuri 當初給他這項工作的任務說明是起因於以前「在義大利這個男性主導的世界裡，女性世世代代被視為魔女」的刻板印象。

同樣在巴黎舉辦的 Junya Watanabe 秀上，前衛化妝師 Isamaya Ffrench 參考聖女貞德的形象，讓模特們展示蒼白光滑的皮膚、幾乎看不到的眉毛和黑色的嘴唇。Ffrench 在 2023 年 10 月時在 YouTube 上還發布教學影片，教大家如何用天然荊棘做眉毛以完成創新的季節性森林精靈妝。

↑ Isamaya Beauty

超濃密睫毛強化了戲劇化的外表。化妝師 Vanessa Icareg 利用 Isamaya French Beauty 的工業風眼影色系 2.0 和狂野之星眼影調色盤中的色彩，打造出了一叢叢且具有焦黑效果的睫毛。誇張的睫毛也出現在維多利亞·貝克漢姆 Victoria Beckham 美妝品牌 在 2024 年春夏秀場上，《Vogue》雜誌報導說，強調該品牌新推出的 Vast Lash Mascaras 濃密睫毛膏產品，可以刷出「很戲劇化像蜘蛛腳那樣又粗又長的睫毛」。

在我們 VML 的《魔幻返潮時代》報告中所探討的，魔女是一個引發爭議的工具，象徵包容著有女性魅力、環境共生精神和具靈性的創新破壞性力量。魔女信仰對文化敘事、美學和美感的影響正在上升。健康品牌，如 Palm of Feronia 和 Kate Moss 的 Cosmoss 都大量援用了神秘的元素。英國香水製造商 Vyrao 甚至邀請了一位靈媒共同創造它的香水《第六感》。

值得關注的原因：
美妝品牌提供產品解決方案，讓消費者可以打造出具叛逆精神的哥德式風格的妝容。此外魔女象徵著對女性力量的肯定，與對現狀的挑戰。事實上有超過 51% 的 Z 世代表現出對於非傳統靈性世界的興趣，這群年輕人在這樣的造型和妝容中得到了慰藉。

53

慢美容

美容品牌們選擇採用永續且謹慎的方法來研製高效的護膚品。

VML

↑ Vintner's Daughter

Vintner's Daughter 在 2023 年推出了第三款產品，Active Renewal Cleanser。這個已有 10 年歷史的美容品牌，以緩慢而細心的方式培育每一款產品。「我創立 Vintner's Daughter 是為了將我在葡萄酒製造的背景中對品質的堅持和工藝的執著融入到護膚產品中」，創始人 April Gargiulo 向 VML 智庫表示。

這三款護膚產品優先考慮全株天然植物為原料，而非合成物和萃取物，每一種產品的製作過程需時三週，這比行業平均速度慢了 66 倍，Gargiulo 解釋道。她相信，高功效標準的產品需要投注大量時間：「精品不僅僅是標價或華麗包裝的問題，更是關乎

↑ Vintner's Daughter

乎原材料的品質,用心的程度,以及將這些原材料組合在一起的精密製程。」該公司經過四年終於完全掌握的最新產品的配方,這使得包括 Gwyneth Paltrow 和 Tracee Ellis Ross 在內的品牌粉絲欣喜不已。

Stella McCartney 和 LVMH 集團於 2022 年夏季推出了美容系列 Stella。McCartney 表示:「我們與 LVMH 集團一起努力工作了近三年,不斷改進,力求達到我認為可能達到的目標:以自然為根基、真正有效且負責任的護膚品。這是一個改變遊戲規則的產品,我希望與大家一起分享。

護膚品新創公司 Dieux 有一個明確的使命:專注於提供優質產品,並且在價格和永續性方面保持透明。此外,該品牌在 2023 年 10 月告訴《Fast Company》,其策略是「更少的銷售產品 Sell Fewer Products」。Dieux 的暢銷產品包括售價 25 美元的 Forever Eyemask (永恆眼膜),正如其名字所示,它與許多其他一次性使用的眼罩不同,可以重複使用。

菲律賓《Vogue》的美容編輯 Joyce Oreña 告訴 VML 智庫,她認為消費者的「良知和道德」標準越來越高,並且「他們不再只關心產品的功效,還關心產品是如何生產出來的」。 這些新的美容標準符合消費者的期望。全球有 83% 的人表示,他們期望品牌在解決氣候變化等挑戰中盡一份力,85% 的人表示,他們希望他們的消費可以用於支持符合其價值觀的品牌上。

值得關注的原因:
Gargiulo 表示:「慢美容是一種更用心的方式,它注重減少浪費、使用更好的原料,以及重質不重量。」考慮到具有生態意識的消費者,美容品牌正在踩剎車,放慢生產速度,試圖改變這個專注於不斷生產銷售產品的行業。

54

品牌SPA

美容體驗是開啟消費者關係的關鍵。

VML

↑ Guerlain Spa at Raffles London at The OWO

高級美容品牌正在開設自身品牌的獨立 Spa 中心，提供一系列的健康服務。這些空間為品牌提供了展示其真正與眾不同之處的機會，同時有助於提升消費者對其專業知識的認知。

2023 年夏天，Sisley-Paris 在紐約米特帕金區首次推出了 Maison Sisley New York，這是該品牌在北美的第一家 Spa。在這個佔地 2,675 平方英尺的空間裡設有四間護理室、化妝空間和一間專門的髮廊精品店，所有這些都是為了提供客戶「一個放鬆身心、照顧自己的地方」。

Guerlain 也加入了這一行列，將於 2023 年在 Raffles London at The OWO 開設 Guerlain Spa。該 Spa 中心占地 27,000 平方英尺，共四層樓，Raffles London at The OWO 所在地是倫敦歷史悠久的舊戰爭辦公大樓。作為 Guerlain 在英國的首家 Spa 中心，為了讓體驗更加獨特，該品牌特地推出一項名為「Spirit of London 倫敦的心靈」的獨家療程。

美容

Guerlain 表示，這是以按摩為基礎「針對與旅行、環境壓力和繁忙生活方式相關的緊張情緒」的身心療程。

2023 年初，Augustinus Bader 在倫敦開設了皮膚實驗室，隨後又在紐約開設了分店。品牌執行長 Charles Rosier 告訴《Glossy》，這些 Spa 中心讓品牌「可以依據我們品牌想要的方式重新規劃從進入中心的感覺開始，到經歷療程的體驗過程。」

值得關注的原因：
美容品牌用策劃自己的整體健康和身心療程滿足消費者對於親身體驗的需求，在獨立的 Spa 中心中進行的體驗，可以增強和擴展他們的品牌理念。

↓→ Augustinus Bader at Lanserhof at The Arts Club London

護膚食品

護膚和營養品融合，創造出利潤豐厚且不斷增長的健康商機。

↑ HyaCera by Ritual

VML

食用美容健康補給品正方興未艾。光是在美國，Mintel 預測到 2027 年健康補給品市場將增長至 450 億美元，其中護膚食品是最令人感到興奮的新商機之一。

現在，營養補給品品牌和護膚化妝品公司用抹去兩個品類間的界限來創新迎合消費者的需求。例如，領先的營養補給品牌 Ritual 於 2023 年 5 月首次進軍美容領域，推出了 HyaCera Daily Skin Hydration 日用皮膚保濕補給品。這種每日服用一次的膠囊由可追溯成分製成，標榜支持皮膚的保濕屏障，幫助減少皺紋。

法國營養美容品牌 Aime 最初是一個皮膚營養補給品品牌，2018 年開始涉足皮膚外用化妝品領域，為消費者提供雙管齊下的護膚方案。Aime 於 2023 年正式在美國上市，目前正積極地向全球發展。

美容研究機構 The Benchmarking Company 的一項調查發現，76% 的美國女性希望美容品牌能夠提供營養補給品，與其外用產品搭配互補，這正恰好是傳統護膚品牌開始做的事情。Murad 是最早推出三種針對抗衰老、除痘和皮膚美白的營養補給品的公司之一，而露得清也邁出了護膚營養補給品的第一步，與 3D 列印維他命組合錠品牌 Nourished 合作在 2023 年消費電子展 (CES) 上首次亮相推出 3D 列印護膚保健補給品，預示了個人化護膚營養補給品的潛力。

↑ HyaCera by Ritual

值得關注的原因：
護膚食品為營養補給品品牌提供了進入美容消費者市場的途徑，同時讓護膚品品牌有機會進一步融入蓬勃發展的健康和保健領域。

美容

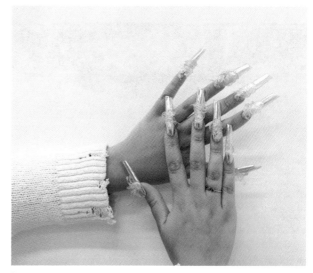

↑ Beauty Tech Art Spa exhibition, courtesy of Izzy Scott

56

美甲時裝

高級的美甲成為最新的時尚配件。

美甲不再是小眾事物，隨著越來越多的顧客湧入美甲沙龍，美甲師們正在用更具創意的美甲技術來提升他們的水平。 在這一流派中最前衛的人物之一，人們可能在普通的美甲沙龍中看不到來自東京 Tomoya Nakagawa 的作品。他的設計充滿奇幻色彩，精緻的水滴從指甲中流淌而出、鑲有金屬和珠寶的指甲、以及類似未來風格帶有紫色設計的腳指甲。根據《Dazed》簡介，他的自然風格設計是透過 CAD、3D 列印和噴槍技術精心製作的。

來自美國的藝術家 San Sung Kim 的作品更為細膩，但也不乏創造力。她的設計涵蓋了萬聖節主題的指甲，上面裝飾著光滑的

VML

↑ Beauty Tech Art Spa exhibition, courtesy of Izzy Scott

黑色蝙蝠翅膀；透明的指甲上夾著一朵玫瑰，帶有並強調「血流」的概念，象徵著「破碎的心」，還有夢幻般的指甲設計，配有金屬滴答作響的鐘針，San Sung Kim 闡述說這是輕微受到西班牙畫家達利的作品《The Persistence of Memory 永恆的記憶》的影響。

從概念的眼光來看美甲沙龍的是 Beauty Tech Art Spa，這是一個於 2023 年 10 月下旬在倫敦自治市鎮開幕的群展，其策展人 Cornershop 稱其為對倫敦各地由不同種族群體經營的美甲沙龍的回應。展覽重點展示了六位女性藝術家的作品，其中包括 Zoë Argires、Hoa Dung Clerget、Athen Kardashian、Nina Mhach Durban，Cornershop 表示，她們「以各自的美

$128.3億美元

2024 年全球美甲沙龍的市場價值
將達到 128.3 億美元。
Grand View Research

學和文化影響對概念美甲店做出了不同的回應」。 這轉化為借鑒「美甲店」的作品，而其他作品，Cornershop 表示，則「喚起了被認知的文化期望」，並將沙龍視為「社區活動的聚集地」。

值得關注的原因：
Grand View Research 預測，2024 年全球美甲沙龍的市場價值將達到 128.3 億美元。這促使美甲沙龍透過比以往更加藝術、精緻和富有創意的創新設計技術脫穎而出。

57

生物芳香

美容創新者正在重新定義香水。

↑ Future Society fragrances, courtesy of Arcaea

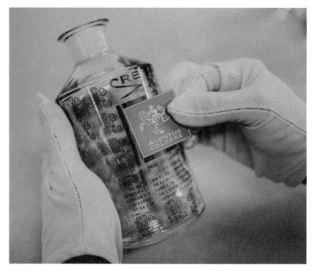

↑ Kering Creed, courtesy of Creed

Arcaea 是一家以生物學為導向的美容公司,其革命性的香味技術已獲得 Chanel 和 Olaplex 等公司的資助,Arcaea 首席執行官 Jasmina Aganovic 表示,我們公司的使命是「讓生物學成為美容領域最受歡迎的技術」。

該公司於 2023 年 10 月推出了新香水品牌 Future Society,從生物學和科學中尋找創作靈感。 Aganovic 說:「科學不僅僅是臨床研究,同時也代表了新的創意工具。首批發布的六款香水是用已滅絕的花朵的 DNA 序列製成的香水系列。」 Aganovic 同時解釋:「香水一直植根於強大的闡述和感官體驗中,我們很高興能展示生物學如何創造新的故事和產品體驗」。

Arcaea 於 2023 年 3 月開發了一款新的技術 ScentArc,這是一種與腋下微生物群一同作用來防止異味的技術。「對於價值 250 億美元的除臭劑品類,其基礎科學依賴於 19 世紀開發的方法:掩蓋氣味、消除或阻止異味散播、吸收汗水」Aganovic 說:「我們透過生物學,利用直到最近才出現的新技術,找到了更好的解決方案。」 這些創新是在香水類別越來越受到主要廠商的關注之際才出現的。 開雲集團於 2023 年 10 月收購了頂級香水公司 Creed。歷峰集團正在加倍關注香水領域,並於 2023 年 9 月成立了新的 Laboratoire de Haute Parfumerie et Beauté 部門,而 LVMH 則於 2023 年 3 月重組了其美妝領導層,以優先發展香水業務。

值得關注的原因:
香水品類正在蓬勃發展,預期有望增加對香水的投資、關注和創新。

58

「非」美麗

誕生於非洲廣闊大陸並受其啟發的美容品牌將其策略推向全球。

Euromonitor 預測，2023 年非洲美容和個人護理市場價值將達到 82 億美元，到 2025 年將增至超過 100 億美元，這顯然是一個值得關注的市場。

為了滿足該地區消費者以及當地居民的獨特需求，本土品牌不斷湧現，將非洲豐富的天然成分與尖端創新相結合。Uncover 是一家總部位於肯亞的新創公司，在肯亞和奈及利亞開展業務，為非洲女性和有色人種女性提供量身定制的護膚和防曬霜。黑人皮膚通常有獨特的需求，例如比白人皮膚更乾燥、更嬌嫩，但很少有產品能滿足其特殊要求。雖然 Uncover 成立於肯亞並受到該地區的影響，但其產品是在韓國製造的，該品牌稱其融合了「創新的韓國美容護膚技術與非洲植物成分」。該系列中的蘆薈隱形防曬乳採用非洲蘆薈、玻尿酸和 SPF 50+ 防護配方，不會給膚色較深的人留下白色印漬。

54 Thrones 由美國人 Christina Tegbe 所創立，她的成長經歷使她受益匪淺，她將其描述為「植根於奈及利亞的文化精髓」。該品牌的產品採用加納和烏干達乳木果油、猴麵包樹油和荷荷巴油等成分，並由「高品質、非洲種植的優秀原料，創造受古老傳統啟發的可持續的美容產品」。品牌的名稱也參考了非洲大陸，向非洲 54 個國家致敬。在彩妝領域，由 Emolyne Ramlov 創立的 Emolyne，她出生於烏干達，在丹麥長大，長期住在倫敦。雖然該品牌是英國品牌，但 Ramlov 在創建該品牌時考慮到了她的非洲傳統，每種指甲和唇彩的配方都適合不同的膚色和底色，每種色調都以不同的非洲地點命名。 其中包括 Fes（柔和的桃色指甲油色調）和 Uganda（深紫紅色唇彩）。

VML

↑ Emolyne cosmetics

值得關注的原因：

除了提供引人入勝的天然成分外，專注於黑人膚色和膚質的非
洲美容品牌，正在這個被預測持續增長的非洲美容市場佔有一
個理想位置。與將其美學引入該地區的全球品牌不同，這些品
牌是根據非洲消費者的需求塑造的。由於它們在黑人膚色需求
方面的專業知識，這些品牌還能夠在全球滿足過去一直被忽視
的黑人群眾的需求。

↑ Emolyne Ramlov, founder of the eponymous cosmetics brand

情商美容學

情緒健康重新定義了美麗。

↑ Body Proud collection by I Am Proud

美容新創公司 I Am Proud 希望向每個人灌輸信心和積極性。該公司於 2020 年推出護膚系列，並於 2023 年推出護髮和身體護理系列。Body Proud 的 NPD 經理 Maria Sarris 告訴 VML 智庫：「Body Proud 的配方採用專利提振情緒的香味技術，經科學證明具有特定的情緒益處。」這些香水花了兩年時間生產，並使用客製化系統「利用神經科學來測試其功效，透過大腦掃描、虹膜辨識和臉部編碼心理學來探索結果，以量化功效」Sarris 表示：「用戶可以選擇感到自信、充滿活力、有力量、或冷靜。」

《改變未來的 100 件事：2023 年全球百大趨勢》中的 Selfmade 正在開闢一條評論美麗的新途徑。「我們使用心理皮膚病學作為了解我們情緒世界的窗。」Selfmade 創始人兼首席執行官 Stephanie Lee 告訴 VML 智庫：「我們使用我們的皮膚作為我們情感世界的數據點，以便真正更深入地照顧自己。」Selfmade 的每一款產品都與一個核心行為概念相匹配，這種直接關聯為消費者帶來新的美容處方。

Priyanka Chopra 的基金會與 Cosmoss 合作於 2024 年 1 月推出了一項名為 NeverAlone.Love 的新計劃，重點關注情緒健康和心理健康，長達一年的系列計劃和活動將使其成為現實。

Glossier 執行長 Kyle Leahy 向 Glossy 講述了該品牌的情感

↑ Body Proud collection by I Am Proud

調和方式。 他表示：「美，對我來說，是一種感覺。我有一個四歲的孩子和一個一歲的孩子。我在想，我希望他們對這個世界有什麼感覺，我希望他們對自己有什麼感覺，品牌如何在提升自信方面發揮作用，尤其是美容公司如何幫助推動這一目標。」

值得關注的原因：
美容品牌正在善用美的優勢，對情感、身份認同和心理健康所能產生的影響，將傳統的產品和美容話題轉化為充滿情感的賦權運動。

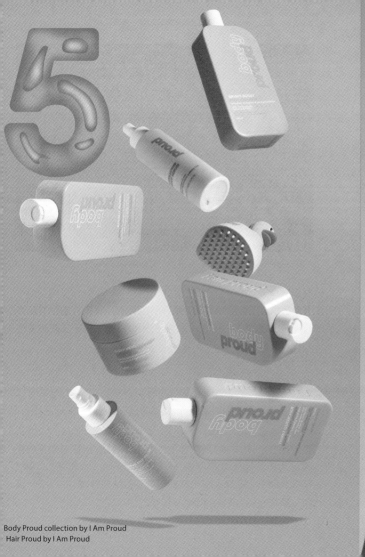

Body Proud collection by I Am Proud
Hair Proud by I Am Proud

↑ Six Senses Rome's modern-day take on the Roman bathing journey

60

身心調和SPAs

生物駭客(Biohacking)的時代已經一去不復返了，
取而代之的是生物調和平衡。

健康教練兼 Chek 研究所創始人 Paul Chek 認為，生物協調是「你了解自己與身體發生的事情的能力」。 健康計劃越來越多地採用這種思維，提供個人化和可衡量的治療方法，並促進身心的長期預防策略。

Six Senses Ibiza's RoseBar 的醫療顧問 Dr. Tamsin Lewis 告訴 VML 智庫：「當涉及生物調和的想法時，我們認為它是比生物駭客更先進的選擇。」 Lewis 實施了一項逐步改進的計劃，為身體意識留出了時間。她認為，實現生物調和可以創造出「真正的健康」，並提供「改善你的生理和心理狀況，同時給你的身體足夠的時間修復和再生」。 羅馬 Six Senses 飯店於 2023 年 3 月開業，其 Spa 中心的靈感源自古羅馬儀式，並與現代護理相結合，遵循與 RoseBar 類似的原則。

VML

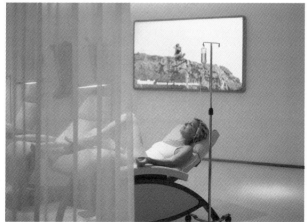

↑ RoseBar at Six Senses Ibiza

Kintsugi Space 於 2023 年 11 月開設一間六層樓的旗艦女性專屬健康中心，邀請會員「休息、修復、重置和更新」。這家會員制俱樂部位於阿布達比的阿爾雷姆島，採取全面的健康療法。其經驗包括阿育吠陀、自然療法、心理學和量子技術，其使命專注於身體和靈魂的治癒和修復。

SHA 健康診所的重點是「為生命增添歲月，為歲月增添生命」。這些計劃旨在提供重新平衡、倡導自然療法和促進情緒健康。SHA 目前僅在西班牙推出，並將於 2024 年擴展到墨西哥和阿拉伯聯合大公國。

值得關注的原因：
快速的健康訣竅正在被水療中心的長期療程所取代，這些療程以緩慢而有序的步驟促進健康長壽（請參閱第 81 章〈長壽渡假村〉）。

零售

零售社團

百貨公司不僅僅是購物場所，還推出了專屬的會員專屬俱樂部。

↑ Gordon Ramsay at Harrods The Residence Shanghai

Harrods 於 2023 年底在上海開設了其首家會員專屬俱樂部「The Residence」。該空間設有酒吧、休息室、私人用餐室和戶外露台，以及由戈登·拉姆齊（Gordon Ramsay）擔任主廚的高級餐廳。它還為會員提供在航空、房地產、室內設計和私人導購等方面的超級服務，以及參加品牌合作夥伴舉辦的私人活動和大師主持的專業課程。

據《女裝日報》報導，入會標準將比其他會員俱樂部更嚴格。「我們想要提供的是依據不同生活方式和興趣，成立各種熱愛不同事物的社群—像是收藏威士忌的、娛樂的、愛好藝術的。」

↑ Selfridges Unlocked, courtesy of Selfridges

Harrods 國際業務發展和通訊總監 Sarah Myler 說:「我們期待的結果是一個提供無與倫比的客戶服務的空間,但是為志同道合的人所設計。」

2023 年 7 月,Selfridges 推出新的忠誠度會員計畫「Selfridges Unlocked」。雖然沒有專用的實體空間,但該計畫為會員提供了類似的好處—解鎖造訪社群活動的權限,如宴餐俱樂部、電影發布和美容大師班。

值得關注的原因:
顧客在尋找的不只是零售商的產品。 Harrods 的餐廳和廚房總監 Ashley Saxton 說:「不僅僅是產品,還有隨之而來的體驗。」

↑ Harrods The Residence Shanghai

62
想像商店

將奇幻的數位空間概念帶入新的營運模式，
讓零售店擺脫實體限制。

VML

數位藝術家 Benjamin Benichou 是社交商務平台 Drop 的創始人兼 CEO，展示了對這一概念最具實驗性的詮釋，想像出了無數由生成式 AI 設計的，在不同地點的 Nike 概念店。在這些突破傳統界限空間中，Benichou 稱之為「不可能商店」，其中一個是以日本傳統建築為基礎設計的未來商店，一個在京都，另一個在火星上；還有一個被想像成是在珠穆朗瑪峰頂上的幾何立方商店。Benichou 告訴 VML 智庫，他相信「這些非傳統的想法可以啟發現實世界的零售設計，鼓勵建築師和設計師超越常規，考慮採用能夠提升零售體驗的新材料、形狀和結構。」此外，Benichou 想像「與 AI 人工智慧合作，我們可以達到創意的新高度，並突破可能性的限制。」

生成式 AI 公司如 Dalle-E 和 Midjourney 所提供的工具承諾可以增強創造力，點燃想像力，而且它們正變得越來越容易使用。Adobe Firefly 於 2023 年 10 月釋出商用版，讓使用 Adobe Creative Cloud 的用戶可以輕鬆地使用簡單的文句指示生成式 AI 做出想要的 AI 視覺效果。Adobe 稱 Adobe Firefly 是你的「想像力的最好的朋友」。Adobe Creative Cloud 的策略開發經理 Chris Duffey 告訴 VML 智庫說：「生成式 AI 對創作者和產出的內容都影響深遠。」Duffey 也觀察到了更廣的生意機會：「我們開始看到生成式 AI 對創意的第二波影響，創意產業正帶出全新的商業模式、全新的策略、全新的創新能力，給創意代理商和公司帶來了全新的可能性。」

除了生成式 AI 之外，品牌還使用元宇宙工具將購物者帶到新的目的地。2023 年 11 月，Bloomingdale 邀請購物者走進一座受 Willy Wonka（"巧克力的冒險工廠"電影中的巧克力工廠主人）啟發的超現實巧克力工廠。Wonka Room 使用 Emperia 的 VR 平台，讓遊客可以進行尋寶、購買系列產品，或者只是享受被各種巨型巧克力包圍的感覺。2023 年夏季，Ralph Lauren 推出了 888 House，這是一家坐落在沙漠景觀中的夢幻虛擬商店。Ralph Lauren 首席品牌與創新長 David Lauren 在接受《Wallpaper》雜誌採訪時表示：「創意創新是 Ralph Lauren DNA 的核心，我們正在踏上一段旅程，以全新的方式讓品牌更加生動活潑，吸引下一代的奢華消費者，他們越來越常在數位空間中做夢與生活。」想深入了解這一主題，請閱讀 VML 智庫的《Into the Metaverse》入門指南。

值得關注的原因：

57% 的千禧世代曾嘗試或希望嘗試虛擬世界中的商店，63% 對 VR 商務感興趣。諸多品牌正因應此趨勢，打造身臨其境、富有想像力的空間，讓消費者能夠走進品牌公司的世界，展示創意的風采，預覽電子商務的未來。

這些非傳統的想法可以啟發現實世界的零售設計，鼓勵建築師和設計師超越常規。

Benjamin Benichou, Drop 創始人兼CEO

↑ AI-generated Nike concept store on Mars, Benjamin Benichou

VML

↑ AI-generated Nike concept store on Mars, Benjamin Benichou

63
下世代收藏家

不要稱他們為奢侈品消費者，應該稱之為精品保管人。

真正奢華的概念正在轉變。《Jing Daily》全球主編 Jing Zhang 告訴 VML 智庫：「稀有性可能正取代價格成為奢侈的象徵，因為高收入消費者越來越希望成為收藏家。」

Jing Zhang 說：「隨著中國的零售、精品和商業帶來更多觸感、文化細節和深度思維。體驗的重要性將超越過去對必敗"單品"的痴迷」。

時尚設計師 Phoebe Philo 深刻領會了這一點，為奢侈時尚品牌提供了一種新的成功配方，將極端稀有與超級悠久配在一起。她備受期待的同名品牌於 2023 年 10 月推出了首發系列，引起了巨大的轟動──但它拒絕遵循奢侈時尚的傳統規則。該品牌不舉辦時裝秀，也不做季節性發佈。

相反，它將發佈限量且無法預測的單品，這些單品應該要隨著時間逐漸收集保存，不鼓勵每個季都用最新設計來把衣櫥裡的都換掉。

「我們的目標是創造一個可以彰顯永恆的產品。」Philo 說道：「Phoebe Philo 的商業模式目標是在生產和需求之間創造一個負責任的平衡。對我們而言，這意味著生產的數量要明顯地少於預期的需求。」

其他奢侈品牌也正在擁抱消費博物館化。「設計師品牌正在將以前的一次性美容產品轉變為收藏品，」《Business of Fashion》於 2023 年 8 月報道。

↑ Future Frequencies: Explorations in Generative Art and Fashion at Christie's

Guerlain 於 2023 年 11 月發佈了一款傳統收藏型香水瓶。這款香水瓶名為 Black Bee Prestige Edition，由法國珠寶商 Lorenz Bäumer 和水晶製造商 Baccarat 精心打造。 此次限量發售 22 瓶，每瓶售價為 25,000 歐元。

Gucci 正與 Christie's 合作進入策展領域，舉辦一場數位藝術拍賣展，名為「未來頻率：生成藝術與時尚的探索」的數字藝術拍賣。該拍賣展示了 21 件 NFT，並於 2023 年 7 月開放競投。藝術家 Claire Silver 在拍賣會上展示了兩件作品，她表示這些

作品的目的是讚揚 AI 時代，包括「文化遺產的深度和未來的光明」。

值得關注的原因：

奢侈品牌的角色正在演變。「奢侈品牌需要充當工藝和起源的守護者，」未來實驗室的前瞻編輯 Fiona Harkin 告訴《Luxury Society》。未來的奢華時代將由收藏而非消費所界定，將品牌和消費者轉變為奢侈品的策展人和管理者。

↑ Kingland initiative in Poole, United Kingdom, supported by LGIM Real Assets

64

社區零售

社區氛圍正在幫助購物區蓬勃發展。

購物區一直在為人流量而掙扎，特別是那些較低層的地區，也就是美國的 Coresight 研究報告顯示低迷入住率的地方。現在，以社區為中心的舉措正在幫助逆轉衰退。

策略是開發商大力投資於並鼓勵獨立商鋪入駐，以營造社區氛圍。在英國普爾，一個富有想像力的項目正在改造 Kingland Crescent。這條曾經沒落的商店街現在是 10 家蓬勃發展的獨立當地零售商店的所在地，包括一家唱片店、一家咖啡烘焙店、一家生鮮魚肉舖和一家珠寶店。這個項目是金融服務公司 Legal & General 的一個專門負責房地產投資的部門 LGIM Real Assets 的點子，從 2021 年開始，向剛嶄露頭角的當地商家提供了為期兩年免租和免稅的單位店鋪。

VML

↑ Airside mall, Hong Kong, by Nan Fung Group, designed by Snøhetta

LGIM 不動產的零售和未來主管 Denz Ibrahim 告訴 VML 智庫，滿足消費者需求的關鍵是提供一個「讓地點有意義的方法」。這些地點還可以通過「整合關鍵可以驅動當地服務的商家」，例如醫療保健、教育和工作空間，成為社區的核心。

Legal & General 提供店面租戶輔導和法律諮詢，希望這種方法可以形成一個發展藍圖，讓其他陷入困境的城鎮和城市可以參考應用。「自從 Kingland 開業以來，我們的店面用戶獲得顯著的成功，他們能夠在那裡學習、成長和擴大規模。」Denz Ibrahim 解釋道。「他們的成長速度之快，甚至要僱用更多人，為當地創造很多新的就業機會。在第一年，Kingland 就額外創造了 220 萬英鎊的消費，營業額每年增長超過 35%。」

在美國，以亞洲顧客為主的購物中心正逆勢崛起，這要歸功於它們獨有的社區氛圍。NBC 報導了亞洲購物中心是個充滿生氣和活力的社交聚會場所，提供娛樂、各種活動和熱鬧的氛圍，從夜市美食和小攤位到舞蹈和 K-pop 韓流商品。

連結的吸引力現在影響著新購物區的設計。在 Snøhetta 設計的香港空側新開發案中，南豐集團提出了完整的概念，邀請「社區聚集在一個可以做自己、與他人和自然相連的地方」。

正如 Denz Ibrahim 所說，能吸引當地人群的互補服務也證明了他們的重要。英國新創公司 Patch 正在建造鄰里共享空間，以增加零售店的客流量。場地的靈感來自於在家附近工作的概念，該概念設想如何在沒有可怕的通勤的情況下改善工作與生活的平衡。創辦人 Freddie Fforde 告訴 VML 智庫，該品牌的使命是「在英國每一條主要街道上，為人們、為工作和為社區創造機會」。

值得關注的原因：
在英國、美國和中國，有 56% 的人說「已經沒有社區感覺了」。零售商圈如果能找到創造性的方式幫助人們重新連接，便可以填補消失的共享公共空間所留下的空白。

Reading room in Patch workspace, High Wycombe, United Kingdom. Photography by Benoît Grogan-Avignon

65
節儉經濟

隨著通貨膨脹持續加劇，零售商必須養成節儉的習慣。

VML

VML 智庫的數據確認，當前生活成本是人們最關心的問題，全球有 64% 的人將其列為面臨的五大迫切問題之一。儘管從長遠來看經濟前景較為光明，消費者在 2024 年仍將感受到經濟壓力。國際貨幣基金組織（IMF）指出：「全球經濟正在艱難地前進，而非快速奔跑，並且大多數國家可能要到 2025 年才能將通貨膨脹降至目標水平。」

全球消費者透過適應更加節儉和更靈活的購物習慣展現出韌性。在中國，「降級消費」成了 2023 年微博上的熱門話題之一，而專注於折扣的電商拼多多的收入同期比增長了 63%。這種心態在全球普遍存在。根據麥肯錫的報告，80% 的美國消費者（包括 88% 的 Z 世代和千禧世代）通過轉向其他產品來尋找價值。

這些購物行為將在 2024 年持續存在，品牌和零售商需要利用低價策略來支持這些更精明的購物者。 加拿大食品配送應用 SkipTheDishes 就是通過其「通膨食譜」雜貨購物工具實現這一點，該工具預測 100 家雜貨店中 400 種受歡迎食材中價格降幅最大的產品，並利用這些數據創建價格合理的「廚師靈感」可購買食譜。在法國，超市巨頭家樂福正將自己定位為消費者的盟友，通過對抗產品減量而價格不變的「縮水通膨」。店內標語直接點名批評採用這種策略的品牌，直到它們同意降低價格。

寵物護理品牌 Wilder Harrier 則在尋求超越價格低廉之外的方式來支持其客戶。該品牌正在建立一個社區寵物食品儲藏室網絡，讓在生活成本危機中掙扎的家庭可以領取捐贈的動物食品。

↑ The Inflation Cookbook by SkipTheDishes

值得關注的原因：

儘管從長期來看經濟前景更加樂觀，但在 2024 年，全球所有市場的消費者將繼續感受到生活成本危機的壓力。通過回應節儉新消費心態，零售商可以滿足對價值優惠日益增長的需求，同時要將自己定位為消費者強大的盟友。

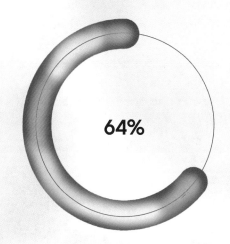

64%

生活成本
是人們最關心的問題，
全球有64%的人
將其列為面臨的
五大迫切問題之一。

VML

66
元宇宙購物

在虛擬世界購買實體商品，不是夢！

亞馬遜正在推出一項新服務，能讓客戶從虛擬世界的商店購買實體商品，包括遊戲、行動應用程式和 AR 擴增實境產品。該服務名為 Amazon Anywhere，於 2023 年 5 月首次推出，最初僅對開發者發出邀請。 Amazon Anywhere 最終將為商家打開新的收入來源，它讓購物者將其亞馬遜帳戶與虛擬體驗相結合，實現在不離開虛擬環境的情況下進行購物。品牌只需在此虛擬體驗中展示產品，亞馬遜則負責訂購、配送和售後服務。

為了推出這款新服務，亞馬遜與 Niantic Labs 合作，發行 Niantic Labs 的擴增實境遊戲《Peridot》。玩家可以在遊戲中購買主題商品，如 T 恤和抱枕，並指定所需的尺寸，而無需離開遊戲。

零售商為其元購物服務，增加虛擬 360 度購物體驗，這次創造了一種能讓粉絲購買 Prime Video 系列和電影商品的體驗。在

VML

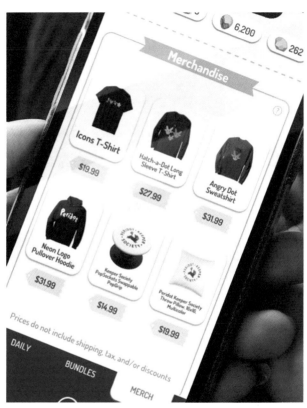

↑ Amazon Anywhere

此次嘗試中，該品牌打造了《Gen V》系列中 Godolkin 大學的身臨其境之旅，該系列講述了美國超級英雄大學的新生的故事。該旅程最終在校園商店結束，位居美國的訪客可以購買 150 種商品中的複製商品。

值得關注的原因：

根據 VML 的 2023 年《未來購物者》報告，11% 的全球購物者表示他們正積極地在元宇宙中購物，但這很可能指的是虛擬物品：如 NFT 或遊戲皮膚和頭像配件。現在的關鍵差異在於，亞馬遜正在發展在虛擬空間購物並收到真實實體商品的能力。透過將服務擴展到其他商家，亞馬遜正在為新時代的元宇宙購物打下基礎。

VML

↑ Dior flagship store

67

精品零售殿堂

超級旗艦店的時代已經來臨。

精品品牌正打造超級旗艦店，讓購物者能完全融入品牌的世界。巴黎奢侈品顧問公司 MAD 的創始合夥人 Delphine Vitry 告訴《女裝日報》：「你不希望 Louis Vuitton 的店面數量跟 Starbucks 一樣多。你需要這種超大型的商店。」

奢侈品零售商正紛紛在美國搶占空間。《華爾街日報》於 2023 年 10 月報導：「Gucci、Chanel 等精品品牌在美國的房地產上大手筆投資。」據房地產投資公司 JLL 表示，自 2022 年 10 月至 2023 年 10 月間，美國的奢侈品牌新租用的空間，總面積達到 65 萬平方英尺，較前一年的 25 萬平方英尺有顯著增加。而且不僅僅是更大的空間，還更加集中：從 2022 年 10 月至 2023 年，精品品牌所簽署租約的平均面積為 5,000 平方英尺或更大，比前 12 個月增長了 28%。

VML

Chanel 在 2023 年 5 月開設了其最大的美國專賣店。這家比佛利山莊的旗艦店橫跨四層，擁有 30,000 平方英尺，是其之前在比佛利山莊的面積的兩倍多。頂樓設有一個名人專屬的 VVIP 閣樓，以及一個面積為 2,690 平方英尺的屋頂露台，面向好萊塢標誌。「對我來說，這攸關於品牌形象，而不僅僅是投資回報的問題，」Chanel 時裝總裁 Bruno Pavlovsky 表示：「我們會繼續在所有網路上保持活躍，但終究精品店內的體驗對於今時的 Chanel 來說，比以往任何時刻更加重要。」

Tiffany & Co 在經過四年的翻新後，新的紐約市旗艦店於 2023 年 4 月開幕。該旗艦店共有 10 層，占地 10 萬平方英尺，是紐約市最大的零售空間之一。頂層有一間僅限收到邀請的 VVIP 才可進入的購物間。

這種轉變並不僅發生在美國。在倫敦，Gucci 於 2023 年 9 月開設了一家五層樓、面積達 15,000 平方英尺的商店，而 Burberry 位於邦德街的三層樓旗艦店則於 2023 年 6 月重新開幕，佔地近 22,000 平方英尺。此外，Dior 位於巴黎馬奈大道的大型旗艦店於 2022 年 3 月重新開業，該店占地超過 107,000 平方英尺，內設餐廳、博物館和酒店套房，同時提供零售服務。

值得關注的原因：
奢侈品牌正大力投入品牌世界構建，以強化其實體存在，打造代表全方位體驗的旗艦店（請參閱第 36 章〈建構品牌世界〉）。

↑ Dior flagship store

零售會員

付費會員制度提供獎勵以獲取忠誠。

VML

↑ CVS pharmacy

來自顧客忠誠度專業公司 Clarus Commerce 的一項調查發現，擁有傳統忠誠計劃的美國零售商中，有 95% 正在考慮推出付費會員制度。這顯示人們越來越意識到了高優質會員計畫能夠為消費者和零售商帶來巨大的好處。

付費會員機制，即消費者支付定期費用以換取折扣和獨家福利，並不是什麼新鮮事。事實上，電子商務數據專家 Yaguara 報告稱，63% 的美國人擁有 Amazon Prime 帳戶。然而，無頭式結帳 (headless checkout) 解決方案 Bold Commerce 的聯合創始人 Jay Myers 表示，付費會員制度仍然是一種極少被使用的策略，只有不到 5% 的線上零售商提供這種服務。

總部位於洛杉磯的健康品牌 Liquid IV 是採用這波新趨勢的公司之一，除了現有的訂閱優惠外，還提供付費會員制度。該公司指出，靈活性是對消費者的一大賣點，消費者可以更自由地在更廣泛的產品中使用折扣，可以隨時隨地購物，並獲得獨家商品，而不受限於品牌所推薦的優惠組合。

美國藥房零售商 CVS 的 CarePass 計劃每月費用為 5 美元，但包含 10 美元的抵用金，作為招攬顧客的誘因來建立忠誠度。CarePass 總經理 Adam Volin 告訴 Retail TouchPoints，會員「購物次數增加且購物籃更大」。麥肯錫的研究支持了這項策略，顯示「付費忠誠度計畫的會員，有 60% 的比例願意在品牌上花費更多」。

對零售商的另一好處是，會員費能提供穩定收入。H&M 旗下的僅限會員品牌 Singular Society 表示，這些費用「讓品牌得以生存」，使其能夠將製造定位在品質和可持續性上。Singular Society 的創意總監兼聯合創始人 Erik Zetterberg 告訴 VML 智庫：「這種轉變使我們能夠開發和製作最高品質的產品，並以傳統方式難以實現的價格銷售。我們的理念是透過讓人們買到更好的產品，以減少不必要的額外消費。」

值得關注的原因：
儘管對消費者和零售商來說都有回報獲利的潛力，但付費會員制度仍然是一個小眾產品。消費者只可能參加少數的付費會員機制，現在是零售商抓住這個有限時機的時候。

VML

69

愉悅零售

**隨著零售商透過歡樂來豐富購物者的生活，
購物的樂趣也隨之增強。**

Ulta Beauty 和作家 Mel Robbins 於 2023 年 9 月啟動了「Joy Project」這項長期計畫，計畫的宗旨是幫助年輕世代，加深與「美」的連結並獲得正向的體驗。Ulta Beauty 行銷長 Michelle Crossan-Matos 表示：「我們知道我們可以發起一場運動，幫助世界各地的人們過上更真實、更快樂的生活。」

Liberty London 正在進行的「Find Joy Within」活動中，五彩笑臉佔據了攝政街商店。該活動於 2023 年初首次推出，包括「讓人感覺良好的時尚」和色彩療法珠寶，帶來愉快的色彩療法體驗。Liberty 的珠寶採購員 Ruby Beales 表示：「佩戴珠寶是一種自我表達的行為，對我來說，這是在你的服裝中添加一些提升心情的亮麗元素的完美方式，想像一下琺瑯的糖果調色板、霓虹珠寶手鐲和色彩斑斕的寶石組合。沒有規則，隨意點綴或疊加對比色調。這一切都是為了享受樂趣。」

今年秋天，電子商務零售商 Terez 在紐約市開設了第一家實體店。當遊客進入商店時，他們會被充滿活力的粉紅色牆壁、異想天開的氣球吊燈以及品牌豐富多彩的時尚系列所吸引。Terez 的使命是「慶祝生活中的美好部分」

值得關注的原因：
品牌透過設計、產品規劃和鼓勵顧客找到內心的快樂，為購物者的生活注入樂趣。

VML

70

AI試裝

科技的進步使虛擬試穿從噱頭變得極為逼真。

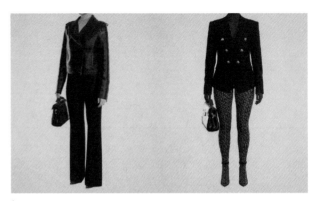

↑ Balmain 3D fitting, Bods

科技先驅們正在開發工具，讓購物者能夠使用更真實的虛擬替身進行線上試穿，甚至能夠模仿服裝在現實生活中的披散和垂墜感。

總部位於洛杉磯的 Bods 正在倡導類似電腦遊戲的虛擬替身作為線上試穿工具。 該公司的 AI 從照片或關鍵測量數據中提取訊息，然後消費者可以調整這些資訊以完全符合自己的身形。2022 年初，該公司在種子輪融資中籌集了 560 萬美元。

2023 年 11 月，Bods 宣布與法國時尚品牌 Balmain 合作，為 Balmain 網站的訪客提供「客製化和虛擬試穿」。 Bods 表示，透過精準的數位呈現，購物者可以讓他們的虛擬替身穿上「Balmain 經典系列和時裝秀設計款」。這些數位呈現「忠實地複製了奢華的面料和色調，以及 Balmain 工作室在手工工藝、裝飾和剪裁方面的專業知識。」

Balmain 的品牌數位長 Simon Cottigny 相信，該技術將為品牌和消費者帶來好處，並表示它將「大大幫助我們的顧客做出更自信的決策」，進而提高轉換率，最終降低退貨率。

2023 年 6 月，Google 首次推出了服裝虛擬試穿功能，該科技巨頭聲稱這項功能「向您展示衣服在不同體型和尺寸的真實模特兒身上的樣子」。為了創造能夠展現真實世界中服裝垂墜、皺紋和摺痕的圖像，該公司建立了一個 Diffusion-Based 的 AI 模型。該工具目前在美國有 Anthropologie、Loft、H&M 和 Everlane 等公司提供。

英國公司 Anthropics Technology 為攝影師和零售商開發軟體，該公司開發了 Zyler，這是一種採用 AI 的虛擬試穿服務。該公司表示，這項服務將轉換率提高了 18%，並可在品牌的網站和店內螢幕上提供虛擬試穿。John Lewis Rental 和 Marks & Spencer 商店目前在英國使用該服務。

值得關注的原因：
由 AI 驅動的虛擬試穿技術變得越來越精確，讓消費者能夠真正看到服裝實際穿著的模樣，藉此提高品牌的轉換率，並減少不必要的退貨。

↑ Balmain 3D fitting, Bods

奢華

歌劇式逃離

**頂尖且浮誇、奢華的室內設計
將帶領豪奢消費者進入另一個新境界。**

↑ Apollo's Muse

奢華的開幕會正從古代享樂主義的解放和揮霍無度的奢華中汲取靈感。2023 年 4 月,倫敦梅費爾區的 Bacchanalia 餐廳後面新開了一家會員俱樂部。這家名為 "阿波羅的繆斯 Apollo's Muse" 的俱樂部被稱為 "最私密的私人會員俱樂部",只允許 500 人入會。康泰納仕的旅遊雜誌《Conde Nast Traveler》稱此俱樂部空間的特點是 "浮誇的華麗"。從地板到天花板的大理石、天鵝絨的吧台椅、訂製的的穆拉諾 (Murano) 酒杯,這僅僅只是開始,俱樂部還收藏了公元一世紀和二世紀的希臘羅馬古董,這些價值連城的古董甚至可媲美一些世界級博物館和美術館。

**人們正在尋找一種
探索和逃離日常的感覺。**

Torquil McIntosh 和 Simon Mitchell,
Sybarite 聯合創始人

VML

← Apollo's Muse. Photography by Johnny Stephens

這家餐廳於 2022 年 12 月開業,被《Standard》形容為「一個歌劇式逃避現實的夢幻之地」。《Guest of a Guest》將其描述為「一個希臘羅馬風格的奢華頌歌」,並在數位媒體公司所稱的「毫不掩飾的奢靡表現」中,餐廳提供價值 500 美元的義大利麵菜餚,由身著古羅馬長袍的服務員提供,裝潢包括巨大的翼獅、獨角獸和希臘神祇的雕像。為了敬希臘和羅馬的奢華,整個牆壁都被一幅由 Thomas Couture 重新演繹的作品《The Romans in Their Decadence》所覆蓋。

在大西洋的另一邊,Bad Roman 將類似的奢靡和放浪不羈帶到了紐約市。該餐廳於 2023 年 2 月開業,被美食雜誌 Eater 譽為「年度最瘋狂的義大利餐廳」,其中「在這裡用餐就是一場奇觀」。這個場地擁有一個穿著霓虹項鍊的野豬雕像、視覺錯覺馬賽克,且在浴室裡有一個的非常大尺寸的噴泉。

值得關注的原因:
設計師們將希臘羅馬式的富麗堂皇運用到現代奢華的室內設計中。設計公司 Sybarite 的聯合創始人 Torquil McIntosh 和 Simon Mitchell 告訴 VML 智庫:「人們正在尋找一種探索和逃離日常的感覺,他們發現到"這樣的空間能將他們帶離並帶入探索的境地"。」

↑ Apollo's Muse. Photography by Johnny Stephens

72

世外聖殿

私人島嶼成為精英人士的天堂渡假勝地。

↑ La Isla Secreta, courtesy of Rosewood Mayakoba

在一個未受污染的珊瑚礁群島的環繞下，有一個占地 1.7 公頃的隱秘療養地，將於 2024 年初開放，供那些準備租下整個島嶼的人使用。沙烏地阿拉伯 Thuwal 私人渡假村是紅海全球公司(Red Sea Global, RSG) 新開發項目的一部分，為希望能享受高度客製化私人渡假的客人提供超豪華服務。遊客抵達島上碼頭後，可以入住三臥室別墅或三間單臥室套房。私人禮賓、管家服務和行政主廚等服務人員將為遊客提供精心策劃的非凡體驗。

紅海全球集團首席執行長 John Pagano 說：「Thuwal 私人渡假村的創立是為了讓顧客有機會擺脫日常生活的壓力，轉而與他們最親密的陪伴重新建立關係。」我們相信：「壯麗的紅海海岸與量身定制的奢華體驗相結合，將為最具鑑賞力的旅行者提供無與倫比的逃離。」

因 1968 年舉辦航運大亨 Aristotle Onassis 和 Jacqueline Kennedy 的婚禮而聞名的希臘私人島嶼 Skorpios 再經過三年的翻新後，將於 2024 年重新開幕，預計耗資 2 億美元將這座希臘小島改造成一個豪華的私人渡假村。這座 VIP 渡假小島最多可容納 50 名遊客，且每週住宿費用將超過 100 萬美元。

墨西哥的玫瑰木瑪雅科巴 (Rosewood Mayakoba) 開設了一個幽靜的新場所，名為 La Isla Secreta──這是渡假勝地內的

↑ La Isla Secreta, courtesy of Rosewood Mayakoba

一個私人、隱密的島嶼，僅可乘船前往。這個「渡假村裡的渡假村」已於 2023 年 1 月開業，為客人提供真正與世隔絕的機會，並讓他們感受到無微不至的呵護。

值得關注的原因：
76% 的高收入者表示，他們更願意將錢花在體驗上，而不是物品上；25% 的高收入者認為，如今的奢華意味著很少有人能做到的體驗。私人島嶼上的高端客製化假期，正吸引著上流社會的人去體驗遠離群眾的獨特體驗。

73

受邀限定

有特定的人脈才能入場享受額外的、有誘人專屬感的豪奢體驗。

↑ Harrods The Residence Shanghai

從專屬會員俱樂部到不尋常的高級精緻餐飲體驗，一種「僅有被邀請的人才能入場參與」的奢華概念正在興起。2023 年底，英國知名的精品百貨 Harrods 在上海開設了一所私人俱樂部—哈羅德公館。據《WWD》報導，該俱樂部是從 Harrods 私人購物邀請制的概念演變而來的。

它初期接受的會員上限 250 名，而未來也只能透過其他會員的提名才有機會加入該俱樂部。他們表示，這是為了確保「完全的隱私和慎重裁量」（請參閱第 61 章〈零售社團〉）。

2023 年初紐約的法國廚師 Yann Nury 首次推出 La Résidence Soho 餐廳，它位於光線充足的 12 樓高層裡，且這是一個僅受邀人士才能進入的空間。Nury 表示：「客人可以在開放又現

↑ La Résidence Soho kitchen. Photography by David Chow

代化的廚房裡中觀賞、見證並且品嚐我們的創作。」此外，空間的美感與美食饗宴同等重要；據《紐約時報》報導，餐廳的閣樓是由法國建築師 Charles Zana 設計，採用義大利大理石工作檯、高級訂製的 Molteni 廚房爐灶，和經典的 1960 年代 Pierre Chapo S11 風格座椅。這家餐廳不提供聯絡電話，唯有透過任何認識「認識 Nury」的人，才有機會進入。

總部位於倫敦的 Caviar Kaspia 餐廳於 2023 年初以「受邀限定」私人俱樂部的方式重新開業。這是一間魚子醬專門店，在世界各地都有分店，但與倫敦不同的是，其他分店是對一般大眾公開的。

值得關注的原因：

根據瑞士信貸（Credit Suisse）的數據，到 2024 年，全球平均成年人的資產將達到 10 萬美元，而到 2026 年，將有 8750 萬人擁有至少 100 萬美元的財富。隨著更多人成為奢侈品消費者，某些「專屬」體驗將不是有錢就可以買到的，還須取決於顧客的人脈關係。

VML

74

奢華新域

隨著全球精品市場放緩，各品牌紛紛向東方尋求成長。

亞洲精品市場正持續升溫，且不僅僅是中國。2023 年 11 月，貝恩諮詢公司 (Bain & Company) 指出：「東南亞國家在全球精品市場呈現正勢力」，而在 2023 年 5 月舉行的英國《金融時報》精品高峰會上，印度、泰國和菲律賓三國也被 BCG 評為精品市場成長之一。現在，精品品牌正增強他們在該地區的影響力。

Dior 成為第一個在孟買舉辦季度時裝大秀的西方大牌，在壯闊的印度門古蹟為背景發佈了其 2023 年秋冬系列。選擇此場地可以凸顯了印度精品消費者日益增長的重要性，更不用說這個國家文化影響力了（請參閱第 33 章〈印度品牌〉）。Knight Frank India 預測，在 2022 年至 2027 年期間，印度財富超過 3000 萬美元的人口數量將增長近 60%。

據彭博社報道，儘管租金飆升，但從 Hermès 到 Christian Louboutin 等精品零售商仍在印度的城市中開設店面。為了掌握市場成長的機會，印度阿達尼集團企業於 2023 年 11 月開設了 Jio World Plaza。該高檔精品購物中心位於孟買的班德拉庫拉辦大樓，匯集了 60 個精品牌，包括 Dior、Gucci、Balenciaga 和 Louis Vuitton，以 及 Manish Malhotra 和 Falguni Shane Peacock 等印度知名設計師品牌。

2023 年 10 月，位於泰國巴吞旺區的暹羅百麗宮 (Siam Paragon) 推出了豪華廳。該店由 Siam Piwat 運營，匯集了 20 個精品牌，包括低調的義大利品牌 Loro Piana 在泰國的首家專賣店，以及 Fendi 和 Louis Vuitton 的男裝系列。泰國精品行業的增長有部分也受惠於觀光旅遊業大量遊客的湧入。

東南亞的發展速度是非常快的。

Jing Zhang,《Jing Daily》全球主編

《Jing Daily》全球主編 Jing Zhang 告訴 VML 智庫:「成都、深圳和曼谷等城市的快速發展,對在倫敦或巴黎的體驗構成了挑戰。」

由於中產階級不斷壯大,越南也被認為是一顆明日之星,預測機構 Statista 預測,至 2023 年底,越南將成為一個價值十億美元的市場。Jing Zhang 將越南描述為「一個充滿活力、人才濟濟的地方」。在河內,四季飯店、費爾蒙飯店、麗茲卡爾頓飯店和華爾道夫飯店等知名品牌新建的高檔飯店和飯店式住宅預計將吸引更多的精品零售商,在這座城市打造一個新的高檔奢侈和購物樞紐。

值得關注的原因:
Jing Zhang 表示:「東南亞和印度為精品產業帶來了重大的新商機,該地區的城市現在可以與傳統的精品之都相媲美。越南和泰國將成為與中國強國並駕齊驅的新星。 在東南亞的發展速度是非常快的,且人們對在曼谷和西貢能找到的東西感到震驚。」

↑ Dior pre-fall 2023 show, Mumbai

VML

↑ Virgin Galactic

75

極致奢華體驗

**奢華旅遊中的一個新興小眾市場，
提供了激發腎上腺素分泌的放縱體驗。**

探險旅遊正在崛起，根據美國市場研究公司 (Grand View Research) 的預測，到 2030 年，全球探險旅遊收入將從 2022 年的 3170 億美元增至 1 兆美元。據《紐約時報》報道，不斷增長的市場需求甚至刺激了對探險保險的新需求，這些保險包含提供撤離和意外傷亡的保障。

維珍銀河公司 (Virgin Galactic) 於 2023 年 6 月將首批旅客送上太空。首航的商用飛機是由義大利空軍資助的一項以研究為重點的任務，為未來尋求刺激的富豪探險者的飛行做準備。該公司已售出約 800 張機票，每張售價 25 萬至 45 萬美元不等。

2023 年推出的 "拉斯維加斯大道跳傘"（Skydive the Strip）可以讓冒險者在天黑後從拉斯維加斯大道上空跳傘，每次跳傘費用高達 3 萬美元。除了高昂的價格外，它的預約席次也非常有限，每年可預約的名額不到 100 個。該公司表示，Skydive the Strip 為的是迎合那些希望能 "體驗不凡" 的腎上腺素上癮

↑ Skydive the Strip

者。聯合創始人 Jim Dolan 告訴《Travel + Leisure》:「生命在於體驗。而這即是獨一無二的體驗。」

Insider Expeditions 是一家專為那些希望能 "突破可能極限" 的億萬富翁旅旅客提供服務的旅行社。據 Skift 報道,該旅行社平均每年舉辦 30 次的舉凡任何想得到的體驗活動,從為約翰 - 麥肯羅 (John McEnroe) 和帕特里克 - 麥肯羅 (Patrick McEnroe) 在塞倫蓋蒂中部建造一個網球場,到在南極洲享受現場演唱會。Insider Expeditions 的創始人 Carl Shephard 告訴 the travel industry 新聞網站:「富豪旅客來到 Insider Expeditions 尋找前所未有的特別體驗。這是 "生命的終極毒藥"。」

值得關注的原因:
2024 年,奢華旅客這些一生一次、令人腎上腺素飆升的終極放縱體驗,能讓他們重振對生活的渴望。

$1 兆美元

到2030年,
全球探險旅遊收入
將從2022年的3170億美元
增至1兆美元。

美國市場研究公司

VML

神秘零售

富裕人士的購物行為變得低調謹慎。

「懂得人，就懂。」一直是精品在服務上的慣用口語。現在，這句話隨著精品品牌為頂端客戶在隱秘目的地提供高規格的保護隱私體驗而更加重要。

Chanel 在北京 SKP 購物中心的店內開設了 31 Cambon，這是一家 VIP 沙龍，其不易辨識品牌的外觀參考了該品牌在巴黎的創始地址和旗艦店。同樣，Chanel 於 2023 年夏季在中國廣州和深圳開設了 Chanel Les Salons Privé。根據小紅書上的圖片，這些僅限邀請才能進入的沙龍極小化了品牌識別，僅能憑黑白外觀的暗示來判斷。

「我們將投資於非常保密的精品店，以極度專屬的方式服務客戶。」據《Jing Daily》報導 Chanel 財務長 Philippe Blondiaux 在 2022 年財務報表的評論說。「我們用盡心力就是要保護我們的客戶，特別是我們的既有客戶。」《Business of Fashion》總編輯 Imran Amed 也指出許多設計師名店外普遍存在的排隊現象，與精品體驗格格不入，因此精品品牌想要為其最尊重的客戶創造更珍稀的體驗並不令人意外。

VML

Gucci 也開始著重於僅對受邀客戶開放的私人沙龍，以滿足最頂級富豪客戶的需求。2023 年 4 月，在洛杉磯的 Melrose Place 和 Melrose Avenue 的轉角處，Gucci 開設了一家佔地 4,380 平方英尺的沙龍。儘管該沙龍建有一個醒目的招牌在建築頂部，但據《WWD》報道，它裝有染色鍍膜玻璃窗，因此 "客戶可以向外一覽無遺，但外面的人看不到裡面"。Kering 集團董事長兼執行長 François-Henri Pinault 在 2 月對分析師表示，其沙龍概念的價格範圍為 40,000 至 300 萬歐元，涵蓋臨時和永久的沙龍空間。 其他奢侈品牌也很青睞這個策略，包括義大利品牌 Brunello Cucinelli，該品牌已經為他們非常重要的客戶開設了七家私人沙龍。

值得關注的原因：
在經濟不確定性的時代，追求高品質生活的消費者開始節制消費，精品品牌因此更著重於服務他們的富豪客戶。──這些客戶的財富，如路透社所說，「幾乎對經濟動盪免疫。」

精品品牌為頂端客戶
在隱秘目的地
提供高規格的
保護隱私體驗
而更加重要。

77

品牌特製宅

從Bentley到Karl Lagerfeld，
一個新的高級品牌住宅等級正在崛起。

↑ Bentley Residences, courtesy of Dezer Development

VML

奢華

當談到要過奢侈生活時，無非就是地點、地點、地點，還要有品牌認證，就只能是邁阿密了，這個擁有陽光島海灘 Sunny Isles Beach 的佛羅里達州的城市，目前是 Porsche Design Tower 和 Armani/Casa 宅的所在地。

預計於 2026 年完工的 Bentley 房產將改變邁阿密的天際線。Bentley 住宅高達 749 英尺，將成為美國最高的海濱大樓。該公司承諾將 "將 Bentley 創新的奢華帶入您的家中"，使人們真正能夠 "生活在品牌之中"。這棟 63 層的大樓包括 216 個住宅單元，並提供包括戶外游泳池、健身房和一個配室內高爾夫的遊戲室在內的眾多設施。

以另一領先品牌為核心的計畫 Aston Martin Residences，也即將在邁阿密市中心營運。根據《紐約時報》的報導，這 391 個單元幾乎已全部售出，包括一個售價為 5900 萬美元的超豪華 Aston Martin 三層閣樓。

時尚住房品牌 Karl Lagerfeld 和阿聯酋房地產公司 Taraf 於 2023 年 10 月宣布將攜手在杜拜開發奢華 villas 別墅。預計在幾個月內開始動工，將擴展 Karl Lagerfeld 的住宅系列組合，該系列已有在西班牙的馬貝拉和馬來西亞等地完成。

在英國，一個新的泰晤士生活專案 Thames Living project 將與豪華汽車品牌的子公司 Porsche Consulting 保時捷顧問合作開展。這個新城鎮將位於泰晤士河沿岸，包括住宅大樓、公園、酒店、餐廳和零售店。

↑ Bentley Residences, courtesy of Dezer Development

值得關注的原因：
精品牌進入價值數十億美元的房地產業務的動作看來很有前景。根據房地產公司 Knight Frank 在 2023 年 7 月的報告，預測從現在到 2026 年，品牌奢華住宅市場每年將增長 12%。此外，透過擴展至房地產領域，精品牌變身為生活方式品牌，為人們提供全方位的品牌體驗。

78
重新分級體驗

頂級奢華體驗要與其他層級隔離開。

↑ Masque restaurant, Mumbai

高端場所和商店正在緊縮紅繩圍欄區，限制除了最體面的客戶之外的人進入。以餐廳為例。2023 年夏季，法國南部地區新聞媒體 Var Matin 報導，St Tropez 當地居民因餐廳的富裕篩選機制被擠在外，一些有意用餐的人聲稱被要求支付高達 5,400 美元的過高價格。

位於倫敦 Hotel Café Royal 飯店內的兩星米其林餐廳 Alex Dilling 在引入每桌最低消費後引起了一些爭議，這導致單人用餐者需支付 330 英鎊的套餐價格。根據《標準晚報》的報導，今年，倫敦兩人用餐的價格首次突破了 1,000 英鎊。而在印度，由頂級廚師和調酒師主導的高檔餐飲體驗趨勢，活動價格高達每人 50,000 盧比，相當於一個家庭的月收入，根據《福布斯印度》報導。一次與紐約 Eleven Madison Avenue 合作，在孟買的奢華餐廳 Masque 舉辦的快閃活動甚至在僅僅九小時內售罄。

VML

飯店服務業正在追隨時尚品牌的腳步，向 1% 的真正奢華消費者展開攻勢，對這群消費者來說，金錢不是問題。依據 Edited 的資料，奢侈品現在的價格比 2019 年平均上漲了 25%。2023 年 Louis Vuitton 推出了 the Millionaire Speedy 百萬富翁包，一個名符其價的包包。

目前的焦點是在那些最富有的客戶身上，他們的消費信心更高。《WWD》引用了 Cushman & Wakefield 副總監 Weiying Guo 的話，她觀察到在中國「如果你的年收入少於 300 萬人民幣，你已不再是目標受眾。」

這是一個精明的策略。在精品領域，最高端消費者極其寶貴，根據 BCG 的精品專家，最富有的兩個消費群體不到 1%，卻貢獻了 10% 的收入。在中國，這一差異更為明顯。根據摩根士丹利的數據，僅 1% 的顧客就占了一些中國精品商場銷售的 40%。

值得關注的原因：
品牌正在將精品的頂峰變得更加尖銳，以安撫那些現在「想要更極端的東西來表達他們的地位」的最富有者，據《Jing Daily》的全球總編輯張靜說。隨著全球中產階級收緊腰帶，超級富豪成為了優先受眾。

VML

1%　　　　　　　　10%

最高端消費者極其寶貴，最富有的兩個消費群體不到 1%，卻貢獻了 10% 的收入。

BCG

79
皇宮住宿

一批超級豪華的新酒店正在吸引那些
想要像現代皇室一樣生活的旅行者。

奢華時尚品牌及珠寶商 Bulgari 於 2023 年 9 月在羅馬開設了新飯店。房價起價 1,500 美元，但最引人注目的是其頂級套房—每晚的費用為 41,000 美元。

在英國倫敦，新開幕的倫敦半島酒店的房間每晚起價 1,600 美元，套房起價剛好低於 4,000 美元。半島套房是「酒店最豪華的住宿」，酒店表示，據報導是倫敦可獲得的最大的私人住宿。面積達 1,400 平方英尺，包括一個正式的餐廳、私人健身房、露台和電影院。「這就像是酒店內的一個小酒店」，半島酒店倫敦分館的管理總監 Sonja Vodusek 告訴《Robb Report》。

許多旅館服務業巨頭正在將舊城堡轉型為富麗堂皇的住宿環境，增添了一份華麗的氣派。2023 年 4 月開幕的 Palazzo Vilòn，「讓客人有機會感受像羅馬貴族一樣生活」，《Travel + Leisure》報導。位於 Palazzo Borghese 的一翼，這是義大利貴族家族的歷史宮殿，別墅被想像為「給阿拉伯酋長、哈里與梅根以及好萊塢皇室的羅馬避風港」，《紐約時報》報導。要租下整座別墅，客人需要支付平均每晚 27,000 美元。

在奧地利，2023 年 4 月開幕的 Almanac Palais Vienna 將一座前宮殿改造成了酒店。而在日本，兩座歷史城堡—大洲城和平戶城—首次開放讓人過夜。

值得關注的原因：
豪華旅遊度假地正將奢華體驗提升至新高度，提供堪比皇室的住宿體驗成為趨勢。

VML

80

奢華運動

極奢健身概念幫助高資產個人HNWIs實現其更高的健康目標。

↑ IV room at Remedy Place, NYC

根據 VML 智庫的數據顯示，當今奢侈生活的最大標誌是「享有長壽而健康的生活」。在這個將最佳健康視為新型財富的新範疇中，超高端健身俱樂部應運而生，為高資產個人提供了一個在充滿先進科技和志同道合人士的環境中追求健康目標的場所，這些場所的設計取材自奢華款待的規範—當然，相對的費用自然不菲。

這種新趨勢由位於洛杉磯和紐約的 Remedy Place 所代表，該機構自稱是世界上第一家社交健康俱樂部。只需支付起價為

VML

2500 美元的月費，會員便能享受到整合了全方位治療師的服務和世界領先的「科技療法」，包括高壓氧艙、淋巴壓縮服以及配備冰浴和紅外線桑拿的私人對照浴。其紐約地點的靜脈注射隧道設計「受到瑞士建築師 Mario Botta 特有的幾何形態風格啟發」，Remedy Place 表示。

由 Kerzner International 推出的 Siro One Za'abeel 酒店，計劃於 2024 年 2 月在杜拜開業，將「整合健身與恢復」概念提升至新層次，拓展了奢華健康與身心靈（Health & Wellness）的傳統定義，結合了世界級營養和健身體驗，專注於恢復和正念。單晚住宿費用約為 1900 阿聯酋迪拉姆（約 517 美元），該酒店提供專業的恢復實驗室以及被稱為 Recovery Cocoons 的客房，配備了創新科技，「以改善身心恢復、緩解時差、提升心情並確保修復性睡眠」。

同樣在杜拜，Seven 健康俱樂部「將奢華與運動相融合」，提供奢華健身體驗。在 2023 年中，與享有生物駭客專業知識聞名的名人廚師 Silvena Rowe 建立的新合作夥伴關係，使得這家俱樂部的內部餐廳推出了以長壽為重點的美食選項。

值得關注的原因：
Statista 估計，到 2025 年，全球健康和身心靈（Health & Wellness）市場價值將近 7 萬億美元，其中很大一部分是由高資產個人（HNWIs）推動的。他們表現出願意為健康和幸福支付高價格，並期望得到最具創新和奢華的地點和體驗。

VML

↑ Siro One Za'abeel, Dubai

健康

81

長壽渡假村

養身勝地正在設計各種方案，
讓活到一百歲甚至更長壽不再得來不易。

VML

↑ Sensei Porcupine Creek. Photography by Chris Simpson
↑↑ Shakti Hall at the Art of Living Retreat Center, North Carolina, courtesy of
　Six Senses

從冷凍艙和熱感應身體構圖，到神經營養計劃及情感力訓練，渡假勝地正在設計各種住宿體驗，幫助旅客活得更久、活得更好。位於加州聖羅莎山山麓的 Sensei Porcupine Creek，是一家占地 230 英畝的健康渡假村。Sensei 的聯合總經理兼營運長 Alexandra Walterspiel 告訴 VML 智庫：「在 Sensei，我們的目標是將幫助人們更長壽、更健康的使命，與我們所有的方案和核心產品服務結合。可提供的方案包括 2023 年 4 月推出的 "休息與恢復"，該方案可幫助客人控管壓力並專注於恢復性睡眠，以及 "最佳健康狀態方案"，該項目包括一名專門的 Sensei 嚮導，該嚮導可根據健康數據和預期目標幫助客人實現客製化化體驗。

Sensei Porcupine Creek 於 2022 年 11 月開幕，穩定吸引著追尋長壽計劃的客人前來體驗。Walterspiel 說：「在疫情之後，越來越多的消費者將個人健康視優先，很明顯地，這個趨勢將持續下去。」

頂級權威抗老集團 CLINIQUE LA PRAIRIE 一直在世界各地開立其長壽渡假村，包括曼谷、杜哈和瑞士日內瓦湖上最初的醫學水療中心。2024 年，CLINIQUE LA PRAIRIE 集團將在中國安吉（請參閱第 28 章〈三大旅遊勝地〉）和沙烏地阿拉伯阿馬伯（Amaala, Saudi Arabia）分別開幕新渡假村。渡假村的每一次長壽之旅都從專門的 "長壽指數" 開始進行評估，將提供保健專家必要的資訊，以便為旅客於整趟旅程期間制定客製化的療程方案。

↑ Six Senses Kaplankaya, Turkey

另一家專注於延長壽命的豪華度假村的公司 Six Senses。它位於土耳其的卡普蘭卡亞渡假村率先推出了長壽計劃，目前在美國也有兩家度假村：北卡羅萊納州的生活藝術渡假中心和田納西州的岩泉渡假中心。在沙烏地阿拉伯，Six Senses Amaal 渡假村將於 2024 年開幕，屆時將設有長壽診所。

值得關注的原因：

在全球，人們的壽命越來越長。在 2020 年，60 歲以上的人口已達到 10 億。世界衛生組織預計，到 2050 年這個數字將翻倍，屆時 60 歲及以上的人口將達到 21 億。此外，全球有 74% 的人表示，他們喜歡活到百歲健康老人的概念，而長壽渡假村即可能是孕育這種可能性的一種方式。

↑ Six Senses Kaplankaya, Turkey

82

迷幻藥管家

隨著使用迷幻藥作為治療性藥物成為主流，
協助指引這些強勁體驗的管家也應運而生。

↑ Psychedelic Passage founders Nick Levich and Jimmy Nguyen

奧勒岡州已於 2023 年成為美國第一個將成人用迷幻藥合法化
的州，而科羅拉多州將從 2025 年起允許專業人士提供迷幻藥
體驗及成人個人使用。在多個美國城市中，也已將使用迷幻藥
除罪化。

來自美國的 Mike "Zappy" Zapolin 自稱是 " 明星的迷幻藥管
家 "，曾與女演員蜜雪兒·羅德里奎茲 (Michelle Rodriguez)
和前職業籃球員拉瑪·歐登 (Lamar Odom) 等人合作，分別指
導他們使用死藤水、K 他命和伊玻蓋因。他向《衛報》解釋自己
的角色時，Zapolin 指出：「飯店的禮賓服務人員不會為你提供
你想吃的食物，他們只是負責協助預訂，而我也是一樣。我根據
最佳實務和協定提供建議，並利用我的人脈找到醫生或專家。
此外，在每次體驗後，藥管家通常還負責為客戶提供心理治療，

VML

在此期間，客戶可以繼續消化他們正經歷的旅程。

總部位於奧勒岡州本德的 Psychedelic Passage 公司稱：「它在客戶的迷幻旅程中扮演著 " 自始至終的隊友 " 和 " 各方之間的聯繫人 " 的角色。」該公司的服務從諮詢電話開始，在進行迷幻療程之前，需先將客戶與預先審查過的迷幻引導者聯繫起來。該公司表示，它已在美國促成了 750 多場迷幻儀式，舒緩了 " 焦慮、抑鬱、創傷後壓力症候群 (PTSD) 和成癮 " 等症狀，同時也促使了 " 個人成長、心靈探索及目標釐清 "。

值得關注的原因：
雖然目前使用迷幻藥的合法性尚不明確，但消費者對這個領域卻十分感興趣—根據 Morning Consult 2023 年在美國進行的一項調查顯示，超過半數的千禧世代受訪者表示：「他們有興趣嘗試迷幻藥來治療心理健康」，這是在所有世代族群中是最多的。而有鑒於這個領域的複雜性，消費者在這個過程中尋求指導也就不足為奇了。

>50%

超過半數的美國千禧世代受訪者表示：「他們有興趣嘗試迷幻藥來治療心理健康。」

Morning Consult

83

恬靜的閒置

無所事事會是讓人生更健康、更快樂的秘訣嗎?

同名慢生活生活風格品牌 Leticia Credido 的創始人 Leticia Credidio 告訴 VML 智庫:「我們都需要一點無聊才能意識到,我們必須尋找能為我們帶來快樂的新鮮事。」該品牌於 2019 年推出了永續睡衣系列,此後,更擴展此系列到提倡慢生活的生活風格產品中。Credidio 解釋說:「慢生活是一種生活方式,它讓我們在如何消費和與他人相處面向做出更明智的選擇。」

《如何「無所事事」:一種對注意力經濟的抵抗》一書的作者 Jenny Odell 認為,無所事事分為兩部分。第一部分是 "脫離注意力經濟",第二部分是 "重新參與其他事情"。2023 年 3 月,奧德爾出版了她的第二本書《節省時間》: 這本書探討了靜坐、維持存在感以及打破時鐘束縛的必要性。

《在壓力的環境中保持平和的心態》在歐洲首次變成了一項比賽。2023 年 8 月,倫敦舉辦了《英國極限放鬆錦標賽》,30 名參賽者在緊張的體驗後,為恢復禪意狀態而展開了激烈的角逐。這項活動由運動心理學家 Jamie Barker 博士首創,他說:「人們越來越需要找到的放鬆方法,以幫助他們從日常壓力和對個人時間需求日益增長中恢復過來。」

在公共場所和工作場合,安靜的空間越來越受歡迎。2023 年 5 月,倫敦 O2 Center 購物中心專門設立了一個寧靜空間,讓人們從繁忙的環境中解脫。Adobe 公司的全球工作場域體驗主管 Eric Kline 告訴《華爾街日報》:「Adobe 公司正在其辦公室裡設置寧靜室,員工在遇到困難的時候可以去那裡獨處、反思或幫助大腦跳脫目前所處無限輪迴。」

VML

↑ Sky Collection by Leticia Credidio

" "

我們都需要一點無聊才能意識到，
我們必須尋找
能為我們帶來快樂的新鮮事。

Leticia Credidio, Leticia Credidio 創始人

VML

↑ Snug Extreme Relaxing Championship

值得關注的原因：

為無聊的時刻留出時間及放空正重新成為生活中健康的必需品，它有可能讓人與自己或與他人建立更有意義的關係。Credidio 說：「在過度工作和忙碌成為現況的世界裡，花時間睡覺、擁抱慢節奏、享受當下即是一種反抗行為。」

84

健康雄心

身心健康不再是雄心壯志祭壇上的犧牲品。

有一群工作者將身心健康放在首位，希望將奮鬥轉為寧靜。在我們的調查中，73% 的受訪者表示工作排在他們生活的第二位，76% 的受訪者稱他們不會接受壓力過大的工作。

2023 年 1 月，紐西蘭總理 Jacinda Ardern 辭職，她承認不再有「足夠的能量」來公正地盡她的職責。此後，加拿大音樂家 Drake、演員 Tom Holland 和蘇格蘭前首席部長 Nicola Sturgeon 等一系列公眾人物都暫停了他們飛速發展的事業。

企業需要制訂策略來解決這個問題。超過半數的受訪者表示，他們經常感到工作倦怠，這顯示想要暫時停工的人數將會增加。

一種解決方案是，公司提供提前休假，即所謂的「工作倦怠假」。雖然這通常更多地提供給已經長時間服務的員工，但像 PayPal、Meta 和 Adobe 這樣的公司開始看到提早提供這一福利的好處，僅在員工工作五年後即可享受。美國一家顧問公司 Sapro 制訂了一項政策，不用告知任何理由，即可為員工提供一到三個月的休假時間，並能享受半薪和全面福利，之後該公司的員工流失率降低至 5% 以下。

然而暫停時間並不能從根本上解決問題。芬蘭公司 Framery 的執行長 Samu Hallförs 在為《Fast Company》撰寫的一篇社論中提出了「倦怠報告」的概念，即公司公開報告健康指標，將健康提升到與財務目標同等的標準，並在這一過程中深化公司的責任感。

VML

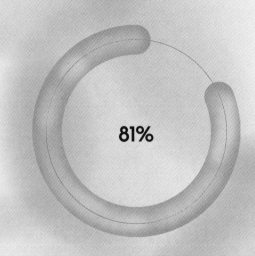

品牌也在積極倡導。在新加坡和馬來西亞，Heineken 繼續其 "工作責任 " 行銷活動，透過 "幽靈酒吧" 來反對有害的生產力，鼓勵員工不要因為過度工作而忽視社交關係。在行銷活動預告片中，酒吧裡的椅子和酒杯會自己移動，藉此展示過度工作的人是如何 "幽靈化" 他們的朋友的。

值得關注的原因：
奮鬥和拼搏不再是人們所追求的理想，因為他們尋求更健康的平衡。品牌可以通過宣揚允許休息的概念，強調正確的休閒價值，為精神健康提供有意義的支持，從而支持人們實現這種平衡；同時，雇主應將對心理健康的有意義支持融入員工體驗中。

81%

**81%的人認為
品牌需要致力於
改善人們的心理健康。**

VML

85

低氧療法

隨著間歇低氧高氧訓練 (IHHT) 在健身房的興起，
高海拔訓練越來越受歡迎。

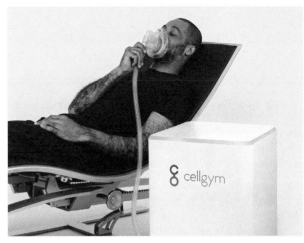

↑ Cellgym

健身房中越來越常見可減少氧氣流量的運動員級缺氧訓練面罩。根據 Wintergreen Research 公司 2020 年的一份報告指出，至 2026 年，缺氧訓練設備的銷售額預計將達到 2.3 億美元，這顯示了這一個產業的實力。

德國健康公司 Cellgym 自 2010 年以來一直專注於間歇低氧高氧訓練 (IHHT)，希望能讓越來越多人都能接受細胞療法。

定期進行間歇低氧高氧訓練 (IHHT) 的好處包括：感覺更有活力、強化免疫系統、改善睡眠品質。Cellgym 的創辦人兼執行長 Rainer Goytia 告訴 VML 智庫：「在過去十年中，有關缺氧的科學研究不斷增加。數以千計的相關研究都取得了正向的成

VML

> ## 間歇性缺氧訓練
> ## 是預防和治療不可或缺的一部分。
>
> Rainer Goytia, Cellgym 創辦人兼執行長

↑ Lanserhof Sylt

VML

果，這表明間歇性缺氧訓練是預防和治療不可或缺的一部分。」Goytia 指出：「這項重大的缺氧發現，該發現於 2019 年獲得諾貝爾生理學或醫學獎，內容是 "細胞如何感知和適應氧氣供應"，這對於提高 IHHT 的可信度至關重要。」

Cellgym 在倫敦的分店 Repose。這家精品健身房店指出，每週定期進行 25 分鐘的缺氧療法療程有很多好處，包括改善皮膚健康、增強心血管功能、提升精力、改善壓力水平以及增強體力和腦力。

德國的 Lanserhof Sylt 提供間歇低氧高氧訓練 (IHHT) 課程，建議每週最多進行三次。其課程規劃將這種訓練描述為 "無副作用的非侵入性細胞刺激"，長久以來一直被專業運動員用來提升表現。

各家飯店也在利用間歇低氧高氧訓練 (IHHT) 設備來提升自己健身中心的水準。紐約的 Aman 飯店、Six Senses 的多家飯店、瑞士的 Gstaad Palace 和倫敦的 Ham's Yard 酒店都擁有自己的低氧室，提供遊客進行高海拔訓練。

值得關注的原因：
健身房和健康中心透過提供間歇低氧高氧訓練 (IHHT) 設備而脫穎而出，這些設施已不再只為專業運動員。

86

未來生育

新興技術正在徹底改變人類的生育方式。

Apple Watch 現在可以做為避孕設備。2023 年 9 月,美國食品和藥物管理局批準 Natural Cycles 使用 Apple Watch 的體溫數據作為一種可行的節育方式。Natural Cycles 是一款利用體溫確定懷孕週期的數位避孕應用程式,它的用戶可以選擇從手錶中導入體溫數據,而不用每天早上手動測量基礎體溫。

位於紐約的初創公司 Gameto 致力於重新定義健康生育。它希望做到這一點的方法是讓卵子凍結和人工受精 (IVF) 更無縫、更少痛苦和更少侵入性。Gameto 的醫生和共同創始人 Dina Radenkovic 博士在接受《紐約客》訪問時表示,她設想未來的試管受精將在「卵子凍結亭 Egg-Freezing Kiosks」中進行。「我幾乎將其視為美容工作室的延伸,那裡積極管理你的生殖和長壽似乎就像是一種自我保養的舉動。」這家新創公司被世界經濟論壇評為 2023 年的科技先鋒。

生物醫學研究的一個新興領域正致力於將幹細胞直接轉化為胚胎,這個過程稱為體外配子法 (IVG)。生技新創公司 Conception 是領銜這項研究的團體之一。體外配子法 (IVG) 將使女性能夠在任何年齡懷上有自己基因的孩子,或在患有像癌症等可能造成懷孕困難的疾病康復後懷孕。它還能讓同性伴侶共同生育自己的親生子女。該公司的首席科學官 Pablo Hurtado 告訴 NPR 說:「我個人認為,我們正在做的事情可能會改變我們所知道的社會的許多方面。」

值得關注的原因:
新創科技將使預計為人父母者更能夠掌握何時、如何以及與誰共同生育孩子的權力,並有能力改變未來家庭的結構。

VML

←Natural Cycles powered by Apple Watch
↓Gameto

VML

87

迷走神經護理

保健專家正在開發利用迷走神經的治療效果。

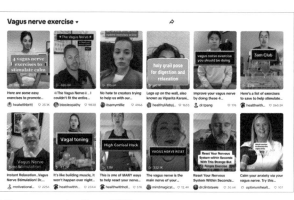

↑ Vagus nerve exercise videos on TikTok

科學界對刺激迷走神經潛力的興趣與日俱增，研究人員正在探索迷走神經在肥胖和憂鬱等疾病中的潛在應用。同時間，許多健康療法以及「TikTok Hacks」，聲稱都可以利用迷走神經的治療和抗焦慮效果。

截至 2024 年 1 月，TikTok 上 hashtag #vagusnerve 的瀏覽量超過 1.8 億次，而「迷走神經運動」的瀏覽量則超過 1.85 億次。分享的做法包括輕彈耳垂、在胸部或臉上放冰塊或深呼吸，目的是減慢心率、鼓勵身體放鬆。

這一趨勢現在正在進入 Spa 療程和美容產品領域。美國護膚品牌 Osea 利用海洋成分的力量，創造了一個迷走神經系列。該系列包括迷走神經油，設計用來輕輕按摩脖子的側面和耳垂後方。成分包括橄欖油、白芒花籽油、迷迭香、薰衣草和杜松油。

倫敦海德公園文華東方酒店於 2023 年推出 Oskia Cryo 臉部冷凍護理療程,其中包括 90 分鐘的 Oskia -30° C 迷走神經重新組織面部護理,其中包括「背部、頸部、臉部和頭皮的感官提升體驗」。該 Spa 中心表示:「cryoblasts 冷炸」會刺激迷走神經,這冷凍療程結合了「淋巴引流和雕塑按摩,以進一步刺激和協助身體的自然排毒過程。」

除了美容療法,刺激裝置也開始進入市場。在 2024 年 1 月舉行的消費電子展 (CES) 上,立陶宛健康科技公司 Pulsetto 展出可以放鬆和緩解壓力的迷走神經刺激裝置。聲稱可以改善睡眠品質並促進身體恢復,利用電刺激技術在四分鐘內「對副交感神經系統進行生物駭客攻擊」。

同樣是在 CES 上,美國生物工程公司 NeurGear 推出的 ZenBud 刺激器採用了先進的超音波技術。它的佩戴方式與傳統耳塞一樣,目的在協助心理平衡和放鬆。

值得關注的原因:
消費者和品牌都渴望將刺激人體迷走神經的好處,納入實踐身心健康作法的一部分,這說明了大腦與身體的連結仍然是一個引人入勝的故事。

↑ Osea Vagus Nerve collection

VML

新診斷術

新創公司正在探索提供侵入性更少的健康診斷方法。

↑ Theblood cofounders Isabelle Guenou and Miriam Santer, courtesy of Theblood

英國初創企業 Daye 於 2023 年 11 月推出了一款可以檢測性傳染病 (STIs) 的衛生棉條。該「陰道微生物群篩檢套件」是一項可在家中進行的性傳染病 (STIs) 診斷服務，同時還可以計算陰道感染和生育併發症的風險。該公司的目標是「讓所有人都能平等地獲得全面的婦科護理」。

由 Isabelle Guenou 和 Miriam Sante 於 2022 年共同創立的柏林新創公司 Theblood 正利用經血提供的洞察力，探索經血到底能發現哪些健康數據。2023 年，該公司籌集了近 100 萬歐元的種子前期資金，以進一步展開研究。目前 Theblood 提供了一個原型測試套件，提供德國消費者使用，以深入了解月經週期和如何控制症狀。

VML

Guenou 告訴 VML 智庫，她自己花了八年時間才診斷出子宮內膜異位症，這也是促使她創立這家公司的部分原因。她說：「我們發現，女性在診斷過程中會受到一些壓力。我們的目標之一就是縮短診斷時間。我們不一定是第一個給出診斷的人，但我們會提供更多數據，以真正找出問題所在。」她補充說，與她交談過的醫生都很支持他們的服務所能帶來的見解。

Guenou 表示，公司最終計劃在其他歐洲國家提供檢測服務，他還指出部分母親正在為她們十幾歲的女兒訂購週期檢測試劑盒。「我可以肯定地說，我們希望為下一代帶來一種全新治療月經的方法。」他說：「你可以從『月經』中獲得實際數據，這不僅僅是每個月都會出現的煩人事情。」

該領域的另一個參與者是美國新創公司 Qvin，該公司將於 2024 年初開始在美國提供週期測試套件。它能檢測客戶月經血中的多種生物標誌物，其中包括用於測量血糖的血紅蛋白 A1c、用於檢測甲狀腺健康和新陳代謝的促甲狀腺激素以及反映生育等級和圍絕經期的 FSH、LH 和 AMH。

VML

↑ Theblood cycle test kit

值得關注的原因：
通過檢測經血，先驅企業表明他們對影響女性健康的獨特因素有了新的認識，從而幫助他們從這種傳統上被視羞於啟齒的穢物中獲得有價值的見解。

89

情感裝置

人們設計自己的個人空間是為了能夠喚起安全感、平靜感和接受等正面的情感。

2023 年 2 月，宜家 Ikea 與設計師 Sabine Marcelis 合作推出了一個雕塑燈飾和家居用品系列。公司表示，Varmblixt 是宜家 Ikea 主張「將照明從純粹功能性轉變為情感性」的長期目標的一部分。這個系列以傳統照明的趣味性為特色，具有豐富的色彩和不尋常的雕塑和形狀，運用直間和間接光線，企圖在家中喚起平靜、情感、寧靜和好奇心。

墨西哥陶瓷工作室 Menat 正在製作設計來安慰和應對悲傷和失去的骨灰罈。一開始是攝影師 Marianna Jamadi 與 Menat 合作設計了 Kunokaiku 骨灰罈給她的父母。這逐漸發展成一廣泛系列作品的骨灰罈，目的是在家中陳列並融入日常儀式中，作為應對和紀念失去的愛人的一種方式。Jamadi 告訴《Wallpaper》雜誌，她認為「在悲傷的時候，擁有一個可以與之互動的物品是很好的，可以讓人感到與失去的親人有所聯繫。」

在 2023 年消費性電子展 (CES) 上，LG 展示了 MoodUp 冰箱，為一款專為反映個人情緒狀態而設計的家用電器。這款冰箱的 LED 門板可以更換和自訂 23 種顏色選項、季節設置、情緒預設設置等。

值得關注的原因：
消費者對情緒健康的追求正在融入日常生活。這些品牌正在對家用電器和家具進行升級，使人們能夠享受舒適和寧靜。

↓ Varmblixt collection designed by Sabine Marcelis for Ikea, courtesy of Ikea

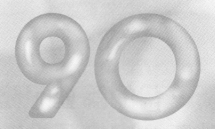

90

未來防護

利用科技來保障未來健康，現在已經成為一種地位的象徵。

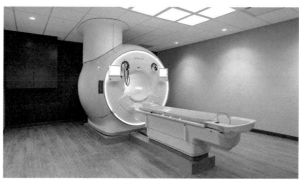

↑ Prenuvo

隨著醫療技術的進步，一些企業正在利用人類渴望保持健康和最大程度延長壽命的需求，開發機器以發現疾病的最初期且最易治療的階段。

2023 年 8 月，金卡戴珊 (Kim Kardashian) 發佈了一張自己站在 Prenuvo 全身掃描儀旁邊的照片，稱其為「拯救生命的機器」，將這一趨勢變成為人們關心的焦點。Prenuvo 是一家由 Andrew Lacy 和放射科醫生 Raj Attariwala 博士創辦的美國公司，在美國用於癌症和其他疾病的早期檢測，在多個地點提供軀幹、全身及頭部加軀幹的掃描服務。2023 年 4 月，該公司在紐約開設了一家門市，此後又開設了 8 家分店，並計劃在不久的將來再開設 11 家分店。

Prenuvo 表示，其服務「與傳統核磁共振 (MRI) 不同，傳統核磁共振 (MRI) 需要數小時且通常需要注射造影劑，而 Prenuvo

↑ Prenuvo founders Andrew Lacy and Dr Raj Attariwala

可掃描 500 多種病症，包括最早可在第一階段檢測到的大多數實體瘤，以及動脈瘤、囊腫等，所有這些無需輻射，在一小時內即可完成。」價格從軀幹掃描的 999 美元到全身掃描的 2499 美元不等。

在倫敦藝術俱樂部的 Lanserhof 診所，醫療服務部門表示，其重點是「預防性醫學」。除了 Lanserhof 在倫敦提供的普通內科、心臟科和營養科服務外，客戶還可以接受該診所的 3T 核磁共振服務，其主要目的為提供最全面、最準確的影像診斷。

值得關注的原因：

雖然一些醫生提醒預防性服務可能會出現誤判和不必要的檢查，但對許多人來說，健康仍然被認為是最大的財富。新一代的篩查服務反映了金字塔頂端客群希望掌握健康和人體不可預測性的願望。

VML

新一代的篩查服務反映了金字塔頂端客群希望掌握健康和人體不可預測性的願望。

創新

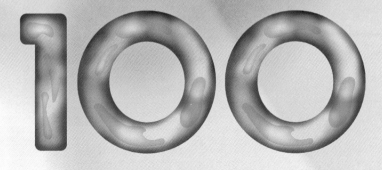

91

超保育

科技是否能夠防止滅絕，甚至扭轉它呢？

↑ Colossal Biosciences

聯合國秘書長安東尼奧·古特雷斯在全球生物多樣性大會（COP15）開幕談話中表示：「人類已經成為大規模滅絕的武器。」根據世界上最全面的滅絕風險數據源—國際自然保護聯盟瀕危物種紅色名錄（IUCN Red List）表示，有超過 40,000 個物種「面臨滅絕威脅」。

生物學家們正在進行一項偉大的嘗試。地球生物基因計畫（EBP）是一項為期 10 年的計畫，將「對地球上所有真核生物的基因組，進行序列、編目和表徵」。換句話說，科學家將評估地球上的每一種植物、動物和真菌，甚至包括那些尚未被識別的單細胞生物，以保護我們星球上的生命。該計畫的規模令人難以置信，它的任務是在短短十年內，對已知的 180 萬種種進行編目。

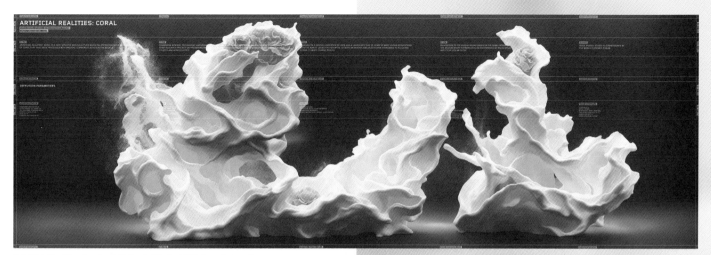

↑ Artificial Realities: Coral by Refik Anadol Studio, 2023. Commissioned by
World Economic Forum

在 EBP 嘗試進行大規模救援的同時,科學家們也在個別物種層面進行研究。BioRescue 旗下的一個由科學家和保育專家組成的聯盟,其宗旨在拯救瀕臨滅絕的北白犀牛。肯亞的一個保護區內只剩下兩隻雌性白犀牛,該計畫目標在利用輔助生殖和幹細胞研究,企圖將這一物種從懸崖邊緣拉回。

與 BioRescue 合作拯救北白犀牛,還有基因和生物技術公司 Colossal Biosciences。該公司專長在於「復活」滅絕物種的顛覆性技術,並正在策劃復育具有像長毛猛獁象、塔斯馬尼亞虎和渡渡鳥等已經滅絕生物特徵的混種。根據英國《金融時報》報道,該公司已經與美國各州就可能的野外放牧地點進行對話,目的是飼養一群猛獁象。

Colossal Biosciences 創辦人兼執行長 Ben Lamm 告訴 VML 智庫,該公司的使命是「揭示生物多樣性危機,同時開發有助於保育的技術」。他們正在有意識地致力於使曾經滅絕的物種重新野化。「我們希望確保能夠以真正有利於環境的方式重新復育動物」拉姆說。

VML

↑ Artificial Realities: Coral by Refik Anadol Studio, 2023. Commissioned by
World Economic Forum

人類記憶的無常性也正在被探索。數位藝術家 Refik Anadol
在 TED 2023 會議上發表了一場名為「AI 藝術如何增強人類的
集體記憶」的演講,其中深刻地想像了我們如何使用花朵或珊
瑚等自然物種的圖像來訓練演算法,以保留對它們的體驗。

Anadol 說:「作為藝術家,我們不僅可以利用這股數位化趨勢
來呈現大自然,還可以記住徜徉在大自然懷抱裡的感覺」。

值得關注的原因:
氣候對話的日益迫切性推動了保護世界自然和文化資產的努力。
儘管未來的世代面臨難以想像的挑戰,但這些計畫將成為潛在
恢復甚至「反滅絕」努力的基礎。

VML

92

百歲未來

長壽專家和追求永生的企業家正在對健康壽命進行醫學3.0的治療。

科技企業家 Bryan Johnson 在《The Diary of a CEO》podcast 中告訴史蒂芬·巴特利特:「我的使命是讓人類生存並茁壯。」1977 年出生的 Johnson 相信,我們所有人都有可能永遠活著,唯一的目標應該是「不死」。他在他的威尼斯海灘家中設立了一家診所,聲稱每年花費 300 萬至 400 萬美元用於補充劑、測試和治療,以將他的生物年齡恢復到 18 歲。

Johnson 自 2021 年以來已將他的生活交托給數據,並在「藍圖計劃 Blueprint」上分享他的日常和研究發現。在 2023 年底,27 歲的 Kate Tolo 被公開介紹為第二位參與嚴格的「藍圖計劃 Blueprint」的人。截至當年 11 月,Tolo 已經承諾參與三個月的「藍圖計劃 Blueprint」,據稱在《時代雜誌》的一次訪談中她「儘管採用這種嚴格的生活方式可能會帶來一些困難或成本,但相對應的健康益處更為重要或更有價值」。有興趣加入「不死誓言」的人可以從 2024 年 1 月開始報名參加「藍圖入門計畫」。

另一家致力於改善生物年齡的公司是風險投資公司 Healthspan Capital,自 2021 年以來一直支持一系列研究長壽生物學的公司。Healthspan Capital 的常務合夥人兼聯合創始人 Sebastian Brunemeier 告訴 VML 智庫:「長壽生物技術將透過醫療控制老化來徹底改變生物醫學」。他預測,「基因和細胞療法等新工具將能夠對生物學進行更精確的重新編程,比較起來,將使我們對藥丸和植物萃取物的歷史顯得像中世紀一樣老舊。」

2023 年,長壽引起了媒體的興趣,為這一領域增添了更多的活力,也為這一話題增添了可信度。《國家地理》發行了一期專門

↑ Blueprint Project, courtesy of Bryan Johnson

討論長壽科學的期刊；《Economist's》的秋季刊物是一份專門報導活到 120 歲的特別報告，深入探討了延緩衰老的方法。8 月，Netflix 發布了一部名為《長命百歲：藍色寶地的奧秘》的紀錄片系列。

Buck 衰老研究所執行長 Eric Verdin 預測，大多數人可以健康地活到 95 歲，並表示：「生活方式對壽命的影響約為 93%，而遺傳因素只佔 7%。」2023 年春季，Peter Attia 博士出版了《超越百歲長壽的科學與藝術》。Attia 認為，醫學和科技領域的領導者應該將注意力轉向他所說的醫學 3.0，為晚年品質提供積極的疾病預防和維護。

值得關注的原因：
全球 73% 的受訪者表示，他們透過飲食來延長壽命，74% 的人喜歡在 100 歲以後過著健康長壽的生活。現在，延長健康壽命的技術和研究，正在實現健康百歲老人常態化的未來。

VML

> "
> **基因和細胞療法等新工具將能夠對生物學進行更精確的重新編程，比較起來，將使我們對藥丸和植物萃取物的歷史顯得像中世紀一樣老舊。**
>
> Sebastian Brunemeier,
> Healthspan Capital 常務合夥人
> 兼聯合創始人

93

AI世代

AI可能對最年輕的一代產生深遠的影響。

↑ TeddyGPT artwork, courtesy of Toymint

↑ TeddyGPT artwork, courtesy of Toymint

AI 將對 2010 年至 2024 年間出生的 Alpha 世代的生活產生巨大影響，就像智慧型手機和社群媒體塑造 Z 世代的生活一樣。 他們與具有情感智能的 AI 夥伴一起成長，例如適合兒童的 Miko 3 和 Roybi AI 機器人，這些機器人的目標在提供教育、建立關係並與他們一起成長。

2023 年 4 月，Toymint 推出了 TeddyGPT，這是一款使用 OpenAI 的玩具，並承諾「滿足每個孩子的獨特喜好和需求」。 這款智慧玩具預計在推出時將提供超客製化互動。 玩具公司偉易達集團執行長 Allan Wong 在接受《金融時報》採訪時表示，他相信到 2028 年，AI teddy 將能夠「為孩子量身打造不一樣的故事，而不是從書籍上讀取」。

對於與 AI 同伴一起成長的一代來說，人際關係將會有所不同，「這是為了在不同的空間中建立人與人之間的聯繫」。未來學家 Ian Beacraft 在 SXSW 2023 的一場有關 AI 的主題演講中說提到：「我們現在必須了解『Alpha 世代』有多少朋友是真的，有多少是虛構的。 坦率地說，這可能重要，也可能不重要。」

AI 也有望塑造職業生涯（請參閱第 20 章〈人工智慧勞動力〉）。AI 公司 Satalia 的執行長 Daniel Hulme 告訴 VML 智庫：「未來的工作已經來臨。」他表示：「我們已經見證了使用 AI 的創造性方法的寒武紀大爆發。」企業使用 AI 來提高商品的創造和分發效率。

如果 AI 承接單調任務的趨勢持續下去，這將為人們提供更多時間專注於創意、道德和社會事業。Hulme 對 Alpha 世代寄予厚望。他說「下一代將配備大量工具來增強他們的創造力」。也許，他們更有機會能在經濟上更自由，為人類做出貢獻。

值得關注的原因：
隨著 AI 的進步，它將帶來更高的效率，並讓人類有更多的時間，做人類真正該做的事。誕生於數位先進世界的 AI 世代可能是迄今為止最具情感投入、最具創造力和目標明確的一代。

94
合成生物學

未來，我們能否像軟體一樣對生物學進行程式設計？

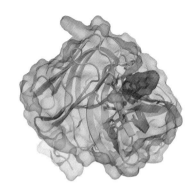

↑ Arzeda

從廣義上來說，合成生物學是將現有生物材料重新編程或重新利用以執行新功能的實踐。簡單來說，「你正在編碼和編程一個細胞來分泌某種物質」Biospring Partners 的聯合創始人 Jennifer Lum 告訴《華爾街日報》，這是一家投資於生命科學技術的成長型股權公司。

根據研究公司 Research and Markets 的估計，到 2022 年，全球合成生物學市場在 2022 年價值僅略超過 110 億美元，預計到 2027 年將達到近 360 億美元，年均增長率近 26%。

根據英國廣播公司 (BBC) 2023 年 9 月報導，合成生物學的最新創新讓科學家在沒有精子或卵子的情況下培育出完整的人類胚胎模型。這項研究背後的魏茨曼研究所團隊表示，他們使用幹細胞製作的胚胎模型，看起來就一個真實 14 天胚胎，如同教科書上的範例。

VML

**" AI 正在加速
像軟體一樣
對身體進行
程式設計的能力。**

AI 正在加速像軟體一樣對身體進行程式設計的能力。「它使我們能夠超越自然所賦予我們的」合成生物學新創公司 Arzeda 的聯合創始人 Alexandre Zanghellini 表示。該公司使用 AI 來設計酶和蛋白質序列。到目前為止，Arzeda 已籌集 5,100 萬美元資金，並正在與聯合利華合作設計洗滌劑酶。

華盛頓大學的生物化學家和計算生物學家 David Baker 正在應用 AI 來創造自然界中找不到的新蛋白質。因為 AI，Baker 估計在過去兩年中，他的領域的創新速度增加了 10 倍。「這完全是科幻小說。我仍然不敢相信會這麼有效」他告訴《華爾街日報》：「在十年之內，這可能會成為醫學的未來。」

值得關注的原因：
自然可能只是未來醫療保健的起點。科技的進步，尤其是 AI，正將我們帶向一個，人們可以從細胞層面重新編程人類健康的未來。

VML

95

虛擬家庭

我們與虛擬人物之間的關係
是否很快就會成為我們最親密的關係之一？

英國 AI 專家 Catriona Campbell 預測，到 2070 年，虛擬兒童可能會變得非常普遍，她表示，這一願景「與我們現在的情況相比似乎是一個巨大的飛躍，但在 50 年內，技術將發展到一個程度，以至於在虛擬世界存在的嬰兒與現實世界中的嬰兒無法區分。」Campbell 補充說，雖然這種「完全數位化的人口統計」可能看起來很「奇怪」，但考慮到它對全球人口和社會變革的潛在影響，它「實際上代表著可能是自青銅時代以來，人類最重要的技術突破之一。」

隨著擴增實境和觸覺技術的進步，Campbell 認為這些虛擬兒童的體驗將更加逼真，甚至能夠在物理環境中感受到和看到這些虛擬兒童。此外，透過機器學習，這些虛擬兒童可以辨認並回應他們的父母，就像真正的孩子一樣。

根據英國廣播公司 (BBC) 科學焦點報道，虛擬兒童的概念目前正被用來培訓成年人如何對有創傷的兒童進行訪談。這些 AI 兒童被編程為「擁有『記憶』並像真正的孩子一樣回答問題。」正如 BBC 所指出的，這些虛擬兒童滿足了寶貴的需求，因為訓練真實的孩子回應有關過去創傷的提問是不道德的。

當談到成人關係時，AI 伴侶變得更加現實。Replika 將自己定位為「關心你的 AI 伴侶」，讓用戶能夠創建自己的栩栩如生的伴侶。 2023 年 2 月，這家美國公司推出了先進的 AI 模式，據

↑ Replika

稱可以提高對話品質和記憶能力。 Replika 的用戶讚揚這款聊天機器人填補了「我在城市孤獨的日常生活中一些過於安靜的角落」，並為「給予了我在以前 AI 中從未見過的安慰和幸福感」而讚譽不已。

值得關注的原因：
未來的家庭正在發生變化（請參閱第 10 章〈共識社區〉）。 隨著我們的數位世界和物理世界不斷融合，預計數位生物將在每個人的生活中變得更加重要。

到2070年，虛擬兒童可能會變得非常普遍。

96

變形城市

自我變形材料將塑造未來的城市。

↑ Creative Differences by the Automorph Network at the London Design Biennale 2023

↑ Creative Differences by the Automorph Network at the London Design Biennale 2023

自然界中隨處可見能夠不斷變形、重塑自身的物質。現在，科學家們正在利用這些特性來使建築物和城市具有適應性和可持續性。

Automorph Network 匯聚了一組跨學科的科學家、建築師和設計師，旨在促進一種新的物質文化；一種基於物質參與自身設計的文化。成員來自全球不同的學術機構，涵蓋了加州大學柏克萊分校的 Morphing Matter 實驗室和耶路撒冷希伯來大學。

在 2023 年的倫敦設計雙年展上，該小組推出了「創意差異」展覽，該展覽從自然世界中汲取靈感，提出了新的變形材料。正如該小組所說：「在空氣、濕度或熱量的觸發下，二維材料變得栩栩如生，成為建造城市、水下或室外人造景觀的立體產品。」概念包括燒製時彎曲的磁磚，扁平包裝材料，無需能源即可在原地自行組裝成立體形狀的平板材料；受潮後可折疊的天然纖維複合材料；以及當水分啟動時會鑽入地下的種子。

康奈爾大學的研究人員也從自然中汲取靈感。他們正領導一個

項目，想像建築和生物學的融合，並借鑒形態發生學——生物形成結構的方式——來設計能夠對環境做出反應的"活"建築。其結果可能是建築外牆可以改變顏色，或者可以按需要形成窗戶，讓建築物自己冷卻下來。

在芝加哥大學，普立茲克分子工程學院的研究人員設計了一種材料，可以透過改變顏色和從固態轉變為液態來自動調節其環境，這有可能為外牆塗料鋪平道路，從而減少對能源密集的暖氣需求、建築物內的通風和空調系統。

在芝加哥大學，普利茲克分子工程學院的研究人員開發了一種材料，它可以透過改變顏色並從固態轉變為液態狀態來自主調節環境，有望為建築中減少對能耗高的空調系統需求的外牆塗料開闢新途徑。

這種變形也延伸到了紡織品。2023 年 11 月，麻省理工學院發布了 FibeRobo 的詳細信息，這是一種基於液晶彈性體的新纖維概念，可隨溫度變化。這將使紡織品在建築和時尚等領域的應用更加靈活：想像一下，窗簾會因熱量而收縮，或者夾克會隨著天氣變冷而變得更厚、更隔熱。

值得關注的原因：
Automorph Network 表示：「自我變形系統可能是我們所有人都需要進行的模式改變，以創造一個更光明、更具適應性和更可持續的未來。」

97

AI身份

AI正在塑造我們的身份識別。

賓州大學華頓商學院行銷學教授,也是該大學 Wharton center AI 聯合主任 Stefano Puntoni 表示:「科技不僅僅反映我們的身份,它塑造我們的身份。」Puntoni 的背景是行為科學,他的研究主要集中在消費者身份及其如何隨著科技發展而演變,這是一個尤為關鍵的主題,尤其是當高階思維不再僅限於人類時。

Puntoni 表示:「對我們的心理健康和行為能力來說,我們對自己的感覺良好非常重要。而實現這一點的一種方式是通過監控我們朝著那些對我們重要的身份的進展。」 他表示,這是天生的,不會改變。將會演變的是「身份的表達和構建方式」,這意味著自動化將改變我們與之產生共鳴的事物的本質,例如成為攝影師或烘焙師。

他說,從積極的方面來看,自動化可能有助於拉近我們的距離,並鼓勵我們減少對差異的關注。他表示:「也許種族、性別或宗教差異將變得不那麼重要,因為我們看到新一波 AI 進入工作場所。」

我們也可能看到人類創造力和勞動力受到重視。在 2023 年《華爾街日報》的一篇文章中,Puntoni 引用了他的團隊的研究,該研究發現「當消費具有象徵意義時,對人工手作的偏好會更強」。一項此類研究發現,消費者更喜歡手工製作的老花鏡鏡框,而對於功能性更強的鏡片,則更喜歡機器製作的鏡片。具有「象徵性」的物品(意味著它們能表達有關其所有者及其所有者身份的資訊)更有可能享受到這種人工價值。

↑ Zach Blas and Jemima Wyman, im here to learn so:)))))), 2017. Exhibited at
Proof of Personhood: Identity and Authenticity in the Face of Artificial
Intelligence, 2023. Courtesy Singapore Art Museum

"

科技不僅僅反映我們的身份，
它塑造我們的身份。

Stefano Puntoni, 華頓商學院教授

Puntoni 說：「展望未來，我們很可能會看到 "技術與人類的某種融合"，從某種意義上說，這種情況已經發生在智慧型手機上，它 "幾乎就像你身體的一部分。你把它靠近你的身體，你每天要觸摸它數百次，更何況我們還與 AI 建立了共生關係」（請參閱第 93 章〈AI 世代〉）。未來，AI 似乎將幫助定義我們。

值得關注的原因：
Puntoni 說，AI 正在改變人類身份的建構和表達方式，而我們現在的不同之處並不在於我們的認知能力，而是更多地根植於「我們的社會情感發展和體認」。

98

復活珍饌

猛獁象肉和渡渡鳥肉正在成為我們的佳餚。

↑ Mammoth meatball by Vow

VML

總部位於澳洲的人造肉公司 Vow 於 2023 年春季推出了世界上第一個由猛獁象 DNA 製成的肉丸。雖然該肉丸尚未可供人類食用，但該計畫旨在展示在食品工業中細胞培養肉的進步及其徹底改變人類生活方式的潛力。

Vow 聯合創辦人 Tim Noakesmit 表示：「我們的使命是通過意想不到的美味風味和難忘的體驗來打破現有的飲食習慣，食物的未來有利於勇於創新的人。」

Vow 最初打算生產渡渡鳥肉，但所需的 DNA 定序並不存在。猛獁肉為培養肉帶來了許多新的可能性。Vow 首席科學官 James Ryall 表示：「這項技術不是簡單地複製現有產品，而是讓我們有機會創造出真正獨特、更好的產品。」

被認為稀有甚至禁止食用的肉類可能很快就會在餐廳和超市貨架上出現。總部位於倫敦的 Primeval Foods 於 2022 年成立，計劃為食客提供人工培育的異國肉類。這家新創公司目前正致力於培育實驗室飼養的虎肉、斑馬肉和獅子肉，以確定對人們來說最佳的口味、質地和營養價值。

VML

細胞培養的食品正在興起，現在涵蓋肉類、乳製品和咖啡。38% 的 Z 世代準備嘗試實驗室種植的食物，27% 的人有興趣嘗試細胞培養的滅絕物種。作為當前供應鏈的可持續替代品，該行業預計將實現增長。Grand View Research 的一項研究顯示，到 2030 年，全球培養肉市場的收入預計將達到 69 億美元，高於 2023 年的 3.731 億美元。

值得關注的原因：
雖然有幾家公司專注於傳統雞肉、豬肉和牛肉等培養肉的升級，但另一些新創公司正在嘗試可以使我們的口味多樣化的機會，並重新思考培養肉的未來。虎肉排，有人要嘗試嗎？

99

擬人AI

規劃未來五年的AI藍圖。

AI 正在為企業帶來變革性的好處。 Satalia 執行長兼 WPP 首席 AI 長 Daniel Hulme 表示，該公司正在開發他所謂的「品牌大腦」——可以創建品牌特定內容的大型語言模型 (LLMs)——以及複製的「受眾大腦」受眾如何感知內容。然而，Hulme 表示，從長遠來看，我們現在擁有的生成 AI 只是「你口袋裡的一個極其興奮的畢業生」。 它 "非常聰明，學得很快"，但未來還有更多。

它也只是一系列複雜技術的一個分支。事實上，WPP 從六個類別的角度來考慮 AI：任務自動化、內容生成、人類表徵、提取複雜的見解、複雜的決策以及擴展人類的能力。Hulme 相信，在接下來的幾年裡，AI 將變得更加複雜，並且更加專業化。「它們將變得更加多模組化——不僅是圖像和文本，還有聲音和影片。」

目前，大多數系統都使用 LLMs，一種人工神經網路。LLMs 非常擅長處理任務，但它們也可能效率低、能源密集，而且難以連續。Hulme 預計，隨著尖端神經網路的興起，各種形態會發生轉變。它們以生物方式傳遞訊息，更接近地模仿我們大腦的工作方式。

Hulme 說：「展望未來，我們的畢業生將快速進步。兩年後，你可能會達到碩士水平的能力，能夠通過對一系列問題進行排序來實現更複雜的目標。」這與 Inflection AI 的 Mustafa Suleyman 的觀點相吻合，他在 2023 年 9 月接受《麻省理工科技評論》採訪時將互動式 AI 視為 AI 的下一階段。史丹佛大學教授 Andrew Ng 在 2024 年 1 月對消費電子展的觀眾表示：「能夠計劃和執行一系列行動的自主代理還只是剛剛起步，但我覺得在研究和商業化方面已經取得了很大進展。」

VML

Hulme 說，從那時起，AI 可能會跳到「博士水平，你可以給它一個非常複雜的假設」。「這個問題以前從未被解決過，但它能夠去那裡進行測試和實驗並嘗試解決它。幾年後，我們的口袋裡可能就會多出一位教授。」「我們口袋裡的教授」是通用 AGI 的另一種說法，它想像技術能夠執行人類可以執行的任何認知任務。 Hulme 說：「我認為真正的通用 AI 可能還需要七、八年的時間。」不過，他補充道，也許我們不應該總是認為人類是智力的頂峰。

值得關注的原因：
AI 的未來充滿希望，但現在是時候以不同的方式思考它了，Hulme 表示，它是一種「讓我們成長並消除低效率的新能源」。同時他補充道，如果可以利用它 "幫助組織實現其目標，企業的集體目標實際上將使我們所有人的未來變得更加美好。"

> ❝
> # AI 的未來充滿希望，但現在是時候以不同的方式思考它，是「讓我們成長並消除低效率的新能源」。
>
> Daniel Hulme,
> Satalia, 執行長兼 WPP 首席 AI 長

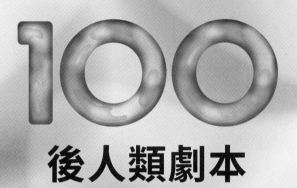

100

後人類劇本

藝術家們正在想像後人類的未來。

↑ Symbiosis, Polymorf

↑ Heterosis, The Greenhouse, Mat Collishaw, 2023 © Mat Collishaw

↑ Nature Always Wins, Universal Everything, 2020

在生態危機的刺激下,藝術家們正在提供去中心化人性的敘事,試圖引導我們在此時此地減少以人類為中心的觀點。

Petrichor 是英國藝術家 Mat Collishaw 於 2023 年 10 月至 2024 年 4 月在英國皇家植物園舉辦的新展,展示了一系列探索人類與自然動盪而複雜的關係的作品。《Even to the End》是一部大型投影作品,帶領觀眾踏上一段令人心酸的旅程,讓他們沉浸在變成被蹂躪的荒地的大自然中。Collishaw 的另一幅作品《溫室》描繪了倫敦國家美術館處於一種被自然拋棄的陰森景象。牆壁上長滿了樹葉,樹木一直延伸到屋頂。

設計團體 Universal Everything 的「Nature Always Wins」作品呼應了同樣的自然收回控制權的願景,該作品於 2022 年底在倫敦 180 Studios 展示,作為展示的一部分。該劇描繪了大自然的肆虐,建築物、道路,甚至一架大型噴射機都被樹葉吞噬了。

在 SXSW 2023 上,體驗設計工作室 Polymorf 和 Studio Biarritz 展示了 Symbiosis,這是一種多感官擴展現實體驗,可將觀眾帶到 200 年後的未來。在這個後人類生物群落中,人類、自然和技術共同演化成混合、共生的生命形式,包括基因改造生物、(化學)機器人、混合技術和自主智慧系統。

> **我們以人為本的立場
> ——僅從人類的角度思考——
> 是不合時宜的，
> 在當前的自然危機中
> 我們無法維持這種立場。**
> Marcel van Brakel,
> Polymorf 創辦人兼首席設計師

其他藝術家正在將注意力轉向我們之後可能發生的事情。 在 2023 年 Ars Technica 動畫節上，題為「數據、身體、空間」的會議展示了思考後人類未來的短片。採用自然紀錄片的風格，哥本哈根設計二人組 Wang 和 Söderström 的《Rehousing Technosphere》呈現了豐富多彩的後人類世願景，其中新的數位生命形式正在建造新的棲息地、挖掘、覓食和繁榮。

值得關注的原因：
想像中的未來生命形式看起來很牽強，但藝術家有更深層的目的：鼓勵尊重其他物種的需求。Polymorf 創辦人兼首席設計師、Symbiosis 聯合總監 Marcel van Brakel 告訴 VML 智庫：「我們以人為本的立場——僅從人類的角度思考——是不合時宜的，在當前的自然危機中我們無法維持這種立場。」

↑ Rehousing Technosphere by Wang & Söderström. Part of the Ars Electronica Animation Festival: Data, Bodies, Space

領域專家的預測與反思

為了紀念10週年「改變未來的100件事」，我們邀請各領域專家為我們分享下列的兩個問題：

2024年，你最期待的一件事是什麼？
過去10年裡，你覺得最大的改變是什麼？

品牌	
	Mark Read, 執行長, WPP
2024	過去10年
展望 2024 年，我們對 AI 和機器學習改變行銷格局的潛力抱持樂觀，讓我們的客戶能夠更好地了解他們的顧客、預測消費行為並以前所未有的規格訂製銷售計畫。	數位平台與科技的興起讓品牌與消費者的連結方式自過去十年來從根本上發了改變。 社交媒體、行動技術和數據分析的提升讓品牌能擁有更精準、個人化和有效的行銷策略，且在正確的時間接觸並吸引正確的消費族群。

奢華	
	Jing Zhang, 全球主編, Jing Daily
2024	過去10年
尋求意義、工藝、慢節奏和真實性——我將這視為對過去十年分析的一種回應。奢侈品牌將努力尋找奢華獨特的屬性、文化和歷史，以區別於其他競爭者。我認為這符合我們在 2024 年將會體驗到的更加慎重的消費觀。	「數位化和對精品世界平民化」。過去的十年中，奢侈品領域日益向公眾敞開，透過數位和社交媒體的方式，奢華品牌以全新方式與粉絲互動。這個行業不再感覺像一個「高牆花園 Walled Garden」，而是發展成為一種更廣泛的文化，即使它仍是社會富裕階層的傳統遊樂場。

旅遊	
	Tom Marchant, 負責人及 聯合創始人, Black Tomato
2024	過去10年
如果你將旅行視為對抗日常生活的解藥或對立面,我認為在 2024 年我們將會看到更多人追求尋找寧靜的旅程。我們正更頻繁地生活在噪音的世界中,因此我們尋求找到寧靜和平靜的時刻,不論是從自然還是環境的角度來看。我並不一定是指寂靜的靜修。更多的是能夠打開一扇門,走出去,然後聽到的只有大地本身。	近年來,人們越來越認識到創造生態可持續性和可恢復性的旅行體驗至關重要,這不僅對客戶,而且對全球各地的社區都是同等重要。

文化	
	Kirsty Sedgman, 傳播博士及 文化研究專家, 布里斯托爾大學
2024	過去10年
我很期待看到一個以更友善的共存方式為核心的新社會契約。在一個惡行無處不在、社會契約似乎正在崩潰的時代,充滿了自私、歧視和不公正,我們認為合理的許多事物都是過去時代的遺物。以正義之名擁抱"不合理"的行為──嗯,這真的是一件壞事嗎?	過去十年來,令人欣喜的變化之一是有更多在戲院裡可以放鬆的表演、親子活動,還有更廣泛的「額外現場 Extra Live」運動的興起。這種變化是由身障社福團體所帶領,目的是為自閉症和其他神經多樣性的患者提供一個更友善的空間,同時也為年輕父母提供更輕鬆的氛圍,因為比在黑暗的戲院裡靜坐不動,他們通常需要更放鬆的環境。

零售	
	Leticia Credidio, 創辦人, Leticia Credidio
2024	過去10年
對於獨立和小型品牌來說，今年將是一個令人振奮的一年，因為消費者要求更透明度和更精緻的工藝。自我照顧和更緩慢步調的選擇現在也進入了人們的優先事項清單。這是作為一個品牌，我們一直期待在零售領域看到的趨勢。	時尚產業和零售格局已經經歷了巨大的變革，隨著大規模製衣業的式微和良知購物興起。在過去的十年裡，我們大多數人一直在學習如何識別環保虛偽行為，並開始選擇可持續品牌和品質，而非追逐時尚趨勢。

食品	
	Alix Cherowbrier, 策略總監, Bompas & Parr
2024	過去10年
我們將會看到更多意想不到的領域和飲食之間的跨界融合，各個領域將相互碰撞，產生真正的創新，從考古調酒到深偽點心。我很興奮看到昔日食材被復活，並透過魔法儀式消費，以及情緒優化的調劑品逐漸普及到主流市場中。	飲食產業已從固定僵化到思考全面。過去十年來，我們看到更高程度的自我意識通過用餐者如何消費食物和飲料而回應，社交媒體的趨勢使我們從餐廳中的旁觀者轉變為互動者。菜單現在是多感官的，讓我們所享用的食物和飲料完全融入自我之中。

美容	
	Kimberley Ho, 創辦人暨執行長, Evereden
2024	**過去10年**
回到重視產品背後的專業知識與科學背書了。因為隨著大量新品牌湧現，美容市場也充斥著大量的行銷噪音，使得消費者感到疲憊。如今，再次渴望在選擇產品時獲得真正的科學支持。	美妝品牌的大眾化與電子商務和社交媒體的崛起相吻合。在過去10年中，這使得新興品牌更快速地增長且取得成功，因為與消費者接觸的門檻降低了。

科技	
	**Daniel Hulme, 執行長, Satalia及AI長, WPP**
2024	**過去10年**
我很期待看到大型語言模型如何使用機器推理變得更加智能和安全。更讓我興奮的是，看到領導階層開始學習 AI 人工智慧，這樣他們就可以實際有效地開始擁抱這些技術，並創造真正的價值。	組織應該如何擁抱人工智慧一直是出於善意的，但有時卻會脫離實際需求。大量投資流向數據湖和數據科學團隊，但這並不總是產生投資回報。現在組織需要專注於直接創造價值的人工智慧技術。比方說，可以利用人工智慧來創造內容，也可以使用虛擬目標群體來快速測試並提供優秀的客戶體驗。

「改變未來的100件事」十週年

我們對100個值得關注的趨勢進行了年度預測來到十週年。這是過去十年中分享的 10 份報告和 1,000 個微觀趨勢。
「改變未來的100件事」目的在於透過結合文化趨勢和消費者對未來創新的期望來激發品牌和個人。

VML

致謝

VML智庫感謝以下專家的時間和提供見解來與我們分享趨勢：

Andrea Ang, digital editor, Vogue Philippines

Sam Bompas, cofounder, Bompas & Parr

Leticia Credidio, founder, Leticia Credidio

Chris Duffey, strategic development manager, Adobe Creative Cloud

Marcus Engman, creative director, Ingka Group

Ranice Faustino, marketing communications head, Vogue Philippines

April Gargiulo, founder, Vintner's Daughter

Kimberley Ho, founder & CEO, Evereden

Daniel Hulme, CEO of Satalia and chief AI officer, WPP

Daniel Hettwer, founder, Hidden Worlds Entertainment

Tom Marchant, owner and cofounder, Black Tomato

Joyce Oreña, beauty editor, Vogue Philippines

Sebastian S Kresge professor of marketing, Wharton School, University of Pennsylvania and codirector, AI at Wharton

Mark Read, CEO, WPP

Kirsty Sedgman, doctor of audiences and cultural studies expert, University of Bristol

Rogier Vijverberg, founder and creative lead, Jimmy

Jing Zhang, global editor-in-chief, Jing Daily

我們也要感謝以下同仁的寶貴意見：

Sasha Grover

Shaziya Khan

Joyce Ling

Sebastian Martinez

Jessica Nuñez Orozco

Maria Pavlopoulos

Ernest Riba

Felipe Ritis

Sophie Robinson

Lydia Tamarat

Darby Waligorski

關於VML智庫(VML INTELLIGENCE)

VML 智庫是 VML 面向未來思考的研究和創新單位。負責觀察剛興起的現象以及未來的全球趨勢、消費型態變化和創新發展模式，並再進一步解讀這些趨勢後，將其見解提供給品牌參考。VML 智庫提供一系列諮詢服務，包括客製化研究、未來趨勢報告和工作坊，也勇於創新，與品牌合作，在品牌框架下引領未來趨勢，並執行新產品和概念。本單位由 VML 智庫的全球總監 Emma Chiu 和 Marie Stafford 帶領。

如欲瞭解更多資訊，請造訪：

vml.com/expertise/intelligence

關於《改變未來的100件事》

這是由 VML 智庫出版的年度預測報告，除了描繪未來一年的樣貌，也呈現了最受歡迎的趨勢，讓您能掌握潮流。這份報告紀錄了十大領域的 100 個趨勢，橫跨文化、科技、旅遊與觀光、品牌與行銷、食品和飲品、美容、零售、奢華及創新。

有關本報告中的數據結果，除非另有說明，其均由 VML 與 SONAR ™ 於 2023 年 9 月調查收集。該研究於 2023 年 9 月 13 日至 10 月 16 日進行，我們市調九個市場，9,000 名成年人(每個市場皆為 1,000 名參與者))。 本研究涵蓋阿根廷、巴西、中國、哥倫比亞、法國、印度、墨西哥、英國和美國。受訪者的年齡、性別和收入方面代表了各自的市場。 經過分析並與全球數據加權後，使五個地區的代表性相同：拉丁美洲 (阿根廷、巴西、哥倫比亞和墨西哥)，歐洲、中東和非洲 (法國和英國)，美國，中國和印度。

VML

聯絡人

Emma Chiu emma.chiu@vml.com
Marie Stafford marie.stafford@vml.com

總編輯

Emma Chiu, Marie Stafford

撰稿人

Emily Safian-Demers, John O'Sullivan, Nina Jones

副編輯

Hester Lacey, Katie Myers
CREATIVE DIRECTOR
Shazia Chaudhry

創意總監

Shazia Chaudhry

封面圖片

Peach Fuzz, Pantone Color of the Year 2024, courtesy of The Development x Almost Studios

字型

Clone Rounded Latin; Dystopian; Snowflake Sans

The Future

100

Trends & change to watch in 2024

VML

A REPORT BY VML INTELLIGENCE

2024 The Future 100
Writer / VML Intelligence

Editor-in-chief / Emma Chiu, Marie Stafford
Writers / Emily Safian-Demers, John O'Sullivan, Nina Jones
Sub editors / Hester Lacey, Katie Myers

Creative director / Shazia Chaudhry

Cover / Peach Fuzz, Pantone Color of the Year 2024,
courtesy of The Development x Almost Studios

Translator and Assistant editor / Evan Teng, Ben Hsu ,
Rita Cheng , Jessica Chien , Sean Hu , Eric Liu , Jeffery Chen ,
Betty Kuan, Tony Liu, Winnie Tung

Publisher / VML Taiwan
Address / 13F - 5, No.8, Sec. 7, Civic Boulevard, Nangang District,
Taipei City, 115, Taiwan
Tel / (02) 3766-1000
Fax / (02) 2788-0260

Agent / China Times Publishing Company
Tel / (02) 2306-6842
Address / No.351, Sec.2, Wanshou Rd., Guisha District.,
Taoyuan City, 333, Taiwan

Retail price / NTD 500
ISBN / 9789869899246

VML
A REPORT BY VML INTELLIGENCE

Foreword

Welcome to the 10th edition of "The Future 100," where a profound and enriching year awaits.

As 2024 unfolds, an intentional slowdown shifts the pace for people and businesses after years of rapid acceleration. At a time when people believe stress, depression, and pollution are the top three challenges for human health, the pursuit of a better quality of life begins with a great deceleration as people opt for a mindful approach to the year ahead.

This slow-living sentiment is evident in Pantone's warm and subdued choice for its Color of the Year 2024, Peach Fuzz (not to be confused with the sparkling Peach Fizz drink). The color forecaster says the shade communicates a message of "compassion and togetherness" (trend #14 Collective recharge). Even gen Zers are fatigued by fast-moving trends on social media that are impossible to keep up with (trend #6 Decelerating hype cycles) and opting for Luddite mode as a coping mechanism (trend #8 Luddite mode). It's not just impacting people—businesses are also taking a measured pace for production (trend #53 Slow beauty), choosing quality over quantity and seeing positive results.

Community and connection at scale are essential to 2024. Mass collective shared experiences are taking place around the world, bringing friends and strangers alike together (trend #05 Prosocial effervescence), while physical stores are bringing community-centric retail to the fore (trend #64 Community-centric retail). Technology is also assisting connection with spatial tech (trend #12 Spatial tech) offering a smoother and more natural immersion. After all, 67% of people agree that community is more important than one individual and 76% believe that technology helps bring people together.

Last year was the year of artificial intelligence (AI) becoming more accessible thanks to OpenAI. This year will show more governance, creativity, and philosophical thinking as people question what it means to be human at a time when advances in tech are leading to very lifelike digital personas (trend #11 Identity economy, and trend #97 AIdentities). Generation alpha are the youngest group still being born and will be hugely influenced by AI, which may allow them to be the most emotionally engaged and purposeful generation to date (trend #93 Generation AI).

This year will dial up on feelings. People want surprise, mystery, awe, and wonder in their lives, making new experiences that engage a wide spectrum of emotions in demand, from emotioneering (trend #01 Emotioneering) to sensory techtopias (trend #13 Sensory techtopias).

For the 10th anniversary edition, we have also included original consumer data surveyed in nine different countries and interviewed experts across various fields to give their takes on the past decade and what to look out for in 2024. Enjoy!

Emma Chiu and Marie Stafford
Global Directors, VML Intelligence
vml.com/expertise/intelligence

Foreword

We are pleased to announce the 10th anniversary of our publication, "The Future, Trends & change to watch in 2024" marking a significant milestone. This year's trend report reveals a desire for a lifestyle centered around slow living, pursuits of quality and shared lifestyle. As we approach 2024, there is a shift towards more thoughtful consumer attitudes, not only on a personal level but also in the operational models of businesses. On the occasion of our 10th anniversary, this report will guide us through exploring the future, discovering new rhythms in life and work.

Speaking of trends, I cannot overlook the development of AI (Artificial Intelligence), which is reshaping the way we work. Thanks to the capabilities of AI, we now have more efficient practices in creative output, image formation, video editing, virtual characters, and even the rapid production of a large volume of advertising materials. You may wonder, "Will AI replace our jobs?" I believe it is already happening. For instance, in our practical operations, tasks such as 3D product imaging, virtual model, retouching, spatial configuration, etc., can all be accomplished through AI, resulting in some people losing job opportunities. However, I remain optimistic about the advertising industry. Because AI can handle and assist many execution tasks, this means we have more time to return to the essence of this industry—ideas—to create more valuable outputs.

This report covers ten categories, including "culture, technology, travel & hospitality, brands & marketing, food & drink, beauty, retail, luxury, health, and innovation." These 10 domains are also exploring their own futures during this decade-long journey. Now brands will embrace AI and machine learning to enhance marketing effectiveness, enabling a better understanding of customers and predicting consumer behavior. Luxury brands seek meaning, craft, slowness, and authenticity, emphasizing unique attributes, culture, and history. Travel is no longer just an antidote to everyday life but also a pursuit of tranquil journeys, and so on. All these signs indicate that we are on the verge of a future where AI, slow living, sustainability, craft, authenticity, and kindness coexist. Let's embrace it.

VML

Evan Teng
VML Taiwan CEO

01

Culture

 11

Technology

21

Travel & hospitality

31

Brands & marketing

41

Food & drink

Beauty

Retail

Luxury

Health

Innovation

By the numbers

Unless otherwise stated, original global consumer data throughout by VML Data. 9,000 18+ adult respondents surveyed in Argentina, Brazil, China, Colombia, France, India, Mexico, the United Kingdom, and the United States. Data collected September–October 2023. For methodology and weightings see page 261.

VML

A gentle optimism is emerging

Despite anxieties, people remain hopeful, especially on a personal level.

How positive or negative people are feeling

Rating of how positive or negative respondents feel about how things are going in their own lives and in the world, on a scale of 1 to 10

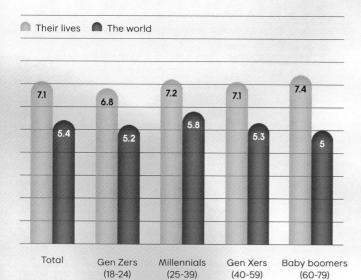

Their lives   The world

People's key emotion about life right now

% selecting each emotion to capture how things are going in life right now

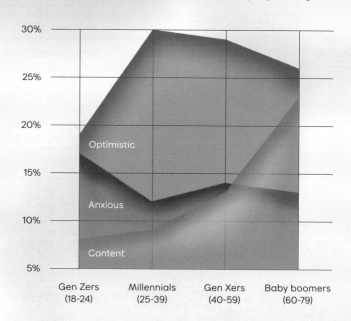

Although challenges persist

People are realistic about ongoing complexity and risk.

The 10 most pressing issues facing society
% selecting in their top five

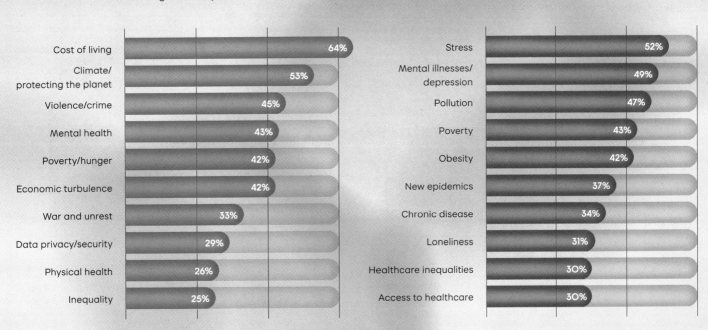

Issue	%
Cost of living	64%
Climate/protecting the planet	53%
Violence/crime	45%
Mental health	43%
Poverty/hunger	42%
Economic turbulence	42%
War and unrest	33%
Data privacy/security	29%
Physical health	26%
Inequality	25%

The top 10 challenges for human health
% selecting

Challenge	%
Stress	52%
Mental illnesses/depression	49%
Pollution	47%
Poverty	43%
Obesity	42%
New epidemics	37%
Chronic disease	34%
Loneliness	31%
Healthcare inequalities	30%
Access to healthcare	30%

VML

Technology inspires us...

Most see its potential for positive impact.

% agree

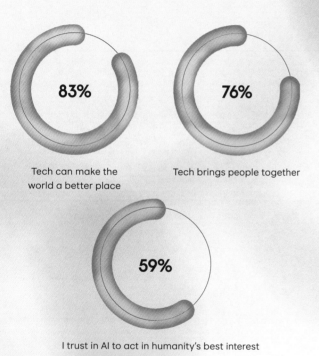

83%

Tech can make the
world a better place

76%

Tech brings people together

59%

I trust in AI to act in humanity's best interest

...but it won't replace us

Humanity, now defined by emotion, will be paramount.

Where technology has potential to outperform humans
% selecting in their top three

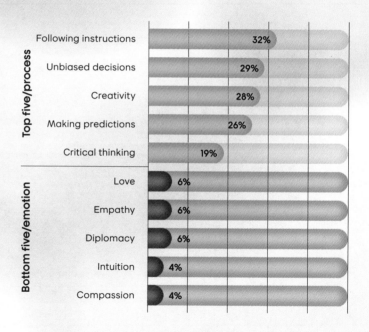

Top five/process

Following instructions	32%
Unbiased decisions	29%
Creativity	28%
Making predictions	26%
Critical thinking	19%

Bottom five/emotion

Love	6%
Empathy	6%
Diplomacy	6%
Intuition	4%
Compassion	4%

VML

People want to reconnect with the world and each other

There's a collective yearning to enrich life through...

Emotions

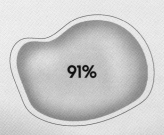

91%

want to feel more emotion in their lives*

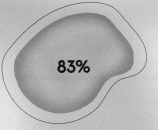

83%

actively seek out experiences that bring joy and happiness*

Experiences

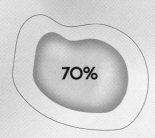

70%

prefer to spend money on experiences rather than things

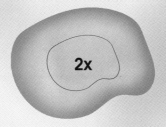

2x

Twice the number of people say spending on experiences (rather than things) makes them happy

Connection

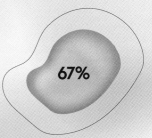

67%

say community is more important than any individual

73%

say spending quality time with others is a motivation when they eat

VML

* VML data 2023, 3,000 adults, China, United Kingdom, United States

Elevating humanity and connection are now key brand opportunities

People expect brands to offer optimism and uplift.

The role of a brand has changed over the past five years

% agree

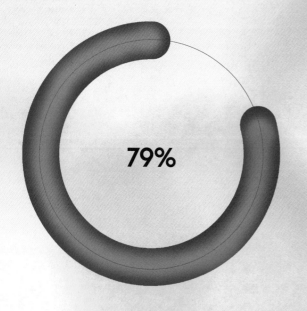

79%

The role of a brand should be to...

% selecting in their top three

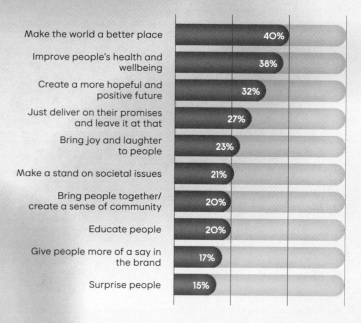

Make the world a better place	40%
Improve people's health and wellbeing	38%
Create a more hopeful and positive future	32%
Just deliver on their promises and leave it at that	27%
Bring joy and laughter to people	23%
Make a stand on societal issues	21%
Bring people together/ create a sense of community	20%
Educate people	20%
Give people more of a say in the brand	17%
Surprise people	15%

VML

Culture

01
Emotioneering

New emotional metrics are in the making for brands.

↑ The Kraken Screamfest VII: Shock Exchange

Two-thirds of people globally say they want brands to help them feel intense emotions, according to VML Intelligence's "The Age of Re-enchantment" 2023 study. The report unpacks an opportunity to stoke imaginations by offering re-enchantment, which celebrates the thrilling, the uplifting, and the awe-inspiring. At a time when people feel burned out, disconnected, and jaded, 77% say they "just want to feel something, to feel alive." There is a spectrum of emotion for brands to explore, and a slew of benefits to doing so.

Psychology tells us fun and joy play a vital role in our physical and mental wellbeing as well as acting as a social lubricant. Feeling awe too is prosocial, and also helps us stop ruminating, look outward, and feel more connected. Surprise can help us connect, as well as reshape self-perceptions. Even difficult emotions have their place, helping us to process challenges and build resilience.

VML Intelligence's data shows that crafting experiences with emotional payback brings mutual reward: consumers are more likely to spend on a brand that makes them *feel*, from joy to surprise, inspiration, and more.

US rum brand The Kraken is leaning in to its dark side. For Halloween 2023 it mounted Screamfest VII: Shock Exchange in selected UK bars. Developed in partnership with the Recreational Fear Lab, it challenged drinkers to try an immersive horror experience wearing a heart-rate monitor: the lower their bpm, the cheaper the cocktail.

Daybreaker, a global wellness brand that hosts uplifting communal morning dance parties, is a pioneer of "emotioneering." Founder and CEO Radha Agrawal tells VML Intelligence that "one of our major key performance indicators at Daybreaker is tears of joy."

Why it's interesting

It's time for brands to disrupt the rational and explore the disruptive power of emotion. In the future, a brand's performance might measure sighs of tranquility, tears of joy, goosebumps, or jaw drops. Consumers will invest in the brands that add emotional value to their lives in the form of re-enchantment.

↑ Daybreaker

VML

02

Collective recharge

Color specialists forecast tones that convey
a warm and nurturing hug.

VML

↑ Peach Fuzz, Pantone Color of the Year 2024, courtesy of The Development x
Almost Studios

Expect to see an increased focus on community.

Laurie Pressman, vice president, Pantone Color Institute

Peach Fuzz is the soft, dewy, and comforting shade that Pantone has selected as its 2024 color of the year. Shifting away from the energetic Viva Magenta of last year, the hue centers around humanity, growth, and peace at a time of instability. "Peach Fuzz brings belonging, inspires recalibration and an opportunity for nurturing, conjuring up an air of calm, offering us a space to be, feel, and heal, and to flourish, whether spending time with others or taking the time to enjoy a moment by ourselves," says Leatrice Eiseman, executive director of the Pantone Color Institute.

The peach swatch imbues a gentle, positive outlook that is dreamy, youthful, and innocuous. Pantone explains that there is a feeling of "tenderness" and a message of "caring and sharing." People are at the heart of the 2024 color decision by Pantone, as the brand expects to see "an increased focus on community, and people across the world reframing how they want to live and evaluating what is important—that being the comfort of being close to those we love," says Laurie Pressman, vice president of the Pantone Color Institute.

↑ Peach Fuzz, Pantone Color of the Year 2024, courtesy of The Development x Almost Studios

UK paint company Dulux echoes a similar sentiment with Sweet Embrace, its 2024 color of the year. The brand described the warm and calming shade as "a kind, delicate tone that brings a feeling of positivity to our lives."

US-based Sherwin-Williams has selected a cool and calming blue shade, Upward, for its 2024 color of the year. The hue evokes a moment of reflection and respite, and Sherwin-Williams describes it as "the color found when we slow down, take a breath, and allow the mind to clear."

Why it's interesting

An enriching, soulful, and cerebral year is in the making, as people are encouraged to slow down to better reconnect with themselves and others. 2024 could be an enlightening year that paves the way for a thoughtful and humancentric future.

VML

↓ Peach Fuzz, Pantone Color of the Year 2024, courtesy of The Development x Almost Studios

Climate-adaptive lives

Extreme climate conditions are changing
every aspect of our lives.

"The era of global warming has ended; the era of global boiling has arrived," United Nations secretary-general António Guterres said in July 2023—which was the planet's hottest month on record. The rise of extreme weather patterns, most notably extreme heat, has far-reaching implications for daily life. "Extreme heat will change us," the *New York Times* avowed.

For workers, extreme heat can have dire consequences. Heatwaves across Europe killed more than 61,000 people in the summer of 2022, according to a study published in *Nature* in July 2023. In the United States, the Occupational Safety and Health Administration is rushing to draft heat standards for workplaces, and President Biden announced new plans to protect workers from extreme heat in July 2023.

While these new weather patterns are undoubtedly dangerous, they are also driving innovation across sectors to help us adapt. UK-based smart clothing business Techniche specializes in thermoregulation technology and is pioneering cooling workwear for construction workers.

US-based Qore Performance supplies cooling vests to enterprises including Boeing, Shake Shack, Chick-fil-A, and FedEx, not to mention the US Air Force, and has seen its business grow by 300% since 2020. The tech powering these vests is IcePlate Curve, "the world's first consumable thermoregulation tool."

Thermoregulation and heat-stress expert James Russell, who predicts a future where workwear is embedded with wearable predictive technology, tells VML Intelligence: "We're currently developing printed biometric sensors that provide low power feedback to blue collar workers and HSSE (health,

VML

safety, security, and environment) teams. The sensors pick up various biometric data points and, with the help of AI, we can then predict if a worker is likely to need medical attention."

In agriculture, new terroirs are reinforming the regions where crops are grown. Some vintners are even spraying their grapes with microbes to protect them from the heat.

To design cities of the future, urban planners need to think about "the thermal comfort of the spaces people are moving through," David Hondula, director of Phoenix's Office of Heat Response and Mitigation, told *The Daily* podcast. Singapore is investing significant resources to radically rethink its sweltering urban areas, the *New York Times* reported. In China, architects are reviving the ancient, naturally cooling concept of skywells—tall, narrow courtyards—in buildings. And architect Vinu Daniel is pioneering climate responsive architecture in India.

Climate-adaptive beauty sees new formulations that protect the skin from environmental irritants. Following the uptick in wildfires, US-based beauty brand Pour Moi launched its Smoke Alarm Drops serum in April 2022 to combat the oxidative stress caused by smoke. In August 2023, Prada debuted a skincare range that uses unique Adapto.gn Smart Technology to help the skin adapt to its environment in real time and promote renewal, regeneration, and reinforcement.

Why it's interesting

"Extreme weather is becoming the new normal," Guterres said. Extreme weather is not going anywhere—and it will continue to reshape our daily lives and drive innovation (see trend #96 Metamorphic cities).

VML

↑ Techniche cooling garments

The era of global warming has ended; the era of global boiling has arrived.

António Guterres, secretary-general, United Nations

↑ Mind your Manners, Netflix, courtesy of James Gourley

The new etiquette

Cultural influencers issue etiquette refreshers for collective experiences.

Bad behavior. Suddenly, it's everywhere. Eighty percent of global respondents agree that people are behaving worse than ever these days. Lurid tales of people getting up to no good in public spaces around the world have made headlines. People are fighting in cinemas; flinging missiles at the headline act at concerts; out-singing the actors at musicals, and even jumping on stage with them in theaters.

"Live performance has always been a canary in the coal mine," Kirsty Sedgman, cultural studies expert at the University of Bristol, tells VML Intelligence. "It's an early warning system when much bigger sociopolitical frustrations and shifts are about to erupt." While some commentators have put riotous behavior down to post-pandemic rustiness, Sedgman sees greater nuance and complexity. She points to the role of what she calls "the disconnection economy" and "a collapsing of the social contract."

VML

↑ Mind your Manners, Netflix, courtesy of James Gourley

"What we have seen is a growing sense of disconnection from each other and a further entrenchment into our echo-chamber bubbles," she says, adding that since people have observed those in power doing as they like without consequence, now "a strong contingent of people seem to be resistant to any authority figure telling them what to do."

Arbiters are stepping up to offer refreshed guidance. One voice is the etiquette expert Sara Jane Ho, founder of China's first finishing school, whose Netflix show *Mind Your Manners* aired in 2023. A book with the same title will be published in 2024, offering Ho's insights on how to present your best self in any situation. In Dubai, Chinese TikTok influencer Ziying Zhou is teaching etiquette and social conduct to UAE residents via workshops and private lessons. In Japan, after people have experienced social isolation and years of mask-wearing, demand for "smiling lessons" is growing. "After three years of COVID-era masking, some Japanese people

feel their facial expressions are a bit rusty," writes the *New York Times*. "Enter Keiko Kawano, smile instructor," whose coaching sessions instruct students on how to smile with genuine feeling and warmth.

Brands are also weighing in. Disney resorts in Florida and California have added a Courtesy section to the visitor preparation guides on their websites, calling on attendees to treat each other with respect. Auto manufacturer Vauxhall has teamed up with decorum expert Debrett's on an etiquette guide for EV drivers, offering advice on respectful queuing and negotiating access to charging points with diplomacy. Businesses are also reiterating codes of conduct: 45% of US companies are offering etiquette classes, reinforcing expectations on everything from attire to navigating conversations in the workplace.

Ho tells VML Intelligence that etiquette is about more than niceties: "In this time of epic loneliness, we need etiquette more than ever as the utmost form of wellness, a way to promote genuine and healthy individual growth—through human connection."

Why it's interesting

In a time when facilitating togetherness holds so much promise, setting guidance on expected behaviors could bring us together. Sedgman's advice to brands is to "think carefully about which rules will actually keep everybody safer and create a fairer, more egalitarian, and more connective form of experience."

05

Prosocial effervescence

Mass collective experiences are fulfilling a yearning for connection and belonging.

Seventy-one percent of people globally agree that loneliness is an epidemic and 66% say there is no sense of community anymore. There is a growing opportunity for brands to engineer collective experiences that promote connection and community at scale with friends and strangers alike.

Collective effervescence describes the energy and harmony released by shared experience, like being part of a choir or a festival crowd. According to Kirsty Sedgman, cultural expert at the University of Bristol, it is important to us "because it really does bring people together from all different kinds of backgrounds and forges strong community bonds." She tells VML Intelligence that "there's so much evidence to suggest that if you can step outside that comfort zone of people who are exactly like you and meet a wider range of people, it leads to massive personal health benefits, and also to stronger communities and better performing economies."

Hence Join My Wedding, a service that allows international tourists to buy tickets to attend the weddings of strangers in India, so they can feel the joy of being a part of the large-scale events. Or The Big Quiet, a mass meditation movement that started with 25-person sessions and has evolved into wellness events with thousands of participants.

It's also why Swedish retailer Ikea is exploring new ways to bring people back together in its stores, starting by hosting nighttime raves during Milan Design Week in 2023. "Ikea is very much about relationships," Marcus Engman, creative director of Ikea franchisee Ingka Group, tells VML Intelligence. The company's philosophy is grounded in *tillsammans*—the Swedish word for togetherness. "That's not just togetherness between Ikea and our customers; it's also among people," he

VML

↑ The Big Quiet. Photography by Felix Kunze
→ Ikea at Milan Design Week 2023. Photography by Ozmoze

VML

says. "So how could we create areas and opportunities for togetherness? This is something that we have worked with from almost the very beginning of Ikea."

As Engman explains, the retailer fulfils the role of facilitator, providing the occasion and the venue, allowing people to do the rest. "When you do a thing like throwing a rave, it's the people together that create the ambience," he says. "We're just the scene for them to create something." And Ikea is not the only retailer exploring the power of connection: department store Selfridges will launch a permanent event space on its fourth floor called The Selfridges Lounge, where visitors can enjoy music and cultural programming.

Why it's interesting
Brands must help people connect with each other, according to Radha Agrawal, founder of mass morning dance event Daybreaker: "The biggest opportunity that brands have is getting people to connect with each other—how this brand can serve a community as a collective rather than the individual inside the community."

05

↑ The Big Quiet

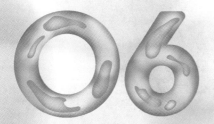

Decelerating hype cycles

The fast-moving trend cycle creates fatigue
and takes a slower turn.

VML

2023 saw a minor rebellion as users, irked by the pace at which new trends are being manufactured and hyped up on TikTok, collectively eyerolled at beauty concepts like "blueberry milk nails," "latte makeup," and "tomato girl summer." "We are not turning light blue into blueberry milk. I refuse," said TikTok user Katie Raymond (@katiehub.org).

In an interview with VML Intelligence, journalists from *Vogue Philippines* agree that concepts presented as trends are not always as novel as they seem. "Latte makeup is steeped in Korean beauty aesthetics, and also in the needs of those with olive skin tones," says digital editor Andrea Ang. Beauty editor Joyce Oreña recommends instead identifying the longer-term shifts that underpin them. "We cannot ignore all these fast-moving trends," she says. "So how do you deal with it? It's really paying attention to the wider tendencies."

In response to the fast-paced hype cycles, there is a simultaneous movement that sees value in slowing down. As we report in Next-gen collectors (trend #63), designer Phoebe Philo is eschewing the standard seasonal approach for her collections, opting instead for limited drops of pieces that are designed for longevity. In beauty, Hermès has opted to produce fewer, more innovative beauty products, while slow skincare brand Dieux has set itself the mission of selling fewer products (see trend #53 Slow beauty).

Clearly there are benefits from a sustainability point of view, and there are also indications that consumers may welcome some respite. According to global research from Ipsos, 73%

↑ Courtesy of Katie Raymond (@katiehub.org) and Sunia Bukhari (@suniabukhari)

wish they could slow down the pace of their life.

There are cultural parallels too: in a September 2023 piece, the *Guardian* describes a shift away from the binge model in TV streaming, and pinpoints shows watched week by week instead as the "new status marker for television."

Why it's interesting

People feel overwhelmed by the sheer pace at which they are urged to consume. Some brands are choosing to decelerate, slow down, and allow time for people to savor experiences before moving on to the next thing.

Brands are choosing to decelerate, slow down, and allow time for people to savor experiences before moving on to the next thing.

VML

07

Lasting ephemera

The beauty of impermanence in artistry that metaphorically echoes the delicacy of nature and humanity is being celebrated.

VML

↑ Condollence. Concept, design and tailoring by Darío Simón Abelló. Photographed at HFBK Photo Studio

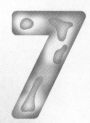

↑ Condollence. Concept, design and tailoring by Darío Simón Abelló.
  Photographed at HFBK Photo Studio

The Met Gala's 2024 theme will capture ephemerality and preservation in fashion, with "Sleeping Beauties: Reawakening Fashion." The accompanying exhibition will showcase approximately 250 archive garments and accessories that are now too delicate to be worn.

"The exhibition endeavors to reanimate these artworks by reawakening their sensory capacities through a diverse range of technologies, affording visitors sensorial 'access' to rare historical garments and rarefied contemporary fashions," said Andrew Bolton, Wendy Yu curator in charge of the Costume Institute at the Met. From May 10, 2024, visitors can explore the reawakened precious artifacts that the museum hopes to revive through the exhibition.

Spanish costume designer Darío Simón Abelló has been exploring volatile materials that change their form when worn. In February 2023, the young artist showcased the Condollence collection at the HFBK 2023 annual graduate exhibition in Hamburg, featuring garments dipped in wax that cracked and crumbled when worn, leaving a trail on the catwalk and changing the outfit's shape. Abelló calls these "shattering garments," and aims to delve into the "fragility and vulnerability" in fashion and humanity.

New York-based fashion designer Prabal Gurung explored the Buddhist concept of "anichya," or impermanence, for his fall 2023 ready-to-wear collection. "This collection is a spiritual awakening through the lens of impermanence and metamorphosis—the ideas that nothing is fixed and all are constantly in flux," Gurung says. "Change provokes a sense of optimism, that everything is ever evolving. This is the beauty of impermanence that rather than fear it, one must embrace it."

Why it's interesting

The fragility of nature and humanity is being reflected in fashion and reinvigorated by artists, showcasing these delicate artifacts and breathing newfound appreciation and life into them.

VML

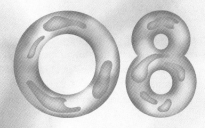

Luddite mode

Gen Z are seamlessly switching between moments of connectivity and digital withdrawal.

VML

↑ Photography by Ellie Adams via Unsplash

The Luddite Club, a New York-based teenage lifestyle group, has attracted much attention in recent years for promoting "self-liberation from social media and technology." Taking its name from the anti-technology Luddite movement of 19th-century England, the group has become synonymous with a gen Z-led rebellion against doom scrolling and social media burnout.

Voxburner's "Youth Trends" report confirms that more than half (54%) of 16-24-year-olds worry about spending too much time on social media. However, rather than committing to the Luddite mentality full time, younger consumers have become adept at switching between moments when they want full connectivity, and crossing into Luddite mode when they need focus or calm.

↑ Nokia 150, courtesy of Nokia

Nokia has reported sustained growth of its "dumb" phones in recent years, driven by their popularity among gen Z. However, according to the *Wall Street Journal*, consumers aren't buying them instead of smartphones, but as "budget second phones." Dumb phones let users swap into Luddite mode on nights out or while relaxing on vacation. In Australia, music label This Never Happened tapped into this mindset with a series of photo- and phone-free events in Melbourne, Sydney, and Brisbane in July 2023, with the prompt: "Experience the moment. Don't record it." For more, see trend #30 Analog travel.

These behavioral changes echo the recent growth in popularity of productivity hack monk mode, which encourages people to cut out all distractions so that they can focus on achieving their core work tasks.

Why it's interesting

While gen Z's mode switching may seem contradictory, brands need to consider whether their products and services can help consumers during moments of connectivity and digital downtime, or if they can help users to seamlessly move between the divergent modes.

09
Nature rights

Legal protections for nature are gaining traction.

VML

A growing global movement that seeks legal rights for nature is gathering momentum in an era beset by climate crisis. According to Katie Surma, writing for *Inside Climate News*, we are in the midst of a litigation boom, with most cases happening in the United States.

In the United States, as in other countries such as Brazil, New Zealand, and Canada, indigenous communities are leading the way. In 2023, tribal leaders in Seattle won a landmark case that guaranteed the rights of salmon to migrate through the city's dams. In other parts of the world, nations are considering enshrining the rights of nature in their constitutions. Leaders across the world from the Philippines and Bolivia to Aruba and the Republic of Ireland are debating following the lead of Ecuador, the first nation to do so back in 2008.

Another approach sees nature granted personhood in law. As the name suggests, this gives rivers and forests the same rights as a human being. The precedent was set by the Maori nation in New Zealand, who secured personhood for the Whanganui river in 2017. Now others are following suit. Successful cases in 2023 earned protections for nature in Brazil (the Komi Memem river) and Spain (the Mar Menor saltwater lagoon), and campaigners are now seeking similar for the river Oder in Poland and the North Sea.

A small number of brands are leaning in to this idea too. Featured in last year's "Future 100," Patagonia and Faith in Nature gave nature a seat on their boards, effectively giving

↑ Mother Nature & Future Generations by Lukas the Illustrator for House of Hackney

nature legal personhood. In November 2023, luxury interiors brand House of Hackney appointed two new directors: mother nature and future generations. "As a business, we think it's imperative we hold ourselves to a high level of legal accountability for our impact on nature and quality of life we're leaving behind for generations to come," says cofounder Frieda Gormley.

Why it's interesting

Mirroring the 20th-century struggle for human rights, the next decade will be defined by a fight for the rights of natural ecosystems.

As a business, we think it's imperative we hold ourselves to a high level of legal accountability for our impact on nature and quality of life we're leaving behind for generations to come.

Frieda Gormley, cofounder, House of Hackney

VML

10

Intentional communities

The traditional family unit is being challenged.

VML

↑ Honeydew eco-community, Italy

Single-person households are on the rise in many regions worldwide, while single-parent households now make up more than a fifth of households in the United States and the United Kingdom. Yet the rise in solo living is juxtaposed by rising loneliness and spiraling housing costs. Enter intentional communities: communities of choice that offer mutual support, enrichment, and companionship in an expanded notion of family.

"Community is the medicine" says the mission statement for Honeydew, a not-for-profit eco-community in Emilia-Romagna, Italy. Founder Benjamin Ramm, a former BBC journalist who escaped solo living in London, hopes to establish a network of multigenerational communities based on a philosophy that prizes mutual care, service, and healing. Ramm tells VML Intelligence that "Honeydew is working to create a new network of intentional communities, grounded in solidarity, sustainability, and mutual care." He explains that the pandemic has spurred urgency "to build collective resilience in the wake of ecological and social crises." He ultimately believes that, despite isolation and despair during this period, "we have been able to nurture social solidarity, and forge a communal identity, in which we are enriched with a sense of mission and purpose."

New Ground is the United Kingdom's first cohousing community for older women. The 26-strong organization is managed by its residents, who each occupy their own home and share communal facilities for recreation and socialization. They are enabled to live independently while also being part of a mutually supportive network. Mutual support is also the idea behind "mommunes," where single

↑ Honeydew eco-community, Italy

mothers and their children share a home. While the concept is not new, it is gaining renewed relevance in the ongoing cost-of-living crisis. Carmel Boss, the founder of a US-based matching service called CoAbode, told the *Today* program in July 2023 that calls to her business have "skyrocketed."

Multigenerational living is another solution. The BBC has reported on a growing number of projects from Canada to the Netherlands that pair students with retirees in shared living quarters.

Why it's interesting

The definition of "family" is evolving as more people opt into communities that provide mutual support and connection. As intentional communities grow, brands need to consider how they cater to and depict the future household.

Technology

20

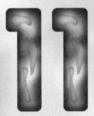

11
The identity economy

A new economy is forming around digital personas.

The Hollywood actors' strike ended in November 2023 after 118 days, with the SAG-AFTRA union celebrating new protections for talent, including guidance on the use of artificial intelligence (AI) in the movie industry. A key stipulation is that studios must seek a performer's consent as well as compensate them for using a digital replica of them or any of their features.

Some actors, including Anil Kapoor, Scarlett Johansson, and Tom Hanks, have already taken legal action over unauthorized uses of their AI likenesses. While legal frameworks are yet to be fully established, this sets us on a path to a new economy around human identity. One emerging service centers on persona creation services, which allow anyone to create their own digital doppelganger.

For content creators and influencers, digital personas can offer unprecedented reach and scale. Chinese influencers are ahead of the game here, commissioning convincing AI clones to enable them to maximize their live-streaming output, churning and earning from content around the clock. A slew of Chinese startups like Silicon Intelligence and Xiaoice can now create deepfake avatars for as little as $1,000, using just one minute of live original video to generate a digital clone.

British AI startup Metaphysic, which shot to fame for its highly convincing deepfake of the actor Tom Cruise (@deeptomcruise), is helping celebrities take control of their virtual personas. Its Metaphysic Pro solution allows users to

VML

↑ Mimio interactive personas

build a portfolio of biometric data that can be used to create a face, voice, and performance that may be licensed and monetized.

San Francisco startup Mimio.ai is building a Personality Engine™ that will allow users to create their own AI persona, adopting their voice, tone, and conversational style. The company foresees applications not just for celebrities and influencers, but also for anyone who might want help handling their email correspondence, and even for elders who might wish to leave behind a digital self for posterity. The company promises that users retain full control of their persona and are free to monetize it as they wish.

VML

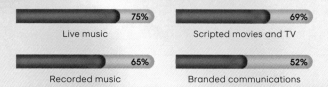

Respondents express a preference for the human over AI when enjoying:

75% Live music

69% Scripted movies and TV

65% Recorded music

52% Branded communications

It seems inevitable that digital clones will become part of our everyday. For now, at least, flesh and blood humanity retains the advantage where artistry is concerned. Respondents express a preference for the human over AI when enjoying live music (75%), scripted movies and TV shows (69%), recorded music (65%), and even branded communications (52%).

Why it's interesting
While ethical and legal guardrails are still to be defined, the identity economy is already thriving. Digital personas offer cost-effective and flexible ways for brands to engage talent, though it's worth noting that the human still carries a premium with audiences. Fewer than one in 10 (8%) respondents say they are looking forward to a future where virtual people are part of everyday life.

12

Spatial tech

Physical and digital worlds continue to blur
with advances in spatial computing.

↑ Vision Pro by Apple, courtesy of Apple

Vision Pro by Apple, courtesy of Apple

Apple will launch its Vision Pro mixed-reality headset in February 2024. For $3,499, buyers will have access to what Apple calls its "first spatial computer." The device promises to "seamlessly blend digital content with the physical world," making it a significant mass-market effort at untethering digital interfaces from screens. The company announced a "guest mode" in January, allowing friends and family to test drive the device.

During the Consumer Electronics Show (CES) 2024, Sony Corporation announced a partnership with Siemens to develop a spatial content creation system. Including an extended-reality headset and controllers, it is due to launch later this year. In October 2023, Chinese augmented-reality company Xreal introduced its Air 2 and Air 2 Pro next-generation lightweight AR glasses, promising "one screen to replace them all."

At CES 2024, Niantic's director of product AR platforms, Tom Emrich, predicted that the contextual advantages of smart glasses and headsets would turn smartphones into a "sidekick" and a "hub for all things wearable devices." According to Emrich, the spatial tech category "is just coming together. But this means that it presents a massive opportunity for app developers, for web developers, for brands and retailers especially to get their feet wet." He added, "I agree with Tim Cook—the spatial computing era has arrived and we're just getting started."

Why it's interesting

As advances in immersive technologies continue to bring the physical and digital worlds closer together, spatial computing will see significant growth. The market is expected to grow from $97.9 billion in 2023 to $280.5 billion by 2028, according to MarketsandMarkets.

13

Sensory techtopias

Creators are leveraging tech to explore the relationship between our senses.

↑ See yourself in sound, Bang & Olufsen

The intriguing synergies and interplay between our senses are the theme for a wave of tech-powered synaesthetic experiences.

Bang & Olufsen's "See yourself in sound" brand campaign turns musical taste into colorful portraits in the form of grooving interactive avatars. The digital experience invites customers to visit a specially designed website where they answer a brief questionnaire or link their Spotify account to receive a unique custom avatar to share across social media.

Aura, another experience making sound visible, was a landmark commission for the 2023 London Design Festival. Designed by Spanish artist Pablo Valbuena in partnership with arts organization Artichoke, *Aura* visualizes the sounds of worship at St Paul's Cathedral. A slender 20-meter column of aluminum studded with custom-made LED lights is

VML

suspended from the dome of the cathedral. The sounds of speech, music, and singing are captured and translated via an algorithm into beams of light, which react to pitch, volume, and intensity.

Mexican-Canadian artist Rafael Lozano-Hemmer's *Atmospheric Memory* makes the spoken word visible. Updated for a November 2023 showing at Sydney's Powerhouse Museum, the exhibit offers a sensory environment inspired by Charles Babbage's conceit that the air around us is a library containing every word, sound, and motion. Visitors walk through a mid-air cloud of text, or see their voice make ripples in a water tank.

Beyond artistic endeavors, the UK artist collective Universal Everything is putting its synaesthetic tech skills and experience to practical use, developing a prototype device that could be used by patients to visualize pain. In Japan, NTT Docomo and collaborating institutions are developing the world's first sensation-sharing technology, which allows users to send movements or tactile sensations digitally. Docomo already has plans to build on its Feel Tech technology, enabling the sharing of other sensations, like taste, hearing, and even emotions.

Why it's interesting

The demand for sensory experience is potent. According to VML Intelligence's research for our "Age of Re-enchantment" report, 63% of consumers want brands to provide them with multisensory experiences, and 72% say that they expect as

many of their senses as possible to be engaged when experiencing something new. The synaesthetic approach adds a new layer of intrigue to sensory experiences, both physical and digital.

↑ See yourself in sound, Bang & Olufsen

↑ Text Stream II, part of Atmospheric Memory by Rafael Lozano-Hemmer. Photography by Zan Wimberley @zanwimberley, courtesy of Factory International and the Powerhouse Museum Sydney

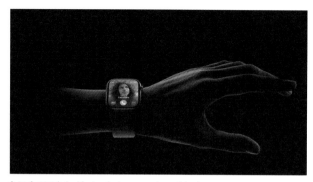

↑ Apple Watch double-tap feature, courtesy of Apple

14

Air gestures

New touchless gestures allow consumers to connect
with devices ever more seamlessly.

VML

During the Consumer Electronics Show (CES) 2024, Finnish startup Doublepoint launched the WowMouse app, allowing Android watch wearers to include air-gesture detection. "We're not just changing the game—we're rewriting the rules for human-computer interaction with our touch-based gesture tracking. It's a leap forward, delivering a natural and powerful user experience for smartwatches and beyond," says Ohto Pentikäinen, CEO of Doublepoint.

In a similar vein, Apple introduced a new double-tap gesture for the Apple Watch Series 9 and Apple Watch Ultra 2 in October 2023. This allows the wearer to simply tap together the index finger and thumb of the hand wearing the watch, to perform actions such as answering a call. Apple notes that the gesture can help the user when their other hand is occupied, such as when they're "walking the dog, cooking, or holding a cup of coffee." This gesture will also be applied to

the company's 2024 release of Vision Pro, its mixed-reality headset.

Neural Lab's AirTouch converts hand and body gestures into commands for any computing device using only a simple webcam, opening up the option for people to include air gestures across different devices.

Google revealed Project Gameface in May 2023, "a new open-source, hands-free gaming mouse that enables users to control a computer's cursor using their head movement and facial gestures." Project Gameface is powered by Google's MediaPipe open-source AI solutions. The company says its technology means that "people can raise their eyebrows to click and drag, or open their mouth to move the cursor, making it possible for anyone to pursue gaming." The company developed the tech with Lance Carr, a quadriplegic video game streamer who has muscular dystrophy. Google notes that while the tool is still in development, the company is "excited about the potential it has to change the lives of people because it's relatively inexpensive to build and maintain."

Why it's interesting

As tech devices become ever more integrated into consumers' lives, companies are pushing boundaries to make them more intuitive and instinctive to use. And alongside this, such hands-free gestures can be crucial for people whose mobility is limited. With just over 12% of US adults living with mobility issues, according to CDC figures, such gestures allow tech companies to make their products and services more inclusive.

↑ Wow Mouse App by Doublepoint

15

Age tech

Technology is tackling the lifestyle and wellness
needs of senior adults.

VML

↑ Nobi smart ceiling lamp

For a growing cohort of elders, technology can be the key to independent living. The Consumer Electronics Show (CES) in January 2024 saw a slew of new devices and tech that deliver enhanced comfort, safety, and emotional support for seniors at home.

Belgian age-tech company Nobi is tackling the problem of falls, a major cause of injury for the elderly. Its smart ceiling lamp can detect when a person has fallen and alert carers for help when needed. The AI-powered tool, initially offered in residential care facilities, will be available to consumers for use in the home later this year.

Focusing on greater comfort, the Lotus wearable ring from US startup Lotus Labs offers accessibility benefits to anyone with reduced mobility. The device, available on pre-order for

shipping in fall 2024, uses infrared technology to control objects in the home simply by pointing, just like a TV remote.

Also thinking of TV, age-related hearing loss can make it difficult for some older people to follow dialog. Japanese venture SoundFun's Mirai Speaker deploys a patented curved speaker design that makes sound clearer and easier to distinguish, meaning everyone can listen at a comfortable volume.

The rise of large language models is ushering in a new wave of devices that offer not just function, but also conversation and companionship.

CES 2024 saw the return of Intuition Robotics' ElliQ, which provides support and enrichment, and facilitates social connections for older people. The tabletop robot keeps users company, offering chat as well as daily engagement and assistance.

The upgraded hardware and AI enhancements in ElliQ 3.0 allow for natural, free-flowing conversation, much of which can now be processed locally for greater privacy, as Intuition Robotics' chief product officer Ronen Soffer explains to VML Intelligence. Over time, the robot builds a relationship with its user by remembering and reflecting on the conversations they share.

Another key focus is facilitating connection to the wider world, whether it's access to the extended community of ElliQ

↑ ElliQ 3.0, Intuition Robotics

users or help with local information and transportation. According to Soffer, the goal of ElliQ is "to understand, enrich and strengthen relationships—and relationships make your life better. Whatever we can connect you to in the real world, we want to do more of."

Why it's interesting

According to the World Health Organization, one in six people globally will be aged over 60 by 2030. As the global population ages, technology catering to the emotional and support needs of this growing cohort holds much promise. (For more on this, see trend #92 Centenarian futures.)

16

Digitized scent

The future of scent is digital.

VML

↑ Osmo aims to give computers a sense of smell

Sight and sound have successfully been digitized—but what about smell? Osmo is one company working to answer this question. The digital olfaction startup hopes to "give computers a sense of smell," the company says. A spinout of Google Research, Osmo aims to create digital representations of smell that change how we capture, transmit, and remember scents.

Osmo cofounder Josh Wolfe sees the company as a digital chemical design company "where people want a very specific odor and we design the chemicals, just like you would design a drug in a biotech or pharma company and then be able to license those," he told *Wired*.

There are other parallels to the world of biotech and pharmaceuticals: "We see AI in drug discovery as a precedent

for ways that AI will revolutionize olfaction," says Osmo CEO Alex Wiltschko. "Similar to how the advent of AI is changing the way drug hunters find new candidates that are more likely to succeed in the clinic, we see AI augmenting the role of synthetic chemists and master perfumers."

Beyond inspiring new perfumes, the technology could be applied to help combat mosquito-borne diseases, the researchers at Osmo say. Wiltschko also points to agriculture, food storage, pandemic tracking, and disease prevention as fields that would benefit from digitizing smell.

Alongside Osmo, Japanese company Revorn uses AI and IoT technologies to reproduce scent and mimic the sense of smell. At the Consumer Electronics Show (CES) 2024, it exhibited odor sensing and reproduction devices.

Luxury perfumers are also exploring digitized scent. In March 2023, Bulgari launched Scentsorial, an immersive multisensory experience in Dubai that linked technology and olfaction. Participants donned a wearable device that measured their brainwaves and heart rate to detect reactions, thoughts, and emotions to scents, then transformed them in real time into generative downloadable collectibles.

Why it's interesting
Advances in technology are changing the way we experience and understand scent, advancing digital sensory toolkits and bringing us one step closer to true multisensory digital experiences, much like Sensory techtopias (see trend #13).

↑ Osmo aims to give computers a sense of smell

17

Omnilingual tech

Instant translation tools create a global village.

VML

↑ Multilanguage audio on YouTube, courtesy of YouTube Official Blog

AI software is unlocking the power of speech in almost any language. A demo video that circulated from fall 2023 on social media shows celebrities including Emma Chamberlain, Elon Musk, and Marques Brownlee speaking an array of languages in a clone of their own voice that both translates and synchs mouth movements in real time. Los Angeles-based HeyGen is the AI video creation startup behind the one-click translation offer. By uploading clips, users can translate a source video instantly into one of 14 languages, with new languages being added every month. HeyGen has added video translation for business to its suite of services, which can handle multiple speakers and supports script editing, long-form content, and brand-specific vocabulary and tone.

Google also demonstrated a universal translator at its I/O developer conference in 2023. Just like HeyGen's technology, it dubs and lip-synchs video into different languages, but for now it is just a concept. Google is exercising caution over how it rolls out the experimental technology, citing concerns over bad actors and the potential for fueling deepfakes.

While Google works to put guardrails on its software, others are pushing ahead. Delaware-based Rask AI offers multilingual voice cloning in 65 languages at the time of writing, retaining vocal characteristics no matter the language.

Translation technology like this offers brands, content creators, influencers, and educators the potential to accelerate revenue by unlocking a truly global audience for the first time. YouTube influencer Mr Beast is well known for his multilanguage strategy, hiring native speakers to

voice-over his videos into multiple languages. In 2023 he tested YouTube's in-house translation tools on 11 of his top videos and told YouTube's Creator Insider that it "supercharges the heck out of the video." Instead of operating multiple language channels, influencers can now translate content from just one. Adam Waheed, another online creator, told *Fortune* that he expects to triple his audience using AI translation.

Spotify is now piloting AI translation for podcasters too, offering a multilanguage experience that it says is more authentic than dubbing. The translations are available on selected podcasts from the likes of Steven Bartlett and Lex Fridman, and access will be extended over time.

Why it's interesting

For companies and brands, AI translation will usher in a new age of global engagement, enabling them to speak freely to any audience without a clunky translation process. As this software progresses inevitably to work in real time, there will be opportunities for customer service, education, training, and more.

18

Supercharging destinations

Next-gen electric vehicle charging stations could transform a chore into an entertainment opportunity.

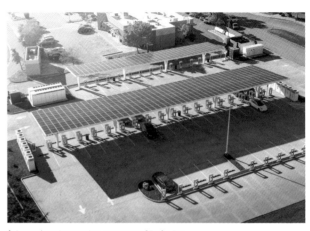

↑ Supercharging station, courtesy of Tesla, Inc

Electric vehicle (EV) use is on the rise. According to the US Bureau of Labor Statistics, which cites research from S&P Global Mobility, US EV sales could reach 40-50% of total passenger car sales by 2030.

This rise in EV use means more demand for EV charging stations and, with charging taking at least 30 minutes for a top-up, companies are dreaming up ways to turn this waiting time into a leisure and entertainment opportunity.

Tesla is currently developing a 24-hour Supercharger station in West Hollywood, complete with 32 charging stalls and a "1950s-style diner and drive-in movie theater." In a tweet previewing the launch, Elon Musk described it as *Grease*

meets *The Jetsons* with Supercharging."

From an entertainment angle, Disney has submitted patents for an in-car entertainment system described by Blog Mickey as an "immersive entertainment pod," into which people could drive their electric vehicle "and be fully surrounded by entertainment while they wait for their car to charge." To illustrate the experience, Disney's patent describes being surrounded by a safari scene rather than simply watching it on a screen.

In September 2023, Shell announced the opening of its largest EV charging station, in Shenzhen, China, with 258 fast-charging points. The space features "Shell Select convenience retailing, Shell Café, vending machines, and a drivers' lounge." Alongside this, Shell also opened its Panlong Integrated Energy Station in Wuhan. The station offers EV charging alongside petrol, diesel, and hydrogen refueling—leisure services span a convenience store, a restaurant, and a drivers' lounge.

Why it's interesting

With EV use forecast to grow, the requirements of these vehicles are creating a new rhythm to driving, in which the longer duration of charging is replacing a quick fill-up at a petrol station. With EV manufacturers, entertainment brands, and energy companies all imagining how to amplify this experience, the concept of charging that combines with entertainment and leisure is an area to watch.

The concept of charging that combines with entertainment and leisure is an area to watch.

↑ Supercharging station, courtesy of Tesla, Inc

VML

19

Symbiotic tech

Our relationship with technology is more human than ever.

↑ Pi chatbot from Inflection AI

VML

Sundar Pichai, the Alphabet and Google CEO, once said, "I've always thought that technology should be adapting to people, not the other way around." With the growing power of AI, this is becoming the reality. Instead of complex processes and commands, we can now use simple gestures and natural conversation. Technology is speaking *our* language.

Pi is a friendly personal chatbot and companion from Inflection AI, a startup helmed by tech entrepreneur Mustafa Suleyman, formerly of DeepMind. Pi, which lives across nine different platforms, including the old-fashioned phone, is an active conversationalist, engaging in back-and-forth chat and asking questions to build deep understanding. In the 100 days following Pi's launch on 2 May 2023, the digital companion exchanged more than a billion messages, according to its founders.

Personality is also a defining feature of the new chatbot Grok from Elon Musk's startup xAI, currently available to verified users of X. Grok "is designed to answer with a bit of wit and has a rebellious streak."

Thanks to a new large language model, Amazon Alexa can now also engage in a more fluid, back-and-forth conversation, initiated by a new command: "Alexa, let's chat." As well as following the thread of the conversation, Alexa can also gather context by using computer vision to identify and track its interlocutor. ChatGPT Plus also has the power of speech, with its latest upgrade offering the choice of five voices. It also has computer vision, enabling it to "see" photos

↑ Humane AI Pin

or diagrams uploaded by a user and give context or analysis.

Could AI one day even know what we are thinking? Although an early experiment at the University of Texas, Austin, managed to decode data from fMRI scans of the brain by matching blood flow patterns with the use of a large language model, the research was laborious and only worked at an individual level. Our thoughts are safe, for now.

Why it's interesting

Personal AI can now see, hear, and speak with us naturally. The more data our digital companions amass, the more symbiotic and human our relationship with them will become, as they adapt to our needs.

20

The AI workforce

The AI-empowered workforce of the future is already here.

VML

Discussions about the risks and potential of artificial intelligence (AI) dominated 2023, with the impact on the global workforce a key focus.

At the first ever global summit on AI at Bletchley Park in the United Kingdom, held in November 2023, Elon Musk referred to AI as "the most disruptive force in history," controversially adding that "there will come a point where no job is needed—you can have a job if you want one for personal satisfaction, but AI will do everything." Musk's speculative view was not shared by all, with British Prime Minister Rishi Sunak asserting: "AI doesn't just automate and take people's jobs. A better way to think about it is as a copilot."

What is clear is that the technology is already making a significant impact on the global workforce. The World Economic Forum (WEF) "Future of Jobs Report 2023" suggests that AI will create 69 million new jobs globally in the next five years, and these positions are already being filled.

In October 2023, there were more than 3,750 job listings posted on Indeed for prompt engineers, who specialize in writing the prompts necessary to elicit the best responses from AI. The ethical concerns facing AI deployment has also created the need for AI ethicists, who make sure that AI integrations are designed to benefit humans, while AI auditors and content moderators now guard against bias and the spread of misinformation.

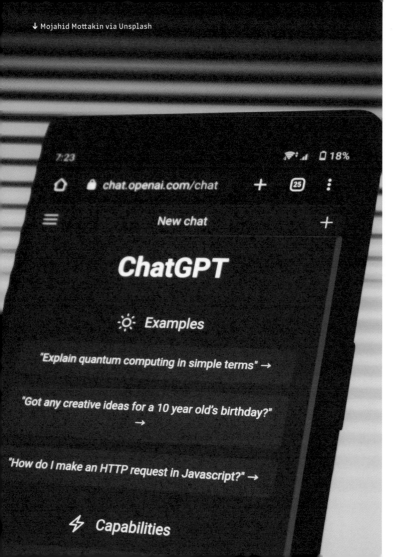

While technical jobs are also abounding for those well versed in AI, existing jobs are being streamlined or even supercharged by the type of AI copiloting that Sunak refers to. Communication technology company Twilio has created a tool using Open AI's GPT-4 that automates the task of filling out request for proposal (RFP) forms. Achieving in minutes what two members of sales staff would take weeks to do, RFP Genie frees up human intelligence for more skilled, creative, or emotionally nuanced tasks.

Proprietary research for this report found that an overwhelming majority (69%) say they are not worried about technology eliminating jobs, while 53% of people say they are already using generative AI tools for research at work. With WEF predicting that the proportion of workplace tasks completed by machines will rise from 34% in 2022 to 43% by 2027, measures are now emerging to protect the human workforce. The agreement that ended the WGA writers' strikes includes amendments that ensure workers remain in charge of AI, while Capgemini creative agency The Works has created "trust marks" to differentiate work done by human creatives.

Why it's interesting

As AI continues to evolve and integrates across industries, work is undergoing a revolution, requiring new skills and reshaping careers. Brands and employees should ready themselves for an AI-powered future where the workforce collaborates seamlessly with intelligent machines (see trend #93 Generation AI on page 229 for more).

VML

21

Travel & hospitality

30

21

Subterranean hospitality

Hotels and spas are finding hidden depths in the search for serenity.

↑ Claridge's Spa, UK, courtesy of Andre Fu Studio

VML

↑ Subterranean spa by Studio Seilern Architects, Lithuania. Photography by Roland Halbe

Zedwell opened a subterranean hotel in London in the summer of 2023. With the help of sleep experts, the rooms have been designed as "underground cocoons" and remove all the distractions of the outside world. With no windows, TVs, or gadgets of any kind, they instead feature noise-reducing walls and lighting based on circadian rhythm, to "create the ultimate sanctuary" and "aid deep rest and restoration," Zedwell says.

In Australia, Victoria's Continental Sorrento hotel opened an underground spa and bathhouse in April 2023, featuring a salt therapy room, cold plunge pools, and geothermally heated mineral baths. "The correlation between health and hotel is deeply rooted," said Nik Karalis, lead architect for the project at Woods Bagot. "Hotels—and the caravanserais, abbeys, and inns that pre-date them—have a long history of being places of refuge and recovery."

Located in the heart of the UK capital, The Londoner descends eight levels below ground and has dubbed itself the city's first "iceberg hotel." The subterranean spaces include a ballroom, cinema, pool, and spa.

Claridge's hotel in London unveiled its underground wellness center in 2022. The renowned destination undertook a five-story excavation to accommodate spa-goers deep beneath the bustle of the city. The 650-square-meter space includes a steam room, pool, sauna, and seven treatment rooms.

UK-based Studio Seilern Architects recently added a subterranean spa to the Boksto 6 complex in Vilnius, Lithuania. The underground spa and swimming pool are built into the UNESCO-protected site's extensive brick cellars, for sequestered peace and quiet.

Why it's interesting
Hotels and spas are offering guests an all-encompassing escape from the hustle and bustle of life above ground.

↓ Claridge's Spa, UK, courtesy of Andre Fu Studio

↑ Black Tomato guests visit Poor Knights Islands, NZ. Photography by Miles Holden, courtesy of Black Tomato

22

Transcendent travel

Self-betterment and life-affirming moments are the new travel requirements.

Debuted in late 2023, travel company Black Tomato's latest experience, See You in the Moment, is "about helping you and your travel companions—be they friends or family (or both)—to savor the world, together. Meaningfully, seamlessly, unforgettably." Forget merely gathering friends to lie on a beach.

One of five Moments categories to choose from, The Challenge includes an itinerary with an expedition to Tierra del Fuego on Argentina's Mitre Peninsula, "where guests will tackle an extreme physical challenge together... against the backdrop of crashing surf at the confluence of the Atlantic, Pacific, and Southern Oceans," Black Tomato says. Among the itineraries for The Journey, guests can choose a trip that sees them travel on a sustainable motor yacht to Poor

VML

Knights Islands, New Zealand, "in search of some of the world's best diving."

Tom Marchant, cofounder of Black Tomato, tells VML Intelligence that the idea for the experiences was born out of the fact that, post-pandemic, people experienced an "urge to connect," coupled with "the desire to do something truly memorable, that you can not only just enjoy, by being present in the moment with [others], but equally something you can reflect back on and you can really savor, that perhaps acts as a catalyst to do more."

Marchant is clear that such experiences bring about transcendent moments. "I think at the heart of it is the ability to take a pause and truly embrace that moment in time— being really present, and disconnected from everything else that's going on in your life," he says. "It could be three hours; it could be three days. But for that period, with those people, it's about just everything else falling away and really savoring that, and leaving feeling contented—full of joy, and inspired, and grateful."

Taking its cue from a similar concept is Black Tomato's Bring it Back service, in which a client's travel itinerary is planned with the notion of bringing back the answer to a question. That could mean a trip to Morocco to ignite creative thinking, or a journey to outer Mongolia to discover new perspectives on family relationships. "The idea was using travel as a vehicle to go out and expose yourself to these communities, to understand how they approach family or business or love…

↑ Black Tomato guests visit Poor Knights Islands, NZ. Photography by Miles Holden, courtesy of Black Tomato

to give you an alternative view. And then bring that back home and pay that into your daily life," says Marchant.

Twenty-six percent of gen Zers and millennials say the reason they select travel destinations is to deepen self-discovery and 32% say they are after personal growth and development.

Why it's interesting
Travelers are keen to throw themselves into experiences that are truly transformative and that will have an impact on their lives beyond the immediate trip. As Black Tomato's Marchant points out: "I think there's an innate part of human nature which is to be curious."

23

Immersive theme parks

The theme park gets an update, reimagined as an all-encompassing experience.

VML

In spring 2024, Japanese marketing and entertainment firm Katana Inc. will open Immersive Fort Tokyo in Odaiba, Tokyo, which the company describes as "the world's first immersive theme park." The 30,000-square-meter site will encompass 12 immersive attractions alongside six shops and restaurants.

The company says Immersive Fort Tokyo will showcase "dramatic events seen in the world of movies, anime, and games."

Katana's CEO Tsuyoshi Morioka told the *Japan Times* on the company's press presentation day in October 2023 that "immersive attractions enable the individual to be more involved in the experience, so the feeling is completely different." Among the examples he cited are visitors being "in attractions where they are the only witness to a murder case, or in the middle of gunfight and have to decide on what action to take." These experiences will unfold within settings that range from a "super-intense, large-scale immersive theatre" to "a terrifying immersive horror experience" and a show that suddenly "erupts in a restaurant," Katana Inc. says.

Arguably the predecessors to these experiences are the interactive digital museums championed by TeamLab. The art collective states that its aim is to "explore the relationship between the self and the world and new forms of perception," and its latest developments include the TeamLab Future Park Okinawa, within the T Galleria by DFS, Okinawa mall, which opened in December 2023. The company describes this space as "an educational project based on the concept of

collaborative creation... an amusement park where people can enjoy creating the world freely with others." The Okinawa space will showcase eight play installations, aimed at children and adults.

Phantom Peak is an immersive theme park experience in London that dubs itself "part escape room, part immersive theatre, part real-life videogame." In this Western-style, steampunk-esque theme park, each guest plays the role of "an explorer and a detective, solving mysteries, haggling with locals, and fishing for platypuses." After Phantom Peak's 2022 opening, cofounder Nick Moran told London publication *Wharf Life* "when you come to Phantom Peak, you're essentially coming to a real-life, open-world, role-playing video game." He noted that "it's not like immersive theatre where you don't know what you're doing—you're guided through the experiences."

Phantom Peak's cofounders are now exploring expanding the experience to the United States, Blooloop reported, with potential locations in Chicago, Atlanta, Denver, Dallas, and San Francisco.

Why it's interesting

Seventy-five percent of people in the United States, the United Kingdom, and China told us they like to be transported to other worlds by stories and narratives, so increasingly visitors to theme parks expect a journey, not just thrills. And whether that's via virtual reality or through performance and storytelling, these expectations are driving theme park experiences to the next level.

↑ Immersive Fort Tokyo visualization
↑↑ Phantom Peak, UK

24

Forage tourism

Travelers are taking to the woods and sea
to dig up unique culinary experiences.

VML

↑ Glen Dye School of Wild Wellness & Bushcraft, Scotland

Following an unusually wet winter in the Pacific Northwest region of the United States, the *New York Times* published a primer for first-time mushroom foragers in February 2023. "This season's boom in mushrooms dovetails with increasing numbers of people interested in plucking them out of the ground," the newspaper wrote, adding that it's "a whole lot of fun, and a fine reason to plan a trip."

Destinations around the world are tapping into the growing interest in forage tourism. In Australia, at Cappella Sydney—

winner of the City Star category in the National Geographic Traveler Hotel Awards 2023—guests can forage for endemic foods with Aboriginal Australian guides.

At the newly launched Glen Dye School of Wild Wellness & Bushcraft in Scotland, visitors can go on a guided three-hour forest-foraging tour to learn how to identify and prepare edible plants.

Luxury travel agency Black Tomato offers multiple foraging excursions, including an afternoon on a traditional 40-foot schooner in the Lofoten Islands of Norway, where participants catch, clean, and prepare cod, and a private truffle-hunting expedition in Italy led by a local forager.

Airbnb offers foraging experiences that include a popular seaweed-gathering trip in California. The 90-minute sea foraging experience teaches basic phycology (marine algae science) and sustainable harvesting techniques. To close out the experience, participants enjoy a bowl of traditional Japanese ramen made with their freshly foraged seaweed.

Why it's interesting

Forage tourism is the latest example in a wave of educational expeditions that see travelers seeking out enriching trips with knowledge-based souvenirs. Emily Fitzroy, owner of Bellini Travel, has seen a spike in requests to learn a culinary skill while on vacation. "Clients want to return home with newfound knowledge," she told the *New York Times*.

This season's boom in mushrooms dovetails with increasing numbers of people interested in plucking them out of the ground—a whole lot of fun, and a fine reason to plan a trip.

New York Times

VML

↑ Glen Dye School of Wild Wellness & Bushcraft, Scotland

25

VVIP lounges

**Upper-echelon travelers reinvigorate
demand for super-exclusive lounges.**

The Windsor Suite, part of Heathrow Airport's VIP service, is where the British royal family fly from—as do celebrities and various world leaders. Using the lounge is part of Heathrow's Black service and costs from £3,025 for three people. In 2023, Heathrow retail director Fraser Brown told Walpole, the official sector body for UK luxury, that demand for the service is on the rise, with a "record number of our guests passing through the Windsor Suite in 2022." As part of the service, guests have a personal chauffeur to and from the lounge, access to a menu designed by Michelin-starred chef Jason Atherton and served by a personal butler, and a personal shopper on hand to help, should they wish.

US company PS describes itself as "a private luxury terminal serving commercial flights at LAX and ATL," offering "the ease, privacy, and security of the private flight experience for commercial travel." The service has been so popular at Los Angeles' LAX and Atlanta's ATL airports that locations at DFW in Dallas, Texas, and MIA in Miami, Florida, are set to be added in 2024. Booking a one-off private suite without a membership at PS costs $4,850, while for an annual fee of $4,850, the same suite costs $3,550.

The invitation-only Qantas Chairman's Lounge is described by Australia's *ABC* as only known to those who are a "politician, judge, business heavyweight, or an A-lister." The British Airways Executive Club Premier Card, also known as its Black Level, is offered by invitation only to those who "control a travel budget which spends at least £2 million per year with British Airways," *Head for Points* reported.

VML

For today's ultra-wealthy, the height of luxury often isn't about visibility, but about moving through the world as seamlessly and privately as possible.

VML

Tel Aviv's Fattal Terminal is a private airport experience that provides check-in, passport control, and security in a space where guests can enjoy private or lounge accommodation, refreshments, and duty-free shopping, and be chauffeured directly to their flight. Prices for the service start at $490.

Why it's interesting
For today's ultra-wealthy, the height of luxury often isn't about visibility, but about moving through the world as seamlessly and privately as possible. From exclusive lounges to private terminals, these haute airport experiences are catering to such travelers' expectations, offering dedicated, discreet spaces amid the hubbub of commercial airports—at a price.

26

Stratospheric journeys

Balloon rides will soon transport visitors to the edge of space.

↑ Céleste from Zephalto

↑ Capsule prototype from Halo Space

By the midpoint of this decade, low-carbon balloon flights will take off, carrying pioneering travelers to the stratosphere and offering transformational views of our planet.

Céleste, a luxury pressurized capsule powered by a giant high-altitude balloon, will offer low-carbon ascents to the stratosphere. Designed by the famed architect Joseph Dirand for the French space travel startup Zephalto, the sleek eco-friendly craft offers space for six travelers in three luxurious "cocoons." From 2025, for the sum of €120,000 each ($132,000), voyagers will depart from Zephalto's French spaceport for a gentle six-hour tailor-made trip. Fine dining and specially selected wines are on the menu, as passengers cruise to contemplate the planet from an awe-inspiring perspective, 25 kilometers up, at the very edge of space. Here, the company says, guests will "admire the curvature of the Earth, its blue halo and the stars."

Céleste will not be the only balloon in the sky. Spanish near-space startup Halo Space has successfully completed its second round of test flights in California's Mojave desert and also hopes to begin commercial flights in 2025. It plans to carry 3,000 passengers a year in its zero-emission balloon by 2029.

Florida-based Space Perspective claims to offer the world's only carbon-neutral spaceship. Its Spaceship Neptune capsule comes with the twist of a splashdown landing at sea. The company is partnering with automotive brand Mercedes-Maybach to offer a truly luxurious experience complete with in-flight meals and cocktails. Arizona-based World View suggests a choice of Seven Wonders launch locations for its balloons, with awe-inspiring views from the start, including the pyramids of Giza, Egypt, and the Great Wall of China. Its Grand Canyon spaceport is already sold out for its first year of operation in 2024.

First to the skies, though, might be the Japanese startup Iwaya Giken, which plans to launch commercial flights in its helium-balloon powered capsule in March 2024. Its four-hour trip will initially be priced at 24 million yen ($166,000) but the company hopes to bring down the price as part of a plan to "democratize space."

Why it's interesting

Stratospheric travel offers a true peak experience, providing the chance to make history while experiencing one of the few remaining untouched locations within reach. Voyagers will be privy to the famed overview effect—the cognitive shift that astronauts report feeling on seeing the beauty and fragility of Earth from afar.

27
Neuroinclusive travel

A movement to make travel more rewarding
for neurodiverse individuals.

VML

↑ Hiking at Usery Mountain, courtesy Visit Mesa

With an estimated 15% of the world's population experiencing some form of neurodiversity, organizations spanning from airlines to tour operators to entire cities are aiming to offer greater accessibility to neurodiverse people.

Mesa, Arizona, became the first autism-certified city in the world in 2019, through the US-based International Board of Credentialing and Continuing Education Standards and Autism Travel. Autism Travel defines a Certified Autism Center as a facility or organization at which at least 80% of staff are highly trained, fully equipped, and certified in the field of autism. Alongside Mesa, the BBC reports that Dubai, UAE; Palm Springs, California; and Toledo, Ohio, are now working toward certification, while the US cities of Visalia, California, and High Point, North Carolina, are both already Certified Autism Destinations.

Operators are also tailoring travel options for neurodiverse people. In 2023 US travel company Explorateur Journeys

announced the launch of its NeuroTripping service, offering "bespoke travel for the neurodiverse." The company says its "fresh and unique planning" helps neurodiverse individuals avoid common travel pain points, such as large crowds and lines; unclear time frames; long periods without rest; and overstimulating locations.

Airlines, too, are striving to be more mindful of neurodiverse travelers' experiences. In October 2023, Emirates announced its collaboration with Dubai International Airport to "improve the travel experience for neurodivergent passengers." As part of this, the airline is facilitating what it calls "travel rehearsals," so neurodivergent people can practice their journey without the pressure of the actual trip.

In the United States, Breeze Airways became the first autism-inclusive network carrier to be certified by US organization Autism Double-Checked, in 2022. As part of its certification, the low-fare airline has instated a training program for its customer-facing staff on how to deliver "a safe and happy travel experience to individuals with autism." The program, developed by Autism Double-Checked, provides flight attendants with training on "identifying and alleviating the stresses of air travel."

Why it's interesting

As neurodiversity diagnoses rise—the US Centers for Disease Control and Prevention in 2023 reported that one in 36 children has autism, versus one in 44 in 2021—the travel industry is making changes now, to ensure it can serve its customers better in the future.

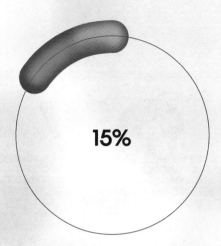

15%

An estimated 15% of the world's population experience some form of neurodiversity.

VML

28

Top three destinations

VML

↑ Half-timbered houses in Bornholm, Denmark, courtesy of Destination Bornholm

1. Bornholm, Denmark

As summers in southern Europe become increasingly unpredictable due to rising temperatures and wildfires, not to mention overtourism in some popular destinations, Scandinavia is being seen as a desirable alternative European destination. Among the region's many captivating destinations is Bornholm, a Danish island in the Baltic Sea, whose fairy-tale landscape spans "rocky cliffs, leafy forests, and bleach-white beaches," as described by *Lonely Planet*. Among its attractions is the two-Michelin-starred Kadeau restaurant, open on the island during summer months, whose low-key, wooden-clad space offers expansive vistas of the Baltic Sea. The island's picturesque towns are another draw. Rønne, the island's principal town, is home to a clutch of design-led stores, while Svaneke, a fishing village, is known for its colorful, half-timbered houses.

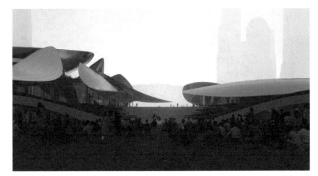

↑ → Anji Culture and Art Center, courtesy of MAD Architects

2. Anji, China

Designated China's first ecological county, Anji in east China was the backdrop to 2000's *Crouching Tiger, Hidden Dragon* movie and is described as a "magical eco-retreat" by the Scott Dunn travel company.

Several new developments are also cementing the region as a destination to watch. The vast Anji Culture and Art Center, designed by Beijing-based MAD Architects, is set to open in 2025. Spanning 149,000 square meters, the space will encompass a grand theater, a conference center, a leisure center, a sports center, a youth activity center, and an art education center. Swiss spa brand Clinique La Prairie is set to open a health resort in Anji, in partnership with China's Sunjoy Group. Simone Gibertoni, CEO of Clinique La Prairie, told *Spa Business* the resort is "set in the perfect location for our guests to experience tranquility."

↑ Our Habitas Atacama, Chile, courtesy of Habitas

3. Atacama Desert, Chile

Consumers are increasingly shifting how they live and travel, in response to a changing climate (see trend #3 Climate-adaptive lives). This is prompting efforts to open travelers' eyes to the stark beauty of drier climates. The Desert Rock development, due to open in 2024, set in Saudi Arabia's granite mountains, makes a feature of the country's "dramatic desert landscapes."

Chile's Atacama Desert is drawing travelers with both its awe-inspiring desert setting and its status as a dark-skies destination—its high altitude, low humidity, and lack of light pollution offer the ideal star-gazing environment. The area is home to several astronomy projects. Making visits for amateur astronomers to the area even more enticing, haute resorts are opening up. Among them is Our Habitas in San Pedro de Atacama, which opened in August 2023. The resort's cozy-meets-luxe, earth-toned rooms are furnished with local textiles. Guests can take part in activities that span hiking, biking, mountaineering, paragliding, and stargazing in what Our Habitas describes as "otherworldly landscapes ranging from salt flats to Mars-like valleys."

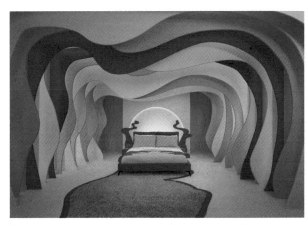

↑ House of Sunny in partnership with Airbnb. Photography by Alix McIntosh

29

Showroom stays

Slumber parties for fashion aficionados are reimagined as showroom doors open for overnight stays.

Indie fashion label House of Sunny invited two guests for an overnight stay in its showroom, in collaboration with Airbnb. The two guests had the opportunity to fully immerse themselves in the whimsical and vibrant world of designer Sunny Williams, in Hackney, east London, in September 2023.

"House of Sunny design and ethos has always been inspired by the intersection of culture, architecture, interior, and our community's love for travel, home, and aesthetics," said Williams. He considers the showroom his home and is leveraging Airbnb to fuse fashion with hospitality to offer a more intimate opportunity for guests to be part of House of

VML

↑ House of Sunny in partnership with Airbnb. Photography by Alix McIntosh

↑ DJ Khaled's room on Airbnb. Photography by Erick Hercules

Sunny. The overnight stay included the chance to try on House of Sunny's latest collection in the Wardrobe of Dreams and a tour of the showroom with the host.

During the 2023 Venice Film Festival this year, fashion consultant Giorgia Viola settled her showroom inside the five-star Nolinski Venezia Hotel, which opened earlier in the year. It was a perfect partnership; in an interview with *Forbes*, Viola describes the symbiotic relationship between couture and high-end hospitality: "Creating a luxury hotel's experience comes back to the same principle as making a made-to-measure couture dress: always being attentive to each

nuance, color shading, choice of fabrics, to the tiniest detail."

In December 2022, DJ Khaled offered a unique Airbnb stay, allowing fans to sleep inside a recreation of his cozy sneaker closet in Miami. Sneakerheads could sleep among his unique sneaker collection, which includes the Jordan 3 Grateful and the Jordan 8 Oregon PE.

Why it's interesting
Fashion and hospitality fuse perfectly, offering guests a uniquely stylish showroom stay.

VML

↑ Ulko-Tammio, Finland. Photography by Annika Ruohonen

30
Analog travel

Intentional travel is reinforced as people ditch smart tech on vacation.

An island in Finland claimed to be the first phone-free tourist destination in summer 2023. Ulko-Tammio, in the Eastern Gulf of Finland national park, launched a campaign to encourage visitors to take a digital fast to better engage with nature. "We want to urge holidaymakers to switch off their smart devices and to stop and genuinely enjoy the islands," said Mats Selin, an expert in island tourism at Visit Kotka-Hamina.

Travel agency Skyscanner, which released its "2024 Travel Trends" report in October 2023, has found that gen Zers are done with incessant social media posting—instead, they are opting for older technology to document their travels. The report shows that 16% of 18-to-24-year-olds in the United Kingdom take a Polaroid camera on holiday, while 13% take a camcorder, and 11% bring a 35mm film camera. This correlates with a generation that is opting for Luddite mode (see trend #8) when traveling.

VML

↑ Ulko-Tammio, Finland. Photography by Annika Ruohonen

Also in the United Kingdom, off-grid digital detox cabins by Unplugged encourage visitors to recharge in nature. The wifi-free zones are just an hour away from major cities including London and Manchester, and guests are required to lock away their tech devices upon arrival, for three days. There is science behind a 72-hour digital detox—research into the "three-day effect" shows that being immersed in nature for three days or more lowers stress levels and improves cognitive function.

Why it's interesting

A VML Intelligence survey that asked people around the world about their personal reasons for traveling found that the top answer is for pure pleasure, closely followed by getting close to nature. This is prompting the return of an analog style of travel that allows travelers to fully engage with their surroundings.

We want to urge holidaymakers to switch off their smart devices and to stop and genuinely enjoy the islands.

Mats Selin, island tourism expert, Visit Kotka-Hamina

VML

Brands & marketing

↑ Burberry Lola bag (left) and BMW iX (right) by Shane Fu, courtesy of Jimmy

31

OOH reimagined

Out-of-home (OOH) advertising takes an intriguing, reality-bending turn.

Digital artists are playing with reality, creating fantastical motion graphics for social media content, with this new, whimsical genre becoming known as faux-out-of-home (FOOH) advertising.

Among the artists driving this playful approach is Shane Fu, a New York-based motion designer from Wuhan, China. Fu says his work incorporates "digital art, AR/VR design, and 3D anamorphic billboards." His pieces include different imagined iterations of the Lola bag for Burberry, with a giant, feathered version set in the middle of a chic London street, and a sequined Lola bag appearing to form from a billowing metallic bubble on a quiet London mews. In another piece for BMW, Fu depicts a BMW iX emerging out of an iridescent, watery bubble.

VML

Fu is a member of Jimmy, a New York-based street art studio of digital artists and creators that aims to "extend reality by mixing real-world footage with 3D assets." Rogier Vijverberg, Jimmy's founder and creative lead, tells VML Intelligence that people are seeking to be entertained in new ways, especially at a time when more people are constantly scrolling on their phones. "The moment you see something which tickles your imagination—making you wonder whether is this real or not, or it has an element that you've never seen it before—that's a moment to stop scrolling and dive deeper."

The Jimmy collective has been gaining traction from brands and positive reception from audiences. In fall 2023, Jimmy collaborated with UK jewelry brand Astrid & Miyu, plotting CGI-created giant snowglobes in New York, Edinburgh, and London. "People really like this type of advertising. They like it because it's not like advertising," says Vijverberg. "There's a sense of wonder."

Another artist creating content that blurs the boundary between the real and the surreal is Origful, the nom de plume of US creator Ian Padgham. Based in France, Padgham is behind content such as a Jacquemus campaign that featured giant versions of the brand's bags on wheels zooming through the streets of Paris. Another of Padgham's creations is social content for Maybelline's Lash Sensational Sky High Mascara, in which London tube trains and buses appear to have giant lashes that get swiped by oversized mascara brushes. For a promotion for Vins de Bordeaux,

↑ Fenty x Puma campaign by Jimmy, courtesy of Jimmy

People really like this type of advertising. They like it because it's not like advertising.

Rogier Vijverberg, founder and chief creative officer, Jimmy

VML

↑ Astrid & Miyu campaign by Jimmy, courtesy of Jimmy

Padgham created spots of a giant bottle of Bordeaux depicted as a train traveling through France, or a boat coasting down the Seine.

While some commenters on Origful's posts appear to think that the stunts are real, Padgham told *Adweek* that he's "never trying to trick anyone. To me, CGI is a sandbox that shows us what could be possible."

Why it's interesting

The reach of social media—coupled with the creative powers of digital art—means that a new reality is being shaped (mentioned in "The Future 100: 2023"). These inventive, reality-pushing FOOH creations illustrate the notoriety-attracting potential of this art form to capture consumers' imaginations.

32
Fanspiration

Vocal fans and influencers are inspiring
their favorite brands to innovate.

"A billion-person focus group": that's how chief product officer at Abercrombie & Fitch, Corey Robinson, referred to TikTok during an interview with the *Wall Street Journal*, adding that "every single merchant and designer" uses it to inform their work. This captures the new social-media-driven R&D paradigm, where brands are parlaying fan hacks and viral influencer content into valuable new product development and innovation opportunities.

In a viral TikTok post in January 2023, creator Samuel Vela (aka @elfisicocuenta) lamented the fact that Colombian fromage frais brand Alpinito only produces 45g tubs. Delighting its nostalgia-craving Gen Z consumers, the brand rose to the challenge and released a limited-edition one-liter Alpilitro strawberry-flavored product in summer 2023. Having sold out within two hours online, it later went on sale across the country. Also in Colombia, Ramo's chocolate-covered-cake brand Chocoramo responded to a viral fan-led social media campaign to launch a new variant, Esquinas de Chocoramo, which includes just the much-loved corners of the cake.

Fan hacks are becoming central to fast-food culture and in 2023 Chipotle responded to the Keithadilla craze—a quesadilla customization popularized by TikTok food critic Keith Lee—by making the dish available at its 3,200 US locations and training more than 100,000 staff in how to create it. McDonald's has also nodded to food hacker culture with its Menu Hacks offering, which made fan creations, such

VML

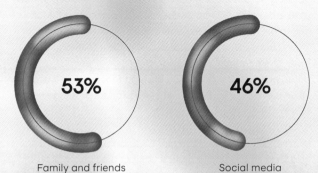

53%

Family and friends

46%

Social media

Social media is the biggest influence on generation Z's purchase decisions, after friends and family.

as the Hash Brown McMuffin, available in store. According to Jennifer Healan, vice president, US marketing, brand content and engagement for McDonald's USA, "This campaign shows that it has never been 'our menu'—the menu belongs to our fans."

Why it's interesting

Brands can satisfy consumer craving for creative influence by tapping into fanspiration, rewarding and delighting fans with real-life innovations based on viral hacks (see trend #39 Co-creative futures).

VML

↑ TikTok creators Keith Lee and Alexis Frost are fans of Chipotle
↑↑ McDonald's Menu Hacks

33

Brand India

India is building hard and soft power to emerge
as a new global powerhouse.

↑ G20 Summit, New Delhi, September 2023, courtesy of the Government of India

2023 was a milestone year for India's boundless growth, as it officially surpassed China as the most populous country in the world. It cemented its position as an emerging global superpower by hosting the G20 Summit in September 2023, and underlined its credentials as a major player in the new space race with missions to the moon and sun.

And India is just getting started. EY predicts it will become the third largest global economy by 2027, while ambitious plans are afoot to make it a leader in tech and innovation. The Indian government is building a semiconductor ecosystem from the ground up to rival that of Taiwan, and Nvidia's CEO Jensen Huang said that the country will be "one of the largest AI markets in the world" at a conference to announce a partnership with Reliance Industries and Tata Group, two of India's largest conglomerates. Apple, Samsung, Kia, Boeing, Siemens, Tesla, and Toshiba are among a slew of

other leading global companies taking advantage of India's manufacturing and tech capabilities. And with Bain & Co predicting its domestic luxury market will "expand to 3.5 times today's size by 2030," brands like Gucci, Cartier, and Louis Vuitton are ramping up their Indian presence.

The potential of India's soft power is also growing. The Offbeat Sari exhibition at London's Design Museum delighted audiences in the United Kingdom, and Bollywood A-listers Alia Bhatt, Deepika Padukone, and Athiya Shetty all became the first Indian brand ambassadors for leading global brands recently when they signed with Gucci, Louis Vuitton, and Laneige respectively. Indian brands like Sabyasachi Calcutta and Forest Essentials are also making their mark around the world by opening retail stores in the United States and the United Kingdom.

Babita Baruah, CEO of VML India says that a confluence of factors explain the rise of Brand India: "While economic growth is an important marker of progress, the combination of talent, technology and grassroot innovation is what is creating something much larger for India; a positive zeitgeist that is making this more than a 'moment' and converting this into a tectonic 'movement'.

Why it's interesting
In September 2023, Huang told the press that this is "India's moment." As its population, domestic market, and tech capabilities continue to grow at pace, it is fast becoming a global political, economic, and cultural powerhouse. This makes it a market that brands, manufacturers, and consumers simply cannot ignore.

↑ Guler sari by Raw Mango at The Offbeat Sari exhibition, UK. Photography by Ritika Shah

↑ The Offbeat Sari exhibition, UK. ©Andy Stagg

34

Creator to consumer (C2C)

The new gateway for brands—creators.

New platforms are allowing creators to build their own storefronts, enticing shoppers with a blend of content, storytelling, and personality, while offering a new discovery channel for brands and retailers.

"Online shopping today is uninspiring, and incentives are misaligned," says Maddie Raedts, cofounder of Bond, a "content-first and creator-led" social commerce experience centered on discovery and personalization. "We are creating the social shopping experience of tomorrow," Raedts tells VML Intelligence.

With Bond's platform, creators curate digital boutiques, assembling hand-picked collections and hosting live streams. Brands enrolled on the platform include Bally, Altuzarra, and Re/Done, while its diverse roster of creators has a combined audience of more than 35 million.

US startup Flagship launched its ready-made storefronts for creators in February 2023, offering the opportunity to promote and earn commission on products from 100 brand partners. Brands sign up with a Shopify account, select the creators they want to work with, and agree a revenue share based on sales. The brand takes care of inventory and fulfilment logistics, leaving creators to focus on the inspiration. There are more platforms in this vein, like Pedlar in Australia, and Canal for Creators and Emcee Studios in the United States.

While creators have been promoting brands on social media

VML

↑ Bond

for some time, the process has always been unwieldy. These new platforms promise to align a mutually beneficial business model. According to Raedts, the benefits for brands are many, including tools "to form partnerships, manage fully automated product seeding/gifting, analytics, and a new sales channel." For creators, the platforms promise better earning potential and a more reliable business model. For the consumer, who gets to buy from people, not search a product, it offers storytelling and human connection.

Major retailers are also finding ways to put creators and content first, albeit tied to their own products. Following the example of Walmart, US retail giant Target launched influencer-led storefronts for the 2023 holiday season, and more than 300 creators opened storefronts within a few weeks of the launch. In May 2023, ecommerce giant Amazon rolled out its new creator platform Inspire to US users.

Now we're seeing this trend extend beyond retail into other categories. Startup Wandr invites travel influencers to create their own booking interface for its inventory of more than a million hotels.

Why it's interesting

Brands can bank on the lure of influencer tastemakers to draw in customers with a blend of personality, storytelling, and enhanced discovery. This trend also speaks to younger cohorts' preference for peer recommendations: 23% of gen Z and millennials already say they are interested in buying directly from influencers.

35

Dopamine packaging

Brands are redesigning their packaging and identities to inject a boost of dopamine—the "feel-good" hormone.

For its first rebrand in a decade, Jell-O updated its packaging in July 2023 with bright colors and punchy graphics designed to spark joy and awe through imagination and play. "We're bringing back the jiggly fun and harnessing the wonder that the brand brings to adults and kids alike," says creative director Rebecca Williams from BrandOpus, the agency behind the rebrand. The new visual identity "unleashes imaginations" by "re-imagining how the flavors can come to life in a playful, sensorial way, transporting customers into the Jell-O world of jiggly goodness," the brand says (see trend #36 World-building brands).

Fanta's April 2023 rebrand includes dynamic, cartoon graphics and vibrant palettes to capture a sense of "playful indulgence." Lisa Smith is global executive creative director at Jones Knowles Ritchie, which developed the identity alongside Coca-Cola. Smith told *Fast Company* that it was the largest spectrum of colors she had ever worked with. The design is intentionally antiprecious and imperfect; the team explored "all the opposites of what formal typography is all about," Smith explained, making the logo "deliberately very, very playful."

"We wanted to portray a brand that values spontaneous play," says Rapha Abreu, global VP of design at The Coca-Cola Company, and "reclaim play as something that people of all ages can embrace and benefit from."

7UP revealed a fresh look in February 2023 that is "all about

↑ 7UP brand identity

being uplifting" and creating a "joyful moment" for drinkers. "UPliftment is a concept that resonates with people globally. Our new visual identity for 7UP was inspired first and foremost by the brand's creation of moments of UPliftment throughout its history," says Mauro Porcini, senior vice president and chief design officer of PepsiCo. "We wanted to create a new fresh look that was more aligned to the time we live in and the positioning of the brand that is all about being uplifting."

Why it's interesting

A 2020 study by London's Science Museum Group concluded that the world is becoming less colorful, based on an analysis of everyday objects in its collections that spanned two centuries. By injecting color into their identities and packaging, brands are delivering emotional uplift. Consumers will actively seek out brands that give them a reason to smile.

VML

36

World-building brands

A brand is no longer a distinct, static entity;
it's an all-encompassing universe.

VML

↑ Barbie, courtesy of Warner Bros

Seventy-nine percent of people agree the role of a brand has changed over the past five years and 88% say that companies have a responsibility to take care of the planet and its people. "Twenty years ago, a brand was really just an icon and colors," Borzou Azabdaftari, founder and chief executive of digital branding agency NickelBronx, told the *New York Times*. But that's changing, he observed. Today, brands are evolving into organic ecosystems. "Creating a more comprehensive brand world has become much more important. They become living, breathing documents that can change and evolve."

Creating a brand means creating the macrocosm that that brand occupies—and inviting consumers into it. "We think of world building as the evolution of brand building," Amplify chief creative officer Jeavon Smith and executive creative director Alex Wilson said in a SXSW 2023 panel.

Isamaya Ffrench's makeup brand is "less about prettification and more about 'world building,'" *Business of Fashion* reports. Under her eponymous brand Isamaya, which launched in June 2022, Ffrench has released three collections that each invent a distinct persona and narrative. Ffrench calls it an invitation "to explore a bigger world."

Mattel turned to Hollywood and brand partnerships to reinvigorate its Barbie brand—sparking a pop culture craze in the summer of 2023 that went far beyond its toys. Referring to the film, "*Barbie* took over the world," *Time* reported in July 2023—thanks in large part to a blitz of merchandising tie-ins

↑ Barbie x Joybird

that let consumers fully immerse themselves in the world of Barbie. To achieve this, Warner Bros and Mattel partnered with brands including Burger King, Pinkberry, Bloomingdale's, Crocs, Gap, Xbox, Ruggable, and furniture brand Joybird for *Barbie*-themed releases. Mattel says the *Barbie* movie is a first step in reinventing how the brand operates. "What you're really starting to see is Mattel as a pop-culture company," Mattel president and chief operating officer Richard Dickson told *Fast Company*.

Why it's interesting

Consumer-brand interactions are moving from distinct, standalone touchpoints to interplay in all-encompassing worlds. Moving forward, Smith and Wilson said, brands will need to "place storytelling at the center of everything they create."

↑ Barbie x Joybird

37
Impactainment

Emotional storytelling inspires positive change.

↑ Hidden Worlds Entertainment

"The outcome that we strive for is to create inspiration at scale in order to make the world a better place." This is the ambition of Daniel Hettwer, founder of Hidden Worlds Entertainment, who has developed "impactainment." The concept blends entertainment with positive action to combat existential threats like the climate crisis or the mental health crisis.

Impactainment is strongly rooted in behavioral science and psychology, and involves creating impactful experiences that inspire mass action and change. It differs from edutainment in that it isn't just about educating participants, but also about galvanizing them to make a difference. "The education element by itself doesn't necessarily create change," Hettwer

VML

> ❝
> # The outcome that we strive for is to create inspiration at scale in order to make the world a better place.
>
> **Daniel Hettwer, founder, Hidden Worlds Entertainment**

VML

tells VML Intelligence. "There's a ton of science out there that highlights the power of story to stimulate certain neurochemistry in your brain. Story has a huge ability to create certain emotions, to create empathy, to motivate. We want to inspire somebody and then help them turn inspiration into action."

An impactainment approach was used for an immersive ocean-positive dining experience with the Bahamas. The event merged art exhibitions, multisensory dining, and 360-degree photography to highlight the conservational successes of the islands, while educating guests about the beauty and plight of the oceans. At the end of the experience, guests were invited to sign up for a beach clean-up, creating what Hidden Worlds Entertainment calls a direct impact.

At launch, Hidden Worlds Entertainment's two focus areas are conservation and mental health, but Hettwer says impactainment can be used for any topic and by brands across all consumer categories. "Our mission is to build the most fun, high-quality guest experiences and leisure, entertainment, and hospitality sectors to promote hope, belief, and innovation," he says.

Why it's interesting

Hettwer believes that impactainment will become "the biggest driver to brand equity and long-term profitability" by providing companies with a fun and authentic way to effect positive change while showcasing their purpose.

38

Brand jesters

It's time for brands to bring back the funny.

↑ Better Climate Store

Data from Kantar's Link+ database shows a steady decline in humorous advertising over the past two decades. Why so serious? Brands have been putting on their solemn faces to tackle purpose and pandemic, but evidence shows that it's laughs, not lectures, that consumers now want.

During 2022 and 2023, Kantar Link+ reported the first uptick in humor in ads for almost 20 years. The laughs have been missed: the "2022 Happiness Report" from Oracle found that 91% of global consumers want brands to be funny, with 90% saying funny brands are more memorable. VML Intelligence data also reveals that the number one reason that people are more likely to purchase from a brand is if it brings them a sense of joy.

Brands are leaning into new comedic sub-genres to give some light relief to consumers. This includes using meta-cringe humor that is designed to make viewers feel uncomfortable. On TikTok, relatable yet awkward #cringetok content now has more than 2.6 billion views. Heavy metal water-in-a-can brand Liquid Death's latest irreverent ad leans heavily into cringe comedy, featuring a blind taste test between its water and the sweat dripping off a man's back.

CEO Mike Cessario shared insights on the brand's focus on humor in an interview with Spy.com, saying, "We knew we could win if we made people laugh. We approach our creative work like an *SNL* writer's room and hold our content to a much higher bar because of that."

And rather than an alternative to purpose, humor can be a vehicle to talk about issues in more approachable ways.

↑ Liquid Death

Ethical marketplace Better Climate Store sells its Greenwash soap with a tongue-in-cheek, self-aware ad that nods to the climate crisis, while gently mocking consumers for making ethical choices just to make themselves feel better.

"Earth clearly has a marketing problem," Ben Becker, cofounder and creative director of Better, tells VML Intelligence, as the planet's "most scientifically equipped advocates aren't necessarily its best brand storytellers. But suppose we can harness attention with entertaining content and products, and divert it towards low-effort climate action from the comfort of one's computer. That's a big win for everyone."

Why it's interesting
Humor can differentiate and engage, while offering some much-needed uplift for consumers still laboring through tough times.

39
Co-creative futures

Brands are giving consumers creative control over their products.

↑ Kiki

Angelina Jolie launched her creative venture Atelier Jolie in summer 2023—a "creative collective" that turns shoppers into designers. "Why simply buy the design of another person, when you can create yourself?" Jolie mused in the official announcement. Instead of selling predesigned pieces, the brand will let consumers pick from deadstock and artisanal fabrics to create made-to-measure garments by in-house tailors. Atelier Jolie will also offer mending services, take-home mending kits, and an in-store "stud-it-yourself activity station" available for free use.

VML

"I don't want to be a big fashion designer," Jolie told *Vogue*. "I want to build a house for other people to become that."

Kiki is embracing cocreation in its product development. The US-based beauty brand, which launched in May 2023, is turning control of its product releases over to its community. "Anybody who wants to be involved in the development of our products has the option to do so," Brendon Garner, cofounder and chief product officer, told *Glossy*. The brand debuted with a single product—a nail polish—and all future product releases will be determined by community voting. "We want to change the dynamic of how a brand, beyond just beauty, should be practiced in the future," cofounder and chief creative officer Ricky Chan told *WWD*.

Golden Goose lets shoppers "cocreate everything, everywhere." At its new co-creation in-store experiences, which debuted in Australia in 2023, shoppers can choose their own design to customize the brand's base products—including sneakers, bags, outerwear, denim, and T-shirts. The design is then executed by on-site artists.

Why it's interesting

Shopping is a form of self-expression, for younger consumers especially—60% of US gen Zers say that their brand choice is an expression of who they are, according to data from VML Intelligence's "Gen Z: Building a Better Normal" report. Brands will need to go beyond product personalization—giving consumers a say in the conception of the products they buy.

VML

↑ Kiki

40

Biodesign brands

Brands harness the power of nature for next-gen fabrics and dyes.

London-based Normal Phenomena of Life is described by its founders as "the first biodesign lifestyle brand." The online platform only features clothing and objects "fabricated with the help of bacteria, algae, fungi, yeast, animal cells, and other biological agents," *Dezeen* reports. This neatly describes the concept of biodesign, which draws on the growth mechanisms of natural organisms to create innovative materials and dyeing techniques. Among Normal Phenomena of Life's products is the Exploring jacket, a technical smock crafted from 100% GOTS-certified silk and batch dyed with wildtype Streptomyces coelicolor, a type of bacteria.

At the 2023 London Design Festival, Danish brand Ganni launched a prototype version of its Bou Bag made from a leather alternative by London biotech company Modern Synthesis, which contains no plastic or petrochemicals. The material is created by growing bacteria on a supportive structure, fed by agricultural waste. The microbes then convert the sugar to nanocellulose. The resulting fiber is eight times stronger than steel and offers natural binding ability.

In 2019 London's Central Saint Martin's unveiled its MA in Biodesign, to "explore bio-informed design strategies as a driver for sustainable innovation." Concepts created by course graduates include Mia Luong's Pearlescence of the Future, which imagines "using bacterial cellulose and nanocellulose to design and reimagine the future of nacre and pearl," in a world where the oysters from which pearls are sourced are extinct.

Why it's interesting
Innovative materials that employ nature's innate generation mechanisms are one way to explore a more sustainable future. While these materials are in their early stages, their potential is compelling and brands are buying in.

VML

↑ Modern Synthesis x Ganni Bou Bag

Food & drink

41

Gen alpha palates

Generation alpha are inspiring a swath of new flavors.

Coca-Cola Y3000 limited edition

International appetites

Gen alpha are on track to overtake gen Z as the most diverse generation to date: data from the US Census Bureau shows that gen alpha will be more diverse than the rest of the US population. It stands to reason that their palates will follow suit. Already, kids' toys are evolving "to reflect more diverse cuisines and up-to-date eating habits," the *New York Times* reported. Kids lifestyle brand Lalo sells toy sushi and charcuterie sets, and Target sells a toy set with plushie sweets from Mexico, India, and Japan.

Exposed to a greater range of cultures and cuisines, gen alpha will pick up where gen Z leave off to drive diversification in dining.

AI flavors

Alongside multicultural meals, digital habits are also offering new sources of flavor inspiration. Rising generations are

VML

↑ Nour: Play With Your Food video game

immersed in digital environments—and it's influencing how they think about and interact with food. Coca-Cola launched its limited-edition Y3000 soda created by AI in September 2023. "We challenged ourselves to explore the concept of what a Coke from the future might taste like," says Oana Vlad, senior director of global strategy at The Coca-Cola Company. To do so, it enlisted the help of AI—a creative collaboration that may become commonplace in gen-alpha kitchens.

Nour: Play With Your Food is a new video game, released in June 2023, that invites users to "rediscover the joy of playing with your food." Nour teaches players "to approach food as if experiencing it for the first time, reveling in the resulting mess and chaos," as reported in the *Financial Times*—celebrating an exploratory, experimental, and imperfect approach to food.

↑ Pringles Crisps and Caviar collection

Digital habits are encouraging eaters to think more creatively and experimentally about food—imbuing rising generations with a sentiment of levity in the kitchen.

Playful pairings

Global palates and digitally enhanced food play are whetting gen-A appetites for playful and unexpected pairings in the world of snacks. Following a viral TikTok trend that paired Pringles with caviar—and garnered more than 10 billion views—Pringles released a Crisps and Caviar collection in September 2023. French's and Skittles partnered to release a mustard Skittles flavor in July 2023. Pepsi introduced Toasty Marshmallow, Chocolate, and Graham Cracker sodas at the end of 2022 that consumers can mix to make their own s'mores soda.

Gen alpha want to have fun with their food—and are challenging brands to look beyond traditional barriers for food and flavor pairings.

VML

42

Dreamscape dining

The latest restaurants and bars are spiriting diners into mythical reveries.

An AI-designed pop-up restaurant in Australia transported diners to a dream realm. In March 2023, Applejack Hospitality launched its Create Your Dream Restaurant competition, inviting entrants to push the boundaries of the restaurant industry by using AI to dream up surreal dining experiences. The winning concept, Luminary by Stephanie Wee, ran for one week in the summer of 2023 at Sydney restaurant Rafi, part of the Applejack Hospitality group. "Best experienced after dark," the concept used hazy, multicolored lighting combined with "atmospheric effects" to create "an ethereal environment that evokes a sense of awe and intrigue," according to the restaurant.

Underbar was designed to be a "landscape of dreams." The pop-up bar, conceived by interior architect Jonas Bohlin and restaurant designer Christine Ingridsdotter for the 2023 Stockholm Furniture Fair, featured felt lamps, a wall of dress shirts, and dim, purple-tinted lighting—all of which combined to create a space evocative of a subconscious fantasy.

Also tapping into the subconscious for inspiration, Hello Sunshine calls itself a "psychedelic inverted cabin." Canadian studio Frank Architecture imagined an "alternate reality" for the Japanese bar and restaurant in Banff, Alberta, taking cues from the "unlikely juxtaposition of Japanese psychedelia meets spaghetti western meets mountain cabin," the studio told *Dezeen*. Much like a dream, "the restaurant isn't immediately visible but is slowly revealed as one moves through space."

Why it's interesting
Diners are looking for a sense of escapism and wonder that takes them out of the mundane and satisfies a yearning for re-enchantment (see trend #1 Emotioneering).

↑ Luminary at Rafi
↑↑ Smoking cocktail at Luminary at Rafi

Diners are looking for a sense of escapism and wonder that takes them out of the mundane and satisfies a yearning for re-enchantment.

Snackification

Small treats are big business as the billion-dollar
snack market continues to grow.

↑ Moonshot climate-friendly crackers are now part of the Patagonia Provisions
brand

↑ Patagonia Provisions crackers

Younger generations are feeling particularly snackish and this may be because 69% of 18-29-year-olds consider snacks the highlight of their day, compared to the global average of 55%. According to the "State of Snacking Report" published in January 2023 by Mondelēz International and The Harris Poll, 71% of global consumers snack at least twice a day, with the growth in this sector attributed to younger generations as millennials and gen Zers consume 10% more snacks daily than older generations due to busier lifestyles.

Kellogg Company has now muscled in by launching Kellanova, a snacking-oriented company, in October 2023. It is composed of popular snacking brands including Cheez-It, Pringles, Rice Krispies Treats, and Pop-Tarts. Kellogg's reports that these snacking brands make up about 70% of its North American snack sales alone. According to market research firm Circana, nearly half of US consumers eat three or more snacks a day. Kellanova has high hopes—the company is forecast to generate approximately $2.25 to $2.3 billion in net sales in 2024.

As appetites for snacking increase, climate-friendly snacks start to see demand. When it comes to eating, 51% of global respondents say they consider the environmental impact and 83% say they expect brands to play their part in solving challenges like climate change.

Patagonia Provisions acquired climate-friendly cracker company Moonshot in March 2023. Julia Collins, founder of the startup, says, "I founded Moonshot with the vision of using the power of food to help tackle climate change. By joining Patagonia Provisions, who recently made Earth their only shareholder, Moonshot now belongs to the planet."

Adding awareness to the cause, Colorado-based Quinn earned Climate Friendly status from American food sustainability rating company HowGood in 2023, to add to its packaging. Quinn aims to "shake up the food industry by reinventing snacks," with products including popcorn kernels and pretzels.

Why it's interesting

Snacks are taking a large slice of the food industry's pie. Global snack sales are expected to pass $675 billion in 2024 and rise to over $831 billion by 2028, according to Euromonitor. Brands will need to cater to the appetites of the younger generation, while upholding the sustainable values that are important to them.

44

Culinary cocktails

Mixologists create concoctions good enough to eat, mixed with a hint of nostalgia and a dash of comfort.

↑ Cold Pizza and Key Lime Pie cocktails at Double Chicken Please, New York City

Cold pizza, Waldorf salad, and French toast can all be found on the menu of Double Chicken Please, located on New York City's Lower East Side—the twist here is that they are all cocktails. The handcrafted drinks served in the venue's Coop room are "based on the approach of hacking design to disassemble culinary dishes and rebuild the flavors into unique cocktail forms," Tako Chang, manager of brand and communications at Double Chicken Please, tells VML Intelligence. Opened in November 2020, the bar has been crowned number one in North America's 50 Best Bars 2023 list and number two in the World's 50 Best Bars 2023 list. Founders GN Chan and Faye Chen's love of food has been the driving inspiration behind the cocktails, which offer an equal blend of innovation and comfort in each glass.

VML

Tucked away in Mexico City's Colonia Juárez neighborhood, Handshake Speakeasy adopts molecular mixology to prepare its cocktails. Expect to find scrumptious desserts on the cocktail menu, including the Strawberry Pancake and the Banana Split, which features banana liqueur, sherry, and a Lego-inspired chocolate filled with banana cream as a special garnish. Ranked third in the World's 50 Best Bars 2023 list, Handshake Speakeasy currently rules the cocktail roost in Latin America.

Those wanting to sample a cocktail take on the sweet and savory tom kha soup should head to Bar Mischief in Austin, Texas. For his Tom Kha cocktail, beverage director Jorge Viana has created a savory mix that includes a mushroom-infused vodka and is topped with a sweet lemongrass and coconut foam.

Why it's interesting

As the cocktail scene evolves, Chan finds that people have gravitated away from flavors that were predominantly sweet, floral, fizzy, and sour. He explains that "over time, as the bar industry expanded its techniques into the culinary domain, guests began to venture into the realm of savoriness."

45

Expedition dining

Fine dining takes to the sea and heads into space.

↑ Iris restaurant, Norway

VML

From 2024, French space tourism company Zephalto will offer fine dining and wine-tasting trips in its luxuriously designed, pressurized Céleste capsule, which will voyage to "the dark of space" attached to a stratospheric balloon. Each journey is open to six guests, who, having dined on a curated menu before the balloon begins its ascent, will be able to taste fine wines during their six-hour flight.

If space is too out-there, avid diners can take a journey across Western Norway's Hardangerfjord to Iris, a restaurant located inside the Salmon Eye floating art installation. Seating only 24 guests, Iris offers a dining experience that it describes as unfolding "a story about challenges, flavors, and possibilities." The experience involves a boat trip from the town of Rosendal, followed by "a pit-stop and welcoming snack at chef Anika Madsen's boathouse on the island of Snilstveitøy." There is then a "multi-sensory underwater experience" held on the art installation, before guests experience the tasting menu in a dining room with views of the fjords and mountain ranges.

To experience the taste of champagne aged in the depths of the Baltic Sea, Veuve Clicquot offers its Cellar in the Sea experience. As part of the event, 14 guests–who must all be experienced divers–are given the chance to dive in the Åland Islands, off the Finnish coast, to a depth of 43 meters to retrieve the sunken champagne bottles. Prices for the diving trip are said to be in the "tens of thousands of pounds." The next expedition will take place in summer 2024.

↑ Iris restaurant, Norway

Why it's interesting

Research indicates that environment affects how tastes are perceived. A 2022 study from China, titled "Does a beautiful environment make food better," found that "food is perceived as tastier, better smelling, and, in certain conditions, better looking in more aesthetically pleasing environments that elicit more positive emotions." These unforgettable fine-dining experiences, which engage the senses on myriad levels, are likely to only enhance the gastronomic experience.

Heritage gastronomy

Countries are actively preserving traditional
cuisine as the food scene diversifies.

Lab-grown meat will not be found on any menus in Italy, and it may remain that way indefinitely. On July 19, 2023, the Senate of the Italian Republic approved a bill that prevents the production and import of cultivated meats and other synthetic foods in a bid to safeguard the nation's culinary heritage. The Italian government hopes to further reinforce the country's food heritage by listing it as a UNESCO Intangible Cultural Heritage asset; UNESCO will rule on this by December 2025.

UNESCO protection for heritage food is not unprecedented. In November 2022, the organization placed the artisanal know-how that goes into making the baguette loaf, known for its four ingredients and specific technique, on the Intangible Cultural Heritage list. The announcement was positively received, with French president Emmanuel Macron describing the baguette in a tweet as "250 grams of magic and perfection in our daily lives." The baguette joins other heritage food on UNESCO's list including Ukrainian borscht, Korean kimchi, and Haiti's joumou soup.

The Middle East is turning to culinary institutions to preserve its rich heritage foods. "Every culinary institution must provide well-structured learning in the ethnic cuisine and foster a deep respect for culinary heritage while innovating," Sunjeh Raja, director and CEO of the International Centre for Culinary Arts Dubai, told *Fast Company*.

Why it's interesting

Rapid developments in cell-cultured food alternatives are being countered by countries eager to double down on preserving their traditional food heritage and reinvigorate the taste, craft, and techniques that define each nation and its culture. After all, 74% of people say food is their way of connecting with their culture and 83% say food is their way of discovering new cultures.

74%

Say food is their way of connecting with their culture.

83%

Say food is their way of discovering new cultures.

↑ Baguette making, courtesy of Frédéric Vielcanet
↑↑ Baguette making, courtesy of Jean-Luc Valteau

VML

Food farmacies

Food is now pivotal to public health.

VML

Fresh produce prescriptions are catching on as research underlines the role healthier food plays in preventing and even reversing chronic disease. Should food brands and retailers now consider themselves healthcare providers?

According to a 2023 study published in *Circulation*, the peer-reviewed journal of the American Heart Association, prescribing produce can unlock multiple health benefits, from lower blood pressure to reduced body mass index.

Physicians in the United States, the United Kingdom, and Australia are among those pioneering "food as prescription" services as a preventive health strategy. Doctors in a number of US states, including Montana, California, and Massachusetts, are now able to issue "produce prescriptions." In London too, GPs are also issuing fruit and vegetable prescriptions to patients on lower incomes as part of a pilot scheme that could ultimately be rolled out across the country.

Typically, participants in prescription programs receive vouchers, loyalty card credits, or debit cards that subsidize or cover the cost of healthy foods at grocery stores and farmers' markets. Other programs distribute healthy supplies in the form of fruit and veg boxes.

Grocery retailers like Kroger and Giant Food are already supporting these programs, and others are leaning in to an industry-wide opportunity to further educate or nudge consumers towards healthier eating habits.

British retailer Tesco has set itself a goal of having 65% of shopping baskets made up of healthy foods and has

pledged to cut 100 billion calories from its own-label range by 2025. In the United States, grocery chain Albertsons has added a digital nutrition tool to its Sincerely Health platform that allows shoppers to measure the nutritional value of their purchases according to the USDA's My Plate guidance.

UK health food retailer Holland & Barrett recently refreshed its food offer, relaunching under the banner "Food that Loves you Back." The store has introduced Plant Points on packaging, a scheme to encourage shoppers to get at least 30 plants a week into their diet.

In contrast, ultra-processed foods (UPFs) are increasingly coming under scrutiny. These foods now make up half the diet in the United Kingdom and the United States, and research published in the *British Medical Journal* says that one in seven adults and one in eight children could be addicted. Expect to see healthier alternatives or reformulations with health-boosting benefits hitting the shelves.

UK grocer Marks & Spencer recently signed an exclusive distribution deal with Modern Baker, creator of the Superloaf. The product of six years of R&D, Superloaf is nutrient-dense and gut-friendly, with fewer calories than a standard loaf. The manufacturer has been granted government funding to expand its research into nutritious formulations for other categories including pastries, ready meals, and breakfast cereals.

Why it's interesting

Alongside national strategies to tackle poor diets, there is an opportunity for food manufacturers and retailers to amplify these efforts, doing more to educate and promote healthier diets, as well as to provide healthy alternatives alongside UPFs.

 Superloaf by Modern Baker
↑↑ Holland & Barrett's healthy groceries

VML

48

Relational dining

People are supping with strangers to combat loneliness and nourish communities.

VML

The *New York Times* calls it "the radical act of eating with strangers": an emerging wave of dining concepts created to encourage community connection.

Dinner With Friends is an intimate dinner party concept that brings eight strangers together over a home-cooked meal. Anita Michaud started Dinner With Friends in May 2022 after moving to New York City and struggling to find community. Since launching, over 800 people have signed up—which equates to a four-year waitlist.

Soup Doula is also connecting communities over food. What started as a soup delivery service for new parents has grown into a facilitator for neighborhood socializing. Creator and chef Marisa Mendez Marthaller hosted weekly "soup shares" at Brooklyn's Nightmoves in February and March 2023, where community members could come together over a bowl of soup on Sunday afternoons. While the service was originally created for new parents, Marthaller says it's for anyone in need of nourishment: elderly parents, the COVID-19 and/or flu-ridden, anyone feeling down or struggling with their mental health, or college or graduate students.

Now the sense of community has never been stronger.

Denise Lefebvre, senior vice president of R&D, PepsiCo Foods

People's social networks decreased in size by an average of 16% during the pandemic, according to research by Marissa King, a professor at the Wharton School of the University of Pennsylvania and the author of *Social Chemistry: Decoding the Elements of Human Connection*. To counteract that pandemic deprivation, people are looking for more than just a good meal when dining out.

"If you look at what our lives were like for a couple of years, we didn't share because sharing was considered dangerous," Denise Lefebvre, senior vice president of R&D for PepsiCo Foods, told the *New York Times*. "Now the sense of community has never been stronger."

Why it's interesting

While the dinner table has always been a place to gather family and friends, it is now deepening those roots, serving up community strengthening and radical reconnection (see trend #10 Intentional communities).

49

Sake boom

Interest in sake food pairings is driving a global boom.

↑ Dassai Blue sake from Asahi Shuzo

The popularity of Asian cuisine and culture has helped introduce international audiences to the refined qualities of sake. Now some are even turning their hand to making it.

Small-batch local sake brewers have been popping up in the United States over the past few years, and there are now more than 20, including Origami sake in Arkansas, which began operating in mid-2023. These upstarts are leaning into their US heritage and terroir to cater better to American palates. Such is their success, Japanese brewers want in on the action. Asahi Shuzo has opened a brewery and tasting room in the Hudson Valley and will launch an American brand, Dassai Blue. It's also joining forces with the Culinary Institute of America to offer a sake educational program.

VML

FOOD & DRINK

→IWA kura (sake brewery) in Shiraiwa, Japan

Locally made sakes from London's Kanpai brewery are on the menu at Evelyn's Table, one of London's buzziest restaurants. Indeed, sake's umami qualities mean it is increasingly paired with food. In Singapore, Rasen sake has been specially crafted to pair with Singaporean dishes. Los Angeles bar and restaurant Ototo serves Cowboy brand sake, which is designed to accompany steak or beef. Even in wine-loving Paris, artisan fromager Taka & Vermo hosts in-store cheese and sake tasting events.

To create more food-friendly tipples, sake brewers are now collaborating with experts from the wine and champagne industry. Richard Geoffroy, a former chef de cave at Dom Pérignon, is now founder-maker at Japan-based sake startup IWA. IWA 5, the first product to launch commercially, is created using the assemblage process, which blends different rice varieties. The beverage is already popular with Michelin-starred chefs like Thomas Keller, who is planning to pair it with caviar at The French Laundry, according to *Robb Report*. "I encourage the followers and lovers of IWA to take an element of risk in experimenting with pairings much as I do," Geoffroy tells VML Intelligence.

Why it's interesting
As international diners learn more about the versatility of sake, experts are predicting it has the potential to rival the most popular Western beverages—even wine.

↑ Moss at the Blue Lagoon resort, Iceland, courtesy of Blue Lagoon Iceland

50

Tundra to table

Arctic cuisine is on the rise.

↑ Hurtigruten Group's MS Kong Harald. Photography by Stian Klo

In Norway, six restaurants received inaugural Michelin stars in 2023, contributing to a growing rank of Arctic eateries elevating the region's culinary standing. In Iceland, Moss at the Blue Lagoon resort received its first Michelin star in June 2023. Alongside regional dishes like Icelandic lamb, Norwegian king crab, and locally caught fish, Moss serves a butter that celebrates its sense of place. Made in house, it is crafted from whipped skyr—Icelandic yogurt—milk from local farmers, dulse seaweed, and sea salt made on site. "The inspiration for our butter comes from our pride in Icelandic skyr," chef Ingi Thorarinn Fridriksson, director of food and beverage at Blue Lagoon, told *Food & Wine.* "We added dulse as a nod to Grindavik, the fishing town where the Blue

Lagoon is located." (At the time of writing, service had been interrupted by volcanic activity in the region.)

"Our local ingredients all have a story to tell. Either you have caught, shot, or collected them yourself—or you know the person who has," Anne Nivika Grødem, CEO of Visit Greenland, told the BBC. "Our food culture is closely linked to our identity."

Arctic travel itineraries are increasingly highlighting the region's cuisine. Two new trips launched in 2023 by cruise operator Hurtigruten showcase Norway's "fjord-to-fork" cuisine, feeding visitors local delicacies like cloudberry honey gathered on the tiny island of Rolvsøy, king oyster mushrooms grown at the family-run Trøndersopp farm, and recipes and ingredients collected from the Indigenous Sámi people.

Appetite for arctic cuisine is spreading to new shores. Three-Michelin-starred Norwegian restaurant Maaemo popped up in Sydney in June 2023 with a $400-per-person tasting menu serving locally hunted deer and smoked reindeer heart. New York City's first Taste of Iceland festival in May 2023 featured a week-long Icelandic pop-up menu at the renowned Coarse restaurant and an Icelandic cocktail class.

Why it's interesting
Chefs from northernmost communities are reviving the overlooked food of the Arctic circle, catering to a growing class of culture enthusiasts and wanderlusters looking for adventurous and hyper-local dishes that fully immerse them in the icy tundra.

↑ Moss at the Blue Lagoon resort, Iceland, courtesy of Blue Lagoon Iceland

Beauty

Gen alpha skincare

The youngest generation are already locking in beauty rituals.

VML

↑ Evereden, courtesy of Evereden

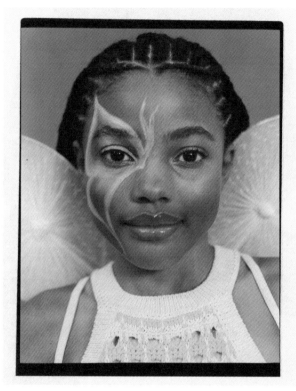

↑ Evereden, courtesy of Evereden

Make way for the skincare-savvy pre-teens taking over social media with tips on cleansing, toning, hydration, and more. Eleven-year-old Riley Curry is described by her mother, actress Ayesha Curry, as having a "full" and "non-negotiable" skincare routine, according to *People*. And 10-year-old North West (daughter of Kim and Kanye) has been dropping videos of her beauty regime on TikTok.

"Many gen alphas have their own skincare routine," Kimberley Ho, founder and CEO of multigenerational skincare brand Evereden, tells VML Intelligence. Growing up as digital natives, this generation are privy to skincare benefits shown on social media. "Whether parents agree with this or not, this generation want their own products," explains Ho. "They want their own routine. They're hugely independent."

Evereden products are "for every age and every stage," and backed by science. The company has pre-teen products that include a Kids Daily 1-2-3 Routine set. It has also expanded into haircare and, more recently, makeup for kids, launching Evereden At Play in September 2023. "Kids aged three to 13 years old are becoming interested in skincare and beauty products at a younger age than previous generations," says Ho. Evereden is using research to meet this group's specific skincare needs.

Proudly, a baby-and-kid-friendly brand tailored for melanated skin, debuted in April 2022. Founders Gabrielle Union and Dwyane Wade created the brand in response to a "lack of options for children of color." Proudly launched its first haircare range in September 2023.

VML

Many gen alphas have their own skincare routine.

Kimberley Ho, founder and CEO, Evereden

Luxury Family Hotels in the United Kingdom is also tapping into gen alpha skincare with its October 2023 addition of Little Ishga, a series of treatments for young customers aged from three to 16, designed to "alleviate stress and encourage self-care from a young age." The brand also wants to encourage the entire family to enjoy its spas together.

As gen alphas approach the world of beauty, they are exchanging learnings in this space with their parents. Ranice Faustino, marketing communications head at *Vogue Philippines*, tells VML Intelligence that as a millennial mother she would often share makeup with her 12-year-old daughter: "She gets my makeup, I get her makeup. I learn a lot from her as well." This sharing culture extends into beauty content, where Faustino would be open to trying influencer recommendations with her daughter.

Why it's interesting

"Gen alpha are engaging with beauty earlier than their siblings and older family," says Ho. As this generation soak up skincare learnings from social media, some are already sharing their regimes with the world, with the full support of their parents, making it a rich market for beauty brands to focus on.

VML

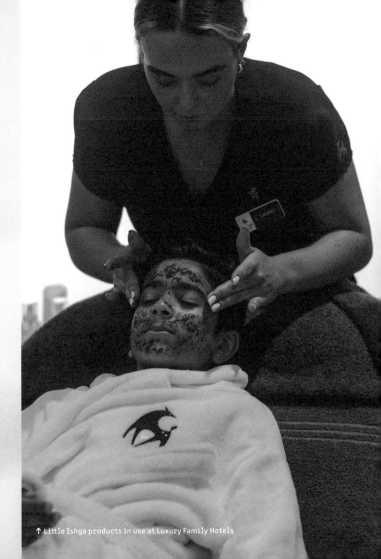

↑ Little Ishga products in use at Luxury Family Hotels

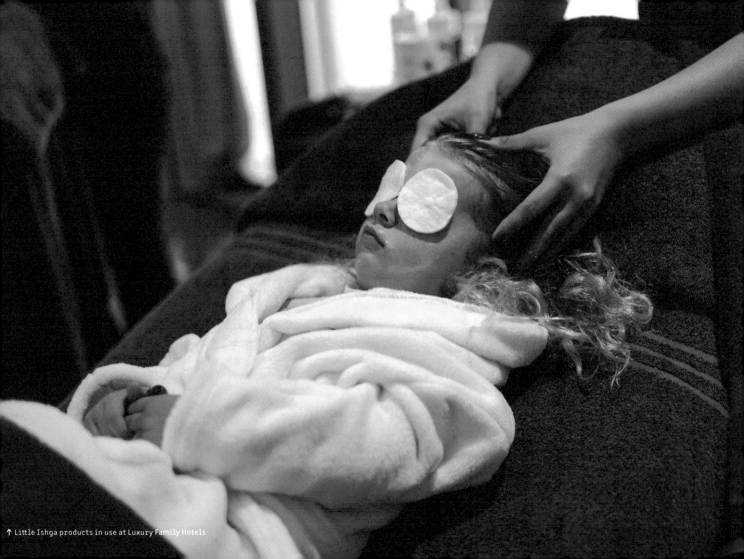

↑ Little Ishga products in use at Luxury Family Hotels

↑ Isamaya Beauty

52

Gothic grace

Beauty now channels the subversive power of witchcraft.

Seasonal runways are serving up gentle gothic glamor for 2024 in the form of dark lips and eyes, and dramatic statement lashes.

The witch was the inspiration behind Dior's show at Paris Fashion Week in September 2023, with models walking with bare lips, delicately stained black, set against luminous skin. Dior Makeup creative and makeup image director Peter Philips told *Harper's Bazaar* that his brief from creative director Maria Grazia Chiuri was informed by "women being seen as witches in a male-dominated world in Italy for generations."

For the Junya Watanabe show, also in Paris, avant-garde makeup artist Isamaya Ffrench channeled Joan of Arc, giving models pale glossy skin, faint brows, and a black lip. Ffrench also posted a YouTube tutorial in October 2023,

VML

↑ Isamaya Beauty

demonstrating an innovative seasonal Woodland Nymph look featuring spiky brows made from natural plant thorns.

Lavish lashes add to the dramatic look. Makeup artist Vanessa Icareg created a clumpy, charred lash effect, showcasing shades from the Industrial Color Pigments 2.0 and Wild Star palettes by Isamaya French Beauty. Extravagant lashes were also at the Victoria Beckham spring/summer 2024 show, highlighting the brand's new Vast Lash Mascara to create "drama that was just the right side of spidery" according to *Vogue*.

As explored in our "Age of Re-enchantment" report, the witch is a tool of provocation, symbolic of a new disruptive power that embraces femininity, ecology, and the spiritual. And witchcraft's influence on cultural narratives, aesthetics, and beauty is on the rise. Wellness brands such as Palm of Feronia and Kate Moss's Cosmoss draw heavily on mystical cues. British perfumer Vyrao has even tapped a psychic to cocreate its scent The Sixth.

Why it's interesting

Beauty brands are serving up the tools for ethereal gothic glam looks that tap into a subversive spirit. The witch stands for an assertion of feminine power, and a challenge to the status quo. Younger cohorts are finding comfort here, with more than 51% of generation Z expressing interest in non-traditional spirituality.

Slow beauty

Beauty brands adopt a sustainable and measured approach to formulating potent skincare.

VML

↑ Vintner's Daughter

Vintner's Daughter released its third product in 2023, the Active Renewal Cleanser. The 10-year-old beauty brand is diligent in nurturing its products with a slow and attentive approach. "I started Vintner's Daughter to apply the same methodical commitment to quality and craftmanship to skincare that I knew from my winemaking background," founder April Gargiulo tells VML Intelligence.

The three skincare products prioritize whole plants over synthetics and extracts, and each bottle takes three weeks to produce, which Gargiulo explains is 66 times slower than industry average. She believes that high-performing standards come with time invested: "Luxury isn't necessarily a price tag or fancy packaging, but it's really about the quality

↑ Vintner's Daughter

of the raw materials, the intentionality, the meticulousness with which those raw materials are put together." The company took four years to master the formulation of its latest release, delighting fans of the brand, who include Gwyneth Paltrow and Tracee Ellis Ross.

Stella McCartney and LVMH launched the beauty line Stella in summer 2022. McCartney says: "We worked hard for almost three years with LVMH constantly evolving and aiming for what I felt was possible: rooted in nature, truly effective, and responsible skincare. It's a gamechanger and I want to share it with everyone."

Skincare startup Dieux has a clear mission to focus on quality products and to be transparent about price and sustainability. In addition, in October 2023 the brand told *Fast Company* that its strategy is to "sell fewer products." Dieux's bestsellers include the $25 Forever Eyemask, which, as the name suggests, is designed to be reused, unlike many other single-use eye masks.

Vogue Philippines' beauty editor Joyce Oreña tells VML Intelligence that she believes consumers are increasingly "conscious and ethical," and "no longer just focus on the efficacy of the product, but also on how it was made." These new beauty standards align with consumer expectation. Eighty-three percent of people globally say they expect brands to play their part in solving challenges like climate change and 85% say they want their money to go to a brand that reflects their values.

Why it's interesting

"Slow beauty is a more mindful approach with a focus on less waste, better ingredients, and quality over quantity," Gargiulo says. With the eco-conscious consumer in mind, beauty brands are pumping the brakes and slowing production down in an attempt to change an industry focused on constantly churning out products to sell.

↑ Guerlain Spa at Raffles London at The OWO

54

Branded spas

Beauty experiences are key to unlocking consumer affinity.

Haute beauty brands are opening standalone branded spas that offer a host of wellness services. These spaces act as an opportunity for brands to showcase what truly sets them apart, while serving to enhance consumers' perception of their expertise.

In summer 2023, Sisley-Paris debuted Maison Sisley New York in the city's Meatpacking District, its first maison in North America. The 2,675-square-foot space offers four treatment rooms, makeup stations, and a dedicated hair boutique, all created with the aim of providing "an escape to take care of yourself," the brand says.

Guerlain has thrown its hat in the ring too, with the 2023 opening of the Guerlain Spa at Raffles London at The OWO. The 27,000-square-foot, four-story spa is located within the new Raffles hotel in what was formerly the city's historic Old War Office building. As Guerlain's first UK spa, the brand has launched an exclusive treatment called Spirit of London to

VML

make the experience even more unique. This mind and body treatment, based around massage, "targets tensions related to travel, environmental stressors, and a busy lifestyle," Guerlain says.

Augustinus Bader opened The Skin Lab in London in early 2023, followed by a branch in New York. Charles Rosier, the brand's CEO, told *Glossy* that the spas allow the brand to "reshape the experience the way we want, from the feeling of entering the location to experiencing the treatment."

Why it's interesting
Beauty brands are responding to the demand for in-person experiences by curating their own holistic health and wellness treatments, carried out within standalone spas that can enhance and expand their brand ethos.

↓ → Augustinus Bader at Lanserhof at The Arts Club London

55

Skingestibles

Skincare and nutrition converge for a lucrative
and growing wellness opportunity.

↑ HyaCera by Ritual

VML

Ingestible beauty supplements are on the rise. In the United States alone, Mintel predicts the supplement market will grow to $45 billion by 2027, with skincare ingestibles emerging as one of the most exciting new opportunities for brands.

Now nutritional supplement brands and cosmetic skincare companies are innovating into the space, blurring category boundaries to meet consumer demand. Leading health supplement brand Ritual, for example, made its first foray into the beauty space in May 2023 with the release of its HyaCera Daily Skin Hydration supplement. Made with traceable ingredients, the once-a-day capsules purport to support the skin's moisture barrier and help minimize wrinkles.

French nutricosmetic brand Aime started originally as a skin supplement brand in 2018, before branching into topical skin cosmetics to offer a two-pronged skincare ritual for its consumers. Aime officially launched in the United States in 2023 and is now on a mission to expand globally.

A survey from beauty research outlet The Benchmarking Company found that 76% of US women expect beauty brands to offer supplements to complement their topical offerings, which is precisely what traditional skincare brands are starting to do. Murad was one of the first, launching three supplements for aging, acne, and skin brightening, while Neutrogena has also taken its first steps into skincare supplements. Its partnership with 3D-printed vitamin stack brand Nourished, which debuted at the Consumer Electronics

↑ HyaCera by Ritual

Show (CES) 2023, hints at the potential of personalization within skincare supplements.

Why it's interesting

Skincare ingestibles offer nutrition brands a way to tap into the beauty consumer, while giving skincare brands an opportunity to embed themselves further into the burgeoning health and wellness space.

56
Nail couture

Elevated manicures become the latest statement accessory.

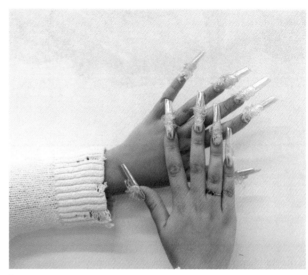

↑ Beauty Tech Art Spa exhibition, courtesy of Izzy Scott

Nail art is no longer a niche affair and as customers flock to salons in greater numbers, artists are upping their game with ever-more inventive nail art. Among the most avant-garde names in this genre—whose work, admittedly, one might not see in the average salon—is Tokyo-based Tomoya Nakagawa. His designs span the fantastical, with elaborate droplets of water emerging from the nails; talons embellished with metal and jewels; and nails that resemble futuristic, purple-toned claws. His nature-inspired designs are crafted via CAD, 3D-printing, and airbrushing techniques, according to a *Dazed* profile.

VML

↑ Beauty Tech Art Spa exhibition, courtesy of Izzy Scott

Taking a more delicate, but no less inventive turn, is US-based artist San Sung Kim. Her designs span Halloween-themed nails adorned with glossy black bats' wings; transparent nails in which a rose appears trapped, with "bleeding" accents, to symbolize "a broken heart"; and a dreamy-looking nail design complete with metal ticking clock hands, which Kim says is "mildly influenced by Dali's *The Persistence of Memory*."

And viewing the nail salon through a conceptual eye is Beauty Tech Art Spa, a group exhibition that opened in late October 2023 at London's Borough Yards, billed by its curator Cornershop as "a response to nail salons across London run by various ethnic groups." The exhibition spotlights the work of six female artists, including Zoë Argires, Hoa Dung Clerget, and duo Athen Kardashian and Nina Mhach Durban, who

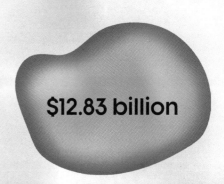

$12.83 billion

The global nail salon market will be worth $12.83 billion in 2024.
Grand View Research

variously "respond to the conceptual nail bar with their own aesthetic and cultural influences," Cornershop says. This translates to works that draw on a "literal nail bar," while others, Cornershop notes, "invoke perceived cultural expectations" and salons as "loci of communal activity."

Why it's interesting

Grand View Research predicts the worth of the global nail salon market will be $12.83 billion in 2024. This is spurring salons to distinguish themselves with innovative design techniques that are more artistic, elaborate, and inventive than ever.

VML

Bio scentsation

Beauty innovators are reimagining fragrance.

↑ Future Society fragrances, courtesy of Arcaea

VML

 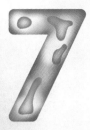

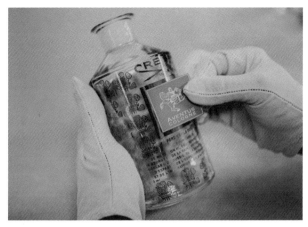

↑ Kering Creed, courtesy of Creed

Arcaea, a biology-first beauty company whose revolutionary scent technology has received funding from the likes of Chanel and Olaplex, is on a mission "to make biology the most desired technology in beauty," according to CEO Jasmina Aganovic.

The company launched a new fragrance brand, Future Society, in October 2023, turning to biology and science for creative inspiration. "Science is about more than clinical studies," Aganovic said. "It also represents new creative tools." The first release is a collection of six perfumes made from the sequenced DNA of extinct flowers. "Fragrance has always been rooted in powerful storytelling and sensory experiences," Aganovic explained. "We are excited to show how biology can create new stories and product experiences."

Arcaea developed ScentArc, a technology that works with underarm microbiomes to prevent odor, in March 2023. "When it comes to the $25 billion deodorant category, the underlying science relies on approaches developed in the 1800s: masking smells, killing odor, or blocking and absorbing sweat," Aganovic said. "We saw a better solution through biology, using technologies that didn't exist until recently."

These innovations come at a time when the fragrance category is garnering increased attention from major players. Kering acquired luxury fragrance house Creed in October 2023. Richemont is doubling down on fragrance with its new Laboratoire de Haute Parfumerie et Beauté division, launched in September 2023, and LVMH reshuffled its beauty leadership in March 2023 to prioritize fragrance.

Why it's interesting
The fragrance category is heating up. Expect to see increased investments in, attention to, and innovation of fragrance.

58

A-Beauty

Beauty brands born on and inspired by Africa's vast continent take their approach global.

With Euromonitor predicting that the African beauty and personal care market will be worth $8.2 billion in 2023, rising to over $10 billion by 2025, this is clearly a market to watch.

And to cater to the unique needs of consumers in the region—and the continent's diaspora—local brands are emerging that combine Africa's wealth of natural ingredients with cutting-edge innovation. Uncover, a Kenya-based startup that operates in Kenya and Nigeria, offers skin care and sunscreen tailored to women in Africa and women of color. Black skin often has distinct needs, such as being drier and more delicate than Caucasian skin, yet few products are tailored to its specific requirements. While Uncover was founded in Kenya and informed by the region, its products are manufactured in Korea, with the brand stating it fuses "innovative K-Beauty skincare technology with African botanicals." Among its range is the Aloe Invisible Sunscreen, formulated to leave no white cast on those with darker skin tones, and infused with African aloe vera, hyaluronic acid, and SPF 50+ protection.

54 Thrones was founded by American Christina Tegbe, informed by her upbringing, which she describes as "rooted in the cultural essence of Nigeria." The brand's products draw on ingredients such as Ghanian and Ugandan shea butters, baobab oil, and jojoba oil, and are composed of "high-quality, African-grown ingredients... to create sustainably made beauty products inspired by ancient traditions." The brand's name also references the continent, nodding to Africa's 54 countries.

↑ Emolyne cosmetics

In the color cosmetics sphere, Emolyne was founded by Emolyne Ramlov, who is Ugandan-born, Denmark-raised, and based in London. While the brand is British, Ramlov created it with her African heritage in mind, with each nail and lip shade formulated to suit different skin tones and undertones, and each of the shades named after a different African location. Among them is Fes, a muted peach nail shade, and Uganda, a deep mauve tone for lips.

Why it's interesting

Alongside offering compelling natural ingredients, African beauty brands that are created with Black skin tones and skin types in mind are in an ideal position to capitalize on the African beauty market's predicted growth. Unlike a global brand bringing its aesthetic to the region, these brands are shaped around the needs of African consumers. And thanks to their expertise in Black skin's needs, these brands are also well placed to cater to the Black community globally, who have historically found themselves underserved.

↑ Emolyne Ramlov, founder of the eponymous cosmetics brand

VML

EQ
beautification

Emotional wellness redefines beauty.

↑ Body Proud collection by I Am Proud

Beauty startup I Am Proud wants to instill confidence and positivity in everyone. The company started in 2020 with its skincare range and launched haircare and bodycare collections in 2023. The Body Proud formulae feature a patented "mood-boosting fragrance technology that is scientifically proven to have specific mood benefits," Maria Sarris, NPD manager at Body Proud, tells VML Intelligence. The fragrances took two years to produce, and use a bespoke system that "leverages neuroscience to test the benefits, exploring the results through brain scans, eye tracking, and facial coding psychology to quantify the benefits," says Sarris. Users can choose to feel confident, invigorated, empowered, energized, or chilled.

Selfmade, featured in "The Future 100: 2023," is paving a new way to talk about beauty. "We use psychodermatology as the window into our emotional world," Selfmade founder and CEO Stephanie Lee tells VML Intelligence. "We're using our skin as data points into our emotional world in order to truly take care of ourselves in a deeper way." Each of Selfmade's products is paired with a core behavioral concept—a direct correlation meant to evoke a new beauty prescription for consumers.

A new initiative called NeverAlone.Love, by Priyanka Chopra's Chopra Foundation in partnership with Cosmoss, launched in January 2024, centered around emotional wellbeing and mental health. A year-long series of programs and events will bring it to life.

↑ Body Proud collection by I Am Proud

Glossier CEO Kyle Leahy spoke to *Glossy* about the brand's emotionally attuned approach. "Beauty, to me, is a feeling. I have a four-year-old and a one-year-old. I [think about] how I want them to feel in the world, how I want them to feel about themselves, how brands can play a role in elevating confidence and how a beauty company, in particular, can help drive that."

Why it's interesting

Beauty brands are harnessing the benefits beauty can have on emotions, identity, and mental wellness, transforming traditional products and beauty talk into an empowering movement filled with feelings.

VML

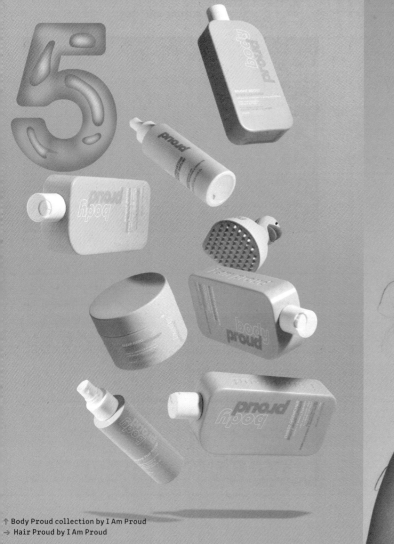

↑ Body Proud collection by I Am Proud
→ Hair Proud by I Am Proud

60
Bioharmonizing spas

Gone are the days of biohacking—instead,
welcome bioharmonized balance.

VML

↑ Six Senses Rome's modern-day take on the Roman bathing journey

Paul Chek, wellness coach and founder of the Chek Institute, considers bioharmonizing "your ability to be aware of what's happening in yourself with your body." Wellness programs are increasingly adopting this thinking by offering therapeutic treatments that are individualized and measured, and promote long-term preventative strategies for the body and mind.

"When it comes to the idea of bioharmonizing, we see it as a more gradual option than biohacking," Dr Tamsin Lewis, medical advisor at Six Senses Ibiza's RoseBar, tells VML Intelligence. Lewis implements a program of gradual improvements, giving time for body awareness. She believes that enabling bioharmony activates "true wellness" and offers "improvements that strengthen your physiology and

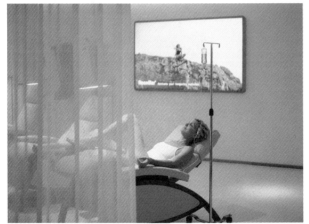

↑ RoseBar at Six Senses Ibiza

psychology, while giving your body enough time to repair and regenerate." Six Senses Rome opened in March 2023, with a spa inspired by ancient Roman rituals paired with modern treatments, following similar principles to RoseBar.

Kintsugi Space opened its six-floor flagship women-only wellness sanctuary in November 2023, inviting members to "rest, repair, reset, and renew." The members-only club is located on Al Reem Island, Abu Dhabi, and takes a holistic approach to health. Experiences include ayurveda, naturopathy, psychology, and quantum technology, in a mission focused on healing and repair for body and soul.

The SHA wellness clinic focuses on "adding years to life, and life to years." The programs aim to provide rebalance, advocating natural therapies and boosting emotional health. Currently only available in Spain, SHA will expand to Mexico and the UAE in 2024.

Why it's interesting
Quick health hacks are being replaced with longer-term treatments at spas that promote healthspans in slow and measured steps (for more on prolonging lifespans, see trend #81 Longevity resorts).

VML

Retail

Retail guilds

Department stores are going beyond shopping, launching exclusive members-only clubs.

VML

↑ Gordon Ramsay at Harrods The Residence Shanghai

Harrods opened its first members-only club, The Residence, in Shanghai at the end of 2023. The space features a bar, a lounge, private dining rooms, and outdoor terraces, as well as a high-end restaurant helmed by Gordon Ramsay. It also offers members ultra-premium services in aviation, real estate, interior design, and personal shopping, as well as access to private events and masterclasses hosted by brand partners.

Criteria for admission will be more discerning than those of other members clubs, *WWD* reported. "It will be based on lifestyle and interests. It's based on a community and that's really what we're trying to deliver—communities of passion, be that for collecting whisky, be that for entertainment, be that for art," said Sarah Myler, international business development and communications director at Harrods. The

↑ Selfridges Unlocked, courtesy of Selfridges

result will be "a space that delivers unrivaled customer service, but is programmed to like-minded people."

In July 2023, Selfridges launched its new loyalty membership program, Selfridges Unlocked. While it isn't affiliated with a dedicated physical space, the program gives members similar benefits—unlocking access to community programming such as supper clubs, film releases, and beauty masterclasses.

Why it's interesting

Shoppers are looking for more than just products from retailers. "It's not just the product," said Ashley Saxton, director of restaurants and kitchens at Harrods. "It's the experience that comes with it."

↑ Harrods The Residence Shanghai

VML

62

Imagination stores

New concepts for fantastical digital spaces unshackle retail stores from physical boundaries.

VML

Showcasing the most experimental take on this idea, digital artist Benjamin Benichou, founder and CEO of social commerce platform Drop, has imagined generative-AI-designed Nike concept stores in myriad locations. Among these boundary-breaking spaces, which Benichou calls Impossible Stores, are futuristic-looking designs in traditional Japanese architecture in Kyoto; another appears on Mars; and another has been imagined as a geometric cube atop Mount Everest. Benichou tells VML Intelligence he believes "these unconventional ideas can inspire real-world retail design by pushing architects and designers to think beyond the norm and to consider new materials, shapes, and structures that can elevate the retail experience." In addition, Benichou imagines "by collaborating with AI, we can reach new heights of creativity and push the boundaries of what's possible."

Generative AI companies such as Dalle-E and Midjourney are promising tools that can enhance creativity and ignite the imagination—and they are becoming more accessible. Adobe Firefly was released for commercial use in October 2023, allowing those with Adobe Creative Cloud to easily generate their own AI visuals using simple text prompts. The company calls Adobe Firefly "your imagination's new best friend." Chris Duffey, strategic development manager for Adobe Creative Cloud, tells VML Intelligence that "generative AI is really having a profound effect on the creators and the outputs as well." Duffey also observes a broader business opportunity: "We're now starting to see the second wave of generative AI's impact on creativity—the business of creativity—where it's

ushering in whole new business models, new reinvention strategies, new innovation capabilities for the creative agencies and companies."

Generative AI aside, brands are transporting shoppers to new destinations using metaverse tools. Bloomingdale's invited shoppers to step into a surreal chocolate factory inspired by Willy Wonka in November 2023. The Wonka Room uses Emperia's VR platform to allow visitors to engage in a treasure hunt, shop the collection, or simply enjoy being surrounded by an assortment of giant chocolate.

In summer 2023, Ralph Lauren unveiled The 888 House, a fantastical virtual store set within a desert landscape. In an interview with *Wallpaper* magazine, David Lauren, Ralph Lauren's chief branding and innovation officer, said: "Creative innovation is at the heart of Ralph Lauren's DNA and we're on a journey to bring our brand to life in new ways to engage the next generation of luxury consumers, who are dreaming and living more and more in the digital space." For more on this theme read VML Intelligence's "Into the Metaverse" primer.

Why it's interesting

Fifty-seven per cent of millennials have tried or would like to try stores in virtual worlds and 63% are interested in VR commerce. In response, brands are creating immersive, imaginative spaces that allow consumers to step into the company's world, and showcase creative flair and a preview of the future of ecommerce.

These unconventional ideas can inspire real-world retail design by pushing architects and designers to think beyond the norm.
Benjamin Benichou, founder and CEO, Drop

↑ AI-generated Nike concept store on Mars, Benjamin Benichou

↑ AI-generated Nike concept store on Mars, Benjamin Benichou

63

Next-gen collectors

Don't call them luxury consumers—call them luxury custodians.

The concept of true luxury is shifting. Jing Zhang, global editor-in-chief of *Jing Daily*, tells VML Intelligence that "rarity could be taking the place of price as the signifier of luxury, as high-net-worth consumers increasingly want to be collectors."

Zhang says: "The importance of experiences will overshadow past obsession with must-have 'it' items, as retail, luxury, and commerce in China come with more texture, cultural nuance, and intellectual thought."

Fashion designer Phoebe Philo is taking this to heart, offering a new formula for luxury fashion brands that pairs extreme rarity with heritage longevity. Her long-awaited eponymous label dropped its first collection in October 2023 to great fanfare—but it is eschewing the traditional rules of luxury fashion. The label will not host fashion shows or adhere to a seasonal release schedule.

Instead, it will release limited and unpredictable drops of pieces that are meant to be acquired over time, discouraging the practice of overhauling wardrobes each season with the latest designs.

"Our aim is to create a product that reflects permanence," Philo says. "The Phoebe Philo business model is designed to create a responsible balance between production and demand. For us, this means producing notably less than anticipated want."

Other luxury brands are also embracing the museumification of consumption. "Designer houses are marketing formerly

VML

↑ Future Frequencies: Explorations in Generative Art and Fashion at Christie's

disposable beauty products into collectibles," *Business of Fashion* reported in August 2023. Guerlain released a heritage collectible perfume bottle in November 2023. Called the Black Bee Prestige Edition, the bottle was crafted by French jeweler Lorenz Bäumer and crystal manufacturer Baccarat. The run is limited to 22 bottles, which will sell for €25,000 ($27,380) each.

Gucci is stepping into the curatorial space with a digital art auction in collaboration with Christie's. Called Future Frequencies: Explorations in Generative Art and Fashion, the auction presented 21 NFTs and was open for bidding in July 2023. Artist Claire Silver, who presented two pieces at the auction, says her works are intended to celebrate the era of AI, including "the depth of cultural heritage and the light of the future."

Why it's interesting

The role of the luxury brand is evolving. "Luxury brands need to act as guardians of craftsmanship and provenance," Fiona Harkin, foresight editor at The Future Laboratory, told Luxury Society. The next era of luxury will be defined by collection, not consumption—turning brands and consumers alike into curators and stewards of luxury goods.

64

Community-centric retail

A community feel is helping shopping districts to flourish.

↑ Kingland initiative in Poole, United Kingdom, supported by LGIM Real Assets

Shopping districts have been struggling with footfall, especially those in lower tiers, where Coresight Research in the United States reports subpar occupancies. Now community-centric initiatives are helping to reverse decline.

One tactic sees developers bet big on independent traders to create a community feel. In Poole, in the United Kingdom, an imaginative project is transforming Kingland Crescent. The once rundown shopping street is now home to 10 thriving independent local retailers, including a record store, a coffee roaster, a fishmonger, and a jewelry store. The brainchild of LGIM Real Assets (a division of financial services company Legal & General) the project offered units to budding local traders rent- and rates-free for a fixed two-year period from 2021. The key to meeting consumers' needs is to offer "an

VML

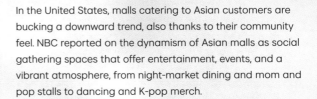

↑ Airside mall, Hong Kong, by Nan Fung Group, designed by Snøhetta

intentional place-based approach," Denz Ibrahim, head of retail and futuring at LGIM Real Assets, tells VML Intelligence. These locations can become the heart of the community by also "integrating key local-service-driven anchors," such as healthcare, education, and workspaces.

Legal & General, which is offering mentoring and legal advice to tenants, hopes the approach can form a blueprint to be adapted for other struggling towns and cities. "Our occupiers have seen huge success since launching at Kingland, where they have been able to learn, grow, and scale up," Ibrahim explains. "They're growing at such a pace that they're employing others and creating new local jobs. In its first year, Kingland generated an additional £2.2 million of spend and we're seeing turnover grow by over 35% year on year."

In the United States, malls catering to Asian customers are bucking a downward trend, also thanks to their community feel. NBC reported on the dynamism of Asian malls as social gathering spaces that offer entertainment, events, and a vibrant atmosphere, from night-market dining and mom and pop stalls to dancing and K-pop merch.

The lure of connection now informs the design of new shopping districts. At the new Snøhetta-designed Airside development in Hong Kong, the Nan Fung Group proposes the concept of wholeness, inviting "the community to gather at a place where you can be yourself and connect to others and nature."

As Ibrahim suggests, complementary offerings that draw a local crowd are also proving their worth. British startup Patch is building neighborhood shared spaces that drive additional footfall to retail locations. Venues are inspired by a work-near-home concept, which imagines how work-life balance could be improved without the dreaded commute. Founder Freddie Fforde tells VML Intelligence that the brand's mission is "to create opportunity for people, work, and community on every UK high street."

Why it's interesting

Fifty-six percent of people in the United Kingdom, the United States, and China say "there's no sense of community anymore." Retail districts that find creative ways to help people reconnect can plug the gaps left by disappearing shared public spaces.

Reading room in Patch workspace, High Wycombe, United Kingdom. Photography by Benoît Grogan-Avignon

65

The thrift economy

As inflation continues to bite, retailers must empower thriftier habits.

VML

VML Intelligence's data confirms that the cost of living is people's top concern today, with 64% globally selecting it as one of the five most pressing issues facing society. While the long-term economic outlook looks brighter, consumers will still be feeling the pinch in 2024. According to the IMF "the global economy is limping along, not sprinting" and "most countries aren't likely to return inflation to target until 2025."

Globally, consumers are showing resilience by adapting to thriftier and more dynamic shopping habits. In China the hashtag "downgraded spending" was one of 2023's trending topics on social media platform Weibo, while discount-focused website Pinduoduo's revenue grew 63% year on year. This mindset is global. According to McKinsey, 80% of US consumers (and 88% of gen Z and millennials) are seeking value by trading down to different products.

These shopping behaviors will continue in 2024, and brands and retailers will need to leverage low-price strategies that support this savvier shopper. Canadian food delivery app SkipTheDishes does this with its Inflation Cookbook grocery shopping tool. This predicts the biggest price drops among 400 popular ingredients across 100 grocery stores and uses the data to create affordable "chef-inspired" shoppable recipes. In France, supermarket giant Carrefour is positioning itself as an ally to consumers by taking a stand against "shrinkflation"—reducing a product's size or quantity while keeping its price stable. In-store signage is naming and shaming brands employing the tactic until they agree to lower their prices.

↑ The Inflation Cookbook by SkipTheDishes

Petcare brand Wilder Harrier is looking beyond low prices to support its customers. It is creating a network of Community Pet Pantries, where families struggling with the cost-of-living crisis can pick up donated food for their animals.

Why it's interesting

While longer-term economic outlooks are more optimistic, consumers in all global markets will continue to feel the pinch of the cost-of-living crisis in 2024. By responding to the thriftier new consumer mindset, retailers can meet the growing demand for value-based offers, while positioning themselves as strong consumer allies.

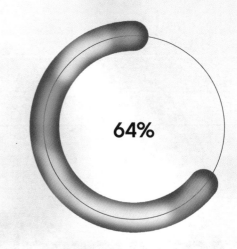

64%

The cost of living is people's top concern today, with 64% globally selecting it as one of the five most pressing issues facing society.

VML

Metaversal shopping

Virtual shoppers can now buy physical items.

Amazon is launching a new service that will allow customers to purchase physical items from stores in virtual store environments, including games, mobile apps, and augmented reality. Launched in May 2023 as an invitation-only offer for developers, Amazon Anywhere will ultimately unlock a new revenue stream for merchants by allowing shoppers to link their Amazon account and make purchases without having to leave their virtual experience. Brands simply display products within their experience and Amazon takes care of ordering, fulfilment, and after-service.

To kick off the launch, Amazon partnered with Niantic Labs, promoting the release of the latter's augmented reality game Peridot. Gamers can stock up on themed merchandise like T-shirts and throw pillows, specifying the size they require, without leaving the game.

The retailer is building out its meta-shopping offer with the

↑ Amazon Anywhere

addition of virtual 360-degree shopping experiences, this time creating an experience that enables fans to buy merchandise for Prime Video series and movies. For its first foray, the brand created an immersive tour of Godolkin University, a key location in the *Gen V* series, which tells the stories of freshmen at America's college for superheroes. The tour culminates at the campus store, where US-based visitors can purchase replica merchandise from a range of 150 items.

Why it's interesting

According to VML's "Future Shopper" report 2023, 11% of global shoppers already say they are actively purchasing in the metaverse, but this is likely to refer to virtual items: NFTs or gaming skins and accessories for avatars. The key distinction now is that Amazon is unlocking the ability to purchase in virtual space and receive a real, physical item. By extending the offer to other merchants, Amazon is building the foundations for a new era of metaversal shopping.

VML

67

Luxury retail temples

The age of the mega flagship is here.

↑ Dior flagship store

Luxury brands are creating colossal flagships that envelop shoppers in the brand's world. "You don't want Louis Vuitton having as many stores as Starbucks," Delphine Vitry, founding partner of Paris-based luxury consultancy MAD, told *WWD*. "You need the mega store."

Luxury retailers are snapping up space in the United States. "Gucci, Chanel, and other luxury retailers splurge on American real estate," the *Wall Street Journal* reported in October 2023. According to real-estate investment firm JLL, luxury retailers in the United States leased 650,000 square feet of new space between October 2022 and October 2023, up from roughly 250,000 square feet the previous year. And it's not just more space—it's more consolidated space: retailers signed leases for space averaging 5,000 square feet or larger from October 2022-2023, which represents a 28% increase from the previous 12 months.

VML

Chanel opened its largest US store in May 2023. The Beverly Hills flagship spans four floors and 30,000 square feet—which more than doubles its previous Beverly Hills footprint. The top floor houses a celebrity VVIP penthouse and 2,690-square-foot rooftop terrace with iconic views of the Hollywood sign. "For me, it's more a question of image than return on investment," said Bruno Pavlovsky, president of fashion at Chanel. "We continue to be active on all digital networks, but at the end of the day the experience in the boutique is more than ever a key moment for Chanel."

Tiffany & Co unveiled its new NYC flagship in April 2023 after four years of renovations. Standing at 10 stories and covering 100,000 square feet, it is one of the city's largest retail spaces. On the top floor is an invitation-only penthouse for VVIP shoppers.

This shift isn't isolated to the United States. In London, Gucci opened a five-story, 15,000-square-foot store in September 2023, while Burberry opened its revamped three-floor New Bond Street flagship, which covers nearly 22,000 square feet, in June 2023. And in March 2022, Dior reopened its sprawling Avenue Montaigne flagship in Paris, which houses eateries, a museum, and a hotel suite alongside retail, across over 107,000 square feet.

Why it's interesting

Luxury brands are leaning heavily into world building (see trend #36 World-building brands) for physical presence, creating flagships that represent an all-encompassing experience.

↑ Dior flagship store

Retail membership

Paid membership schemes offer a rewarding route to loyalty.

VML

↑ CVS pharmacy

A survey from customer loyalty specialist Clarus Commerce found that 95% of US retailers with traditional loyalty programs are considering launching paid-for membership schemes. This speaks to the growing awareness that the premium programs can offer strong benefits to both consumers and retailers.

Paid-for membership schemes, where consumers pay a regular fee in exchange for discounts and exclusive perks, are nothing new. Indeed, ecommerce data specialist Yaguara reports that 63% of the US population has an Amazon Prime account. However, paid membership remains a vastly underused tactic, with less than 5% of online retailers offering it, according to Jay Myers, cofounder of headless checkout solution Bold Commerce.

Los Angeles-based wellness brand Liquid IV is one of the new wave of companies now offering paid membership in addition to its existing subscription offers. It cites flexibility as the big selling point for consumers who, rather than being tied to curated selections, have more freedom to use their discounts across a wider range of products, can shop whenever they want, and gain access to exclusive merchandise.

US pharmacy retailer CVS's CarePass program costs $5 per month, but includes $10 credit, acting as a loss-leader to build loyalty. Adam Volin, general manager of CarePass, told *Retail TouchPoints* that members "make more trips and their baskets are larger." Research from McKinsey backs up this tactic, revealing that "members of paid loyalty programs are 60% more likely to spend more on the brand."

Another benefit for retailers is the guaranteed revenue provided by the membership fee. H&M-owned members-only brand Singular Society says the fees "keep the brand alive," allowing it to orient its manufacturing around quality and sustainability. Erik Zetterberg, the creative director and cofounder of Singular Society, tells VML Intelligence: "This shift enables us to develop and craft products of the highest possible quality and sell them at prices that would not have been possible traditionally. Our idea is to help people buy less by enabling them to buy better."

Why it's interesting

Despite the potential rewards for consumers and retailers, paid membership programs remain a niche offering. As consumers are only ever likely to commit to a handful of paid memberships, now is the time for retailers to pounce on this limited-time opportunity.

Euphoric retail

The pleasure of shopping heightens as retailers enrich
the lives of shoppers by deploying joy.

The Joy Project by Ulta Beauty and author Mel Robbins launched in September 2023. The long-term initiative aims to help future generations deepen their connection with beauty and have positive experiences. "We know we can ignite a movement that will help people everywhere live more authentic, and joyful lives," said Michelle Crossan-Matos, chief marketing officer of Ulta Beauty.

Liberty London's ongoing Find Joy Within curation sees multicolored smiley faces take over the Regent Street store. First started in early 2023, the collections include "feel-good fashion" and colorful mood-boosting jewelry that delivers cheerful chromotherapy. "Wearing jewelry is an act of self-expression and for me, the perfect way to add some mood-boosting brights to your outfit," says Ruby Beales, Liberty's jewelry buyer. "Think candy palettes of enamel, neon beaded bracelets, and juicy stone combinations. There are no rules: sprinkle it on or stack up contrasting shades. This is all about having fun."

In the fall, ecommerce retailer Terez launched its first physical store in New York City. As visitors enter the store they are struck by the vibrant pink walls, a whimsical balloon chandelier, and the brand's colorful fashion collections. Terez's mission is to "celebrate the good parts of life."

Why it's interesting

Brands are giving shoppers a euphoric boost by instilling fun, through design, product curation, and encouraging customers to find their inner joy.

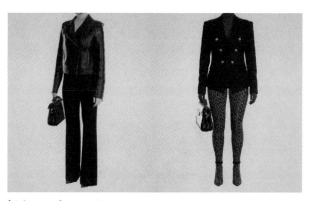

↑ Balmain 3D fitting, Bods

AI try-ons

Advances in tech take virtual try-ons from gimmicky to ultra-realistic.

Tech pioneers are developing tools that allow shoppers to virtually try on clothes with avatars that better reflect their own image, and even mimic the way clothes drape and fall in real life.

Los Angeles-based Bods is championing computer-game-like avatars as a virtual try-on vehicle. The company's AI extracts information from photos or key measurement data, which the consumer can then adjust to exactly match their shape. In early 2022, the company, which counts Karlie Kloss among its investors, raised $5.6 million in a seed funding round.

In November 2023, Bods announced a partnership with French fashion house Balmain, to provide visitors to Balmain's website with a "customized and virtual fitting." Shoppers can dress their custom avatar in "precise digital recreations of Balmain house signatures and runway designs," according to

VML

Bods. These "faithfully replicate luxury fabrics and tones, as well as the Balmain atelier's expertise in artisanal construction, embellishing, and tailoring."

Simon Cottigny, chief digital officer at Balmain, believes the technology will bring benefits for both brand and consumer, saying it will "greatly assist our Balmain customer in making more confident decisions," in turn improving conversion rates, and ultimately lowering return rates.

In June 2023, Google debuted its virtual try-on for apparel, a feature that the tech giant said "shows you what clothes look like on real models with different body shapes and sizes." To create images that convey how clothing drapes, wrinkles, and creases in real life, the company has created a diffusion-based AI model. The tool is currently available in the United States from brands such as Anthropologie, Loft, H&M, and Everlane.

British company Anthropics Technology, which creates software for photographers and retailers, has developed Zyler, a virtual try-on service that employs AI. The company says the service increases conversion rates by 18%, and offers it both on brands' websites and on in-store screens. John Lewis Rental and Marks & Spencer stores currently use the service in the United Kingdom.

Why it's interesting
AI-powered virtual try-ons are becoming more sophisticated, allowing consumers to literally visualize designs, improving conversion rates for brands, and minimizing wasteful returns.

↑ Balmain 3D fitting, Bods

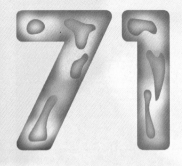

Luxury

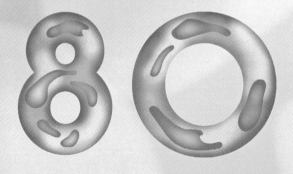

71
Operatic escapism

Over-the-top, extravagant interiors are transporting luxury consumers to another world.

↑ Apollo's Muse

Luxury openings are taking inspiration from the hedonistic abandon and unrestrained extravagance of antiquity. In April 2023, a new members' club opened behind the Bacchanalia restaurant in London's Mayfair. The club, Apollo's Muse, is billed as the "most private of private members' clubs," and will grant membership to only 500 people. The space is characterized by "overstated magnificence," *Conde Nast Traveler* said. Floor-to-ceiling marble, velvet bar stools, and custom Murano wine glasses are just the start—the club also houses a collection of priceless Greco-Roman antiquities from the first and second centuries AD, rivaling some of the world's top museums and galleries.

People are looking for a sense of discovery and escapism from the everyday.

Torquil McIntosh and Simon Mitchell, cofounders, Sybarite

VML

←Apollo's Muse. Photography by Johnny Stephens

The restaurant itself, which opened in December 2022, has been described as "a fantasy land of operatic escapism" by the *Standard*. Guest of a Guest describes it as "a Greco-Roman ode to opulence" and, in what the digital media company calls a "shameless display of debaucherous decadence," the restaurant offers diners $500 pasta dishes served by waiters dressed in togas, with décor including larger-than-life statues of winged lions, unicorns, and Greek gods. In an on-the-nose nod to Grecian and Roman luxury, a floor-to-ceiling painting reimagines Thomas Couture's The *Romans in Their Decadence*.

Across the pond, Bad Roman is bringing a similar spirit of decadence and playful irreverence to New York City. Opened in February 2023, it was dubbed by *Eater* "the year's most unhinged Italian restaurant" where "dining is a spectacle." The space features a sculpture of a wild boar wearing a neon necklace, trompe l'oeil mosaics, and a full-sized fountain in the bathroom.

Why it's interesting
Designers are applying Greco-Roman opulence to modern luxury interiors. People "are looking for a sense of discovery and escapism from the everyday," Torquil McIntosh and Simon Mitchell, cofounders of design agency Sybarite, tell VML Intelligence—and they're finding it in "spaces that transport them away and take them on an adventure."

↑ Apollo's Muse. Photography by Johnny Stephens

72

Secluded sanctuaries

Private islands become the go-to paradise retreat for the elite.

VML

↑ La Isla Secreta, courtesy of Rosewood Mayakoba

↑ La Isla Secreta, courtesy of Rosewood Mayakoba

Surrounded by a pristine coral archipelago rests a 1.7-hectare secluded retreat, opening in early 2024 for those prepared to hire out the entire island. Part of new developments by Red Sea Global (RSG), the Thuwal Private Retreat in Saudi Arabia centers on uber luxury for guests wanting a highly personalized and private vacation. After arriving at the island's jetty, visitors will be able to stay at the three-bedroom villa or three one-bedroom suites. Private concierges, butler services, and executive chefs will be part of the crew available to offer a curated and exceptional experience.

"Thuwal Private Retreat has been created to allow guests the chance to disconnect from the stresses of daily life, and instead reconnect with their closest companions," says John Pagano, group CEO of Red Sea Global. "Our belief is that the sublime Red Sea coast combined with tailored luxury experiences will deliver a peerless escape for the most discerning travelers."

In Greece, the private island Skorpios, known for hosting the wedding of shipping tycoon Aristotle Onassis and his bride Jacqueline Kennedy in 1968, will reopen in 2024 after three years of renovation and an estimated $200 million to transform the tiny Greek island into a lavish private resort. The VIP complex can accommodate up to 50 visitors and will cost over $1 million per week to rent in its entirety.

Rosewood Mayakoba in Mexico has a secluded new venue, La Isla Secreta—a private, undisclosed island within the resort, accessible only by boat. The retreat within a retreat, opened in January 2023, offers guests the chance to truly disconnect and feel pampered.

Why it's interesting

Seventy-six percent of high-income earners say they prefer to spend money on experiences rather than things and 25% agree that luxury today means experiences very few people will achieve. High-end, personalized vacations on private islands are luring the upper echelons to unique experiences away from the masses.

73

Invite-only spaces

Luxury access focuses on who you know for an additional, tantalizing layer of exclusivity.

VML

↑ Harrods The Residence Shanghai

From exclusive members' clubs to idiosyncratic fine-dining experiences, invitation-only luxury concepts are on the rise. In late 2023 Harrods opened The Residence in Shanghai, a private members' club that, *WWD* reported, evolved out of the retailer's invitation-only personal-shopping concept. The Residence will initially accept no more than 250 members and will only consider additional members in the future through peer nomination—according to Harrods, this is to ensure "total privacy and discretion" (see trend #61 Retail guilds).

In early 2023, New York-based French chef Yann Nury debuted La Résidence Soho, an invitation-only space on the

↑ La Résidence Soho kitchen. Photography by David Chow

light-filled 12th floor of a SoHo building, where Nury says guests can "witness the artistry of our culinary team in an open, state-of-the art kitchen as well as taste their creations." The aesthetics of the space are just as important as the culinary experience, with the loft designed in collaboration with French architect Charles Zana and decked out with Italian marble worktops, a custom Molteni stove, and 1960s Pierre Chapo S11 chairs, the *New York Times* reported. There is no contact phone number—*Air Mail* noted that "instead, like with anything good in the city, you have to know somebody who knows Nury."

London-based restaurant Caviar Kaspia reopened in early 2023 as a private, invitation-only club. The establishment focuses on the art of caviar and has locations around the world that, unlike London, are open to the public.

Why it's interesting

By 2024 the global average adult will be worth $100,000 and by 2026 there will be 87.5 million people with a minimum of $1 million in wealth, according to Credit Suisse. As more people become luxury consumers, exclusivity will not only be based on wealth, but also accredited to connections.

VML

New luxury frontiers

As the global luxury market slows, brands look east for growth.

VML

Asian luxury is hotting up, and it's not just about China. In November 2023, Bain & Company noted that "Southeast Asian countries experienced positive momentum" in the global luxury market, while India, Thailand, and the Philippines were among BCG's picks for growth at the FT Luxury Summit in May 2023. Now luxury brands are now looking to ramp up their presence in the region.

Dior became the first major Western label to host a seasonal runway show in Mumbai, unveiling its pre-fall 2023 collection against the dramatic backdrop of the Gateway to India monument. The location choice underlines the growing significance of the Indian luxury consumer, not to mention the nation's cultural heft (see trend #33 Brand India). Knight Frank India forecasts that the number of people in the country with more than $30 million in wealth is set to grow by almost 60% between 2022 and 2027.

Luxury retailers from Hermès to Christian Louboutin are opening stores in Indian cities despite spiraling rents, according to *Bloomberg*. To capitalize on growing interest, Indian conglomerate Reliance Industries opened the Jio World Plaza in November 2023. The upscale luxury mall, situated in Mumbai's Bandra Kurla Complex, hosts 60 luxury brands including Dior, Gucci, Balenciaga, and Louis Vuitton alongside leading Indian designers such as Manish Malhotra and Falguni Shane Peacock.

In Thailand, in October 2023, the Siam Paragon complex in Pathum Wan launched Luxe Hall. Operated by Siam Piwat, the space hosts 20 luxury brands, including the first Thai store for understated Italian label Loro Piana, as well as

The pace of growth within Southeast Asia is really fast.

Jing Zhang, global editor-in-chief, *Jing Daily*

men's collections from Fendi and Louis Vuitton. Thailand is enjoying growth in its luxury sector thanks in part to an influx of tourism. Jing Zhang, global editor-in-chief of *Jing Daily*, tells VML Intelligence that cities like Chengdu, Shenzhen, and Bangkok are developing so fast that they are "presenting a challenge to the experience you get in London or Paris."

Vietnam is also tipped as a rising star thanks to a growing middle class, and forecaster Statista predicts a billion-dollar market by the end of 2023. Zhang describes it as "an incredibly dynamic place with a lot of talent." In Hanoi, a slew of new upscale hotels and branded residences from leading names such as Four Seasons, Fairmont, Ritz-Carlton, and Waldorf Astoria are expected to lure more luxury retailers, creating "a new upscale luxury and shopping hub in the city."

Why it's interesting

Southeast Asia and India present significant new opportunities for luxury, with cities in the region now rivaling traditional luxury capitals, according to Zhang, who tips Vietnam and Thailand as the new stars alongside the China powerhouse. "People are shocked at what you can find in Bangkok and Saigon," says Zhang. "The pace of growth within Southeast Asia is really fast."

↑ Dior pre-fall 2023 show, Mumbai

VML

75

Lux-treme experiences

An emerging niche in luxury travel offers adrenaline-fueled indulgence.

VML

↑ Virgin Galactic

Adventure tourism is on the rise: it is expected to generate more than $1 trillion of revenue globally by 2030, up from $317 billion in 2022, according to Grand View Research. The growing market is even fueling a new demand for adventure insurance, with some policies offering evacuations and coverage for accidental death or injury, the *New York Times* reports.

Virgin Galactic took its first customers to space in June 2023. The inaugural commercial flight was a research-focused mission funded by the Italian Air Force, in preparation for future flights that will carry wealthy thrillseekers. The company has already sold around 800 tickets, priced at $250,000 to $450,000 each.

Skydive the Strip, launched in 2023, lets daredevils skydive over the Las Vegas strip after dark—for upwards of $30,000 per jump. Alongside the steep price tag, it's also highly limited, offering fewer than 100 reservations per year. Skydive

↑ Skydive the Strip

the Strip caters to adrenaline junkies who want to "experience the extraordinary," the company says. "Life is about experiences," cofounder Jim Dolan told *Travel + Leisure*. "And this is one of a kind."

Insider Expeditions is a travel agency for billionaire travelers who want to "push the barrier of what is possible." The agency hosts an average of 30 experiences per year, which can be anything from creating a tennis court in the middle of the Serengeti with hosts John and Patrick McEnroe to taking in a live concert in Antarctica, *Skift* reports. Wealthy travelers come to Insider Expeditions looking for "something very special that's never been done before," founder Carl Shephard told the travel industry news site. It is "the ultimate drug of life," he said.

Why it's interesting
The ultimate indulgence for luxury travelers in 2024 is once-in-a-lifetime, adrenaline-pumping experiences that reinvigorate their thirst for life.

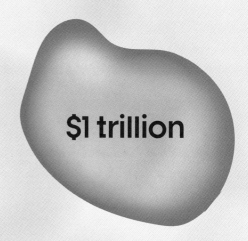

$1 trillion

Adventure tourism is expected to generate more than $1 trillion of revenue globally by 2030.

Grand View Research

VML

76
Clandestine retail

Shopping gets discreet for the wealthy.

"If you know, you know" has always been a luxury mantra. Now that maxim carries even more weight with the emergence of luxury brands offering hyper-private experiences for select clients at under-the-radar destinations.

Within its store in Beijing's SKP mall, Chanel has opened 31 Cambon, a VIP salon whose subtle branding references the house's founding address and flagship in Paris. Similarly, Chanel opened its VIP salons, Chanel Les Salons Privé, in the Chinese cities of Guangzhou and Shenzhen in summer 2023. According to images posted on Xiaohongshu, these invitation-only salons are minimally branded, with just a black and white exterior hinting at what's inside.

"We're going to invest in very protected boutiques to service clients in a highly exclusive way," commented Philippe Blondiaux, chief financial officer at Chanel, in a 2022 earnings release, *Jing Daily* reported. "Our biggest preoccupation is to protect our customers and in particular our pre-existing customers." With the *Business of Fashion*'s editor-in-chief Imran Amed having called out the ubiquity of queueing systems outside designer stores, and how at odds it is with a luxury experience, it's no surprise that luxury labels are creating more

VML

rarefied experiences for their most valued clients.

Gucci, too, is turning to invitation-only private salons to cater to its most affluent, top-tier clients. In April 2023, Gucci opened a 4,380-square-foot salon at the corner of Melrose Place and Melrose Avenue in Los Angeles. While the salon does have a prominent Gucci billboard atop the building, it also, *WWD* reports, has tinted windows, so "clients can see out, but prying eyes can't see in." François-Henri Pinault, chairman and chief executive officer of Kering, told analysts in February that prices in its Salon concepts, set to encompass both temporary and permanent spaces, would range from €40,000 to €3 million ($43,000 to $3.3 million). The strategy is being favored by other luxury marques including Italian label Brunello Cucinelli, which has opened seven private salons for its very important customers.

Why it's interesting

As aspirational customers rein in their spending amid an uncertain economic climate, luxury brands are lavishing more of their attention on their highest-spending clients—whose fortunes, Reuters points out, are "largely immune to economic turbulence."

VML

Luxury brands are offering hyper-private experiences for select clients at under-the-radar destinations.

77

Branded residences

From Bentley to Karl Lagerfeld, a new class of high-end branded homes is emerging.

↑ Bentley Residences, courtesy of Dezer Development

VML

When it comes to location, location, location for luxury living with a branded seal, Miami is the place to be. The city of Sunny Isles Beach in Florida is currently home to the Porsche Design Tower and Residences by Armani/Casa.

Scheduled for completion in 2026, the Bentley of real estate will alter the Miami skyline. Standing 749 feet tall, Bentley Residences is set to be the tallest oceanfront building in the United States. The company promises to "bring the innovative luxury of Bentley into your home" allowing people to literally live the brand. The 63-story building comprises 216 residential units and a host of amenities, including an outdoor pool, a gym, and a gaming room featuring indoor golf.

Branded around another leading marque, Aston Martin Residences is set to open its doors in downtown Miami. According to the *New York Times*, the 391 units are almost completely sold out, including the ultra-luxurious $59 million Aston Martin triplex penthouse.

Fashion house Karl Lagerfeld and UAE real estate firm Taraf announced in October 2023 that they would join forces on a project to create luxury branded villas in Dubai. Expected to break ground in the coming months, the project extends Karl Lagerfeld's branded residence portfolio, which already exists in Marbella, Spain, and Malaysia.

In the United Kingdom, a new Thames Living project will commence in collaboration with Porsche Consulting, a

↑ Bentley Residences, courtesy of Dezer Development

subsidiary of the luxury auto brand. The new town will be located along the River Thames and consist of residential buildings, parks, hotels, restaurants, and retail.

Why it's interesting

The motivation for luxury brands to enter the billion-dollar real estate business looks promising. According to a July 2023 report by real estate company Knight Frank, the market for branded luxury residences is predicted to grow 12% each year between now and 2026. In addition, by expanding into real estate, luxury brands become lifestyle brands, providing people with an all-encompassing brand experience.

78

Restratified experience

Top-tier luxury experiences are pulling away from the rest of the pack.

↑ Masque restaurant, Mumbai

Upscale venues and stores are tightening the velvet rope as brands restrict access to all except the most well-heeled customers. Take restaurants. In the south of France in summer 2023, reports surfaced in regional news outlet *Var Matin* that locals in St Tropez were being priced out of eateries because of wealth screening. Prospective diners claimed to have been quoted exorbitant set prices of up to €5,000 ($5,400) for tables.

London's two-Michelin-star Alex Dilling restaurant at the Hotel Café Royal ruffled a few feathers when it introduced a minimum spend per table, which would see single diners paying £330 ($410) for a set menu. This year, the price of a meal for two breached £1,000 ($1,244) for the first time in London, according to the *Standard*. And in India, a trend for upscale dining experiences fronted by top chefs and mixologists has seen events priced up to Rs 50,000 ($601) per head, equivalent to the monthly household income for a family,

VML

according to *Forbes India*. One pop-up, in collaboration with New York's Eleven Madison Avenue at the luxury restaurant Masque in Mumbai, even sold out in just nine hours.

Hospitality is following the path of fashion brands and courting the 1%—true luxury spenders, for whom money is no object. Luxury goods now cost more, with price tags up on average by 25% since 2019 according to data provider Edited. 2023 was the year Louis Vuitton launched the Millionaire Speedy: a bag with a price to match its name.

For now the focus is on the very wealthiest customers, who are spending with more confidence. *WWD* quotes Weiying Guo, associate director at Cushman & Wakefield, who observes that in China "if your annual income is less than ¥3 million ($414,100), you are not the target audience anymore."

It's a savvy strategy. In luxury, the highest spenders are enormously valuable, with the top two wealthiest buying clusters making up less than 1% of customers and delivering 10% of revenue, according to BCG's luxury experts. In China, the distinction is yet more stark. According to Morgan Stanley, just 1% of customers account for 40% of sales in some of China's luxury malls.

Why it's interesting

Brands are sharpening the peak of luxury to reassure the wealthiest, who now "want something more extreme that can express their status" according to Jing Zhang, global editor-in-chief of *Jing Daily*. As the middle class tightens its belt the world over, the super-rich are the priority audience.

VML

1%   10%

The highest spenders are enormously valuable, with the top two wealthiest buying clusters making up less than 1% of customers and delivering 10% of revenue.

BCG

79

Palatial stays

A new crop of uber-luxe hotels is courting travelers who want to live like modern royalty.

Luxury fashion house and jeweler Bulgari opened its new Rome hotel in September 2023. Room rates start at $1,500, but the crowning jewel is its premier one-bedroom suite—which costs €38,000 ($41,000) a night.

In the UK capital, rooms at the newly opened Peninsula London hotel start at $1,600 per night, and suites start at just under $4,000. The Peninsula Suite is "the hotel's most palatial accommodation," the hotel says—and reportedly the largest private accommodation available in London. At 1,400 square feet, it includes a formal dining room, a private gym, terrace, and cinema. "It's like a hotel within a hotel," Sonja Vodusek, managing director of The Peninsula London, told *Robb Report*.

Upping the opulence with an added dose of grandeur, many hospitality moguls are transforming old castles into majestic accommodations. Palazzo Vilòn, opened in April 2023, "gives guests the chance to live like Roman nobility," *Travel + Leisure* reports. Located in one wing of the Palazzo Borghese, the Italian noble family's historic palace, the villa was imagined as "a Roman refuge for Arab sheikhs, Harry and Meghan, and Hollywood royalty," the *New York Times* reports. To rent the entire villa, guests will need to shell out an average of €25,000 ($27,000) per night.

In Austria, the Almanac Palais Vienna, opened in April 2023, transformed a former palace into a hotel. And in Japan, two historic castles—Ozu Castle and Hirado Castle—are opening their doors to overnight guests for the first time.

Why it's interesting

Uber-luxe destinations are upping their indulgence with accommodations fit for royalty.

↑ IV room at Remedy Place, NYC

Athluxe

Ultra-luxury fitness concepts are helping HNWIs achieve their heightened health goals.

VML Intelligence's data reveals that the number one signifier of luxury today is "living a long, healthy life." In this new paradigm where optimum health is the new wealth, ultra-premium fitness clubs are emerging where HNWIs can get serious about their health goals surrounded by cutting-edge technology and like-minded people, in locations that borrow from the design codes of luxury hospitality—with a price tag to match.

The new approach is exemplified by Remedy Place in Los Angeles and New York, which refers to itself as the world's first social wellness club. For an all-access monthly fee starting from $2,500, it merges access to holistic practitioners with world-leading "tech remedies" that include

VML

hyperbaric oxygen chambers, lymphatic compression suits, and private contrast suits with ice baths and an infra-red sauna. The design of the IV Tunnel at its New York location is "inspired by Swiss Architect Mario Botta's signature idiom of geometric forms," Remedy Place says.

The Siro One Za'abeel hotel from Kerzner International, which is set to open in February 2024 in Dubai, is an "integrated fitness and recovery" hotel that broadens the traditional definition of luxury health and wellness, merging world-class nutrition and fitness experiences with a focus on recovery and mindfulness. With one-night stays costing in the region of AED 1,900 ($517) it offers a specialist Recovery Lab as well as guest rooms, referred to as Recovery Cocoons, with innovative technology "to improve physical and mental recovery, mitigate jet lag, enhance mood and ensure restorative sleep."

Also in Dubai, the Seven wellness club "blends opulence with athleticism" for a luxury fitness experience. In mid-2023, a new partnership with celebrity chef Silvena Rowe, renowned for her expertise in biohacking, saw longevity-focused cuisine on the menu at the club's in-house restaurant.

Why it's interesting

Statista estimates that the global health and wellness market will be worth almost $7 trillion by 2025, driven in large part by HNWIs. They are showing a willingness to pay a premium for health and wellness, and expect the most innovative and opulent locations and experiences in return.

↑ Siro One Za'abeel, Dubai

Health

81

Longevity resorts

Wellness destinations are designing programs that make living to a centenary and beyond a reality.

VML

↑ Sensei Porcupine Creek. Photography by Chris Simpson
↑↑ Shakti Hall at the Art of Living Retreat Center, North Carolina, courtesy of Six Senses

From cryotherapy chambers and thermal body mapping to neuronutrition plans and emotional strength training, resorts are curating stays that help guests live longer and age better. Situated in the foothills of the Santa Rosa mountains in California is Sensei Porcupine Creek, a 230-acre health retreat. "At Sensei, we aim to weave our mission of helping people live longer, healthier lives into all of our programming and core offerings," Alexandra Walterspiel, copresident and chief operating officer at Sensei, tells VML Intelligence. Programs available include Rest and Recover, introduced in April 2023, which helps guests manage stress and focus on restorative sleep, and the Optimal Wellbeing Program, which includes a dedicated Sensei Guide who helps personalize the experience based on health data and desired goals.

Sensei Porcupine Creek opened in November 2022 and has seen steady footfall from people seeking longevity plans. "Following the pandemic, more consumers are prioritizing their personal wellness and it's clear this trend is here to stay," says Walterspiel.

Clinique La Prairie (CLP) has been expanding its longevity resorts around the world, with locations including Bangkok, Doha, and the original medical spa on Lake Geneva, Switzerland. In 2024, CLP will be opening two new destinations, one in Anji, China (see trend #28 Top three destinations) and the second in Amaala, Saudi Arabia. Every longevity journey at the resort begins with a proprietary Longevity Index assessment, which provides wellness experts with the necessary information to create a personalized

↑ Six Senses Kaplankaya, Turkey

treatment plan for the guest's entire stay.

Another luxury resort operator with a focus on boosting lifespan is Six Senses. Its Kaplankaya, Turkey, location was the first to introduce a longevity program, and two are now available in the United States—the Art of Living Retreat Center in North Carolina, and Rock Springs Retreat Center in Tennessee. In Saudi Arabia, the Six Senses Amaala resort is due to open in 2024 and will feature a longevity clinic.

Why it's interesting

Globally, people are living longer. In 2020, there were 1 billion people aged 60 years plus. This is expected to almost double by 2050, when 2.1 billion people are expected to be 60 years and over, according to the World Health Organization. In addition, 74% of people globally say they like the idea of living to be a healthy centenarian and longevity resorts may be one way to nurture that possibility.

Six Senses Kaplankaya, Turkey

82

Psychedelic concierges

As therapeutic use of psychedelics goes mainstream, concierges are emerging to help navigate these powerful experiences.

↑ Psychedelic Passage founders Nick Levich and Jimmy Nguyen

The heightened interest in psychedelic services follows Oregon becoming the first US state to legalize the adult use of psilocybin in 2023, while Colorado is set to allow professionals to offer psilocybin experiences from 2025, alongside adult personal use. Several US cities have also decriminalized the use of psilocybin.

US-based Mike "Zappy" Zapolin describes himself as "psychedelic concierge to the stars," having worked with figures including actress Michelle Rodriguez and former professional basketball player Lamar Odom, guiding them through the use of ayahuasca, and ketamine and ibogaine, respectively. Explaining his role to the *Guardian*, Zapolin noted that "a hotel concierge does not get you the food

VML

you're going to eat; they just make the reservation. It's the same with me: I'm advising based on best practices and protocols, and using my network to find the doctor or expert." In addition, after each experience, concierges are also typically responsible for facilitating therapy sessions, during which clients can process the journey they have been on.

Psychedelic Passage, based in Bend, Oregon, says it acts as "an ally from start to finish," and "a liaison between parties," on its clients' psychedelic journeys. Its service begins with a consultation call to connect clients with pre-vetted psychedelic facilitators before a psychedelic session is undertaken. The company says it has facilitated more than 750 psychedelic ceremonies in the United States, to alleviate conditions such as "anxiety, depression, PTSD, and addiction," while promoting "personal growth, spiritual exploration, [and] clarity of purpose."

Why it's interesting

While the legality of psychedelic use is currently patchy, consumer interest in this area is strong—according to a 2023 survey from Morning Consult in the United States, "more than half of millennials surveyed said they were interested in trying psychedelics to treat their mental health, the most of any generational demographic." Given the complexity of this field, it's no surprise that consumers are seeking guidance in this process.

VML

>50%

More than half of US millennials surveyed said they were interested in trying psychedelics to treat their mental health.

Morning Consult

83

Idyllic idleness

Can doing nothing be the secret to a healthier and happier life?

"We all need a bit of boredom to realize that we must seek new things that could bring us joy," Leticia Credidio, founder of her eponymous slow-living lifestyle brand, tells VML Intelligence. The brand launched in 2019 with a sustainable sleepwear collection and has since expanded to lifestyle products that promote slow living. "Slow living is a way of being that allows us to make more conscious choices on how we consume and relate to others," Credidio explains.

Jenny Odell, author of *How to Do Nothing: Resisting the Attention Economy* suggests there are two halves of doing nothing. The first is "disengaging from the attention economy" and the second is to "reengage with something else." In March 2023, Odell released her second book, *Saving Time: Discovering a Life Beyond the Clock*, which explores the need to sit still, remain present, and defy the constraints of the clock.

Being at peace in stressful situations has been turned into a competition for the first time in Europe. In August 2023, London held the Extreme Relaxing UK Championships, where 30 contestants battled it out to resume a Zen-like state after tense experiences. The event was pioneered by sport psychologist Dr Jamie Barker, who says there is "an ever-growing need for people to find ways to relax to aid recovery from everyday stress and increasing demands on individuals' time."

In public spaces and the workplace, quiet rooms are rising in popularity. In May 2023, the O2 Centre shopping mall in London dedicated a quiet space to allow people to

VML

↑ Sky Collection by Leticia Credidio

↑ Snug Extreme Relaxing Championship

"

We all need a bit of boredom to realize that we must seek new things that could bring us joy.

Leticia Credidio, founder, Leticia Credidio

disconnect from the busy environment. Adobe is reported to be in the process of installing quiet rooms in its offices where "employees dealing with harder moments can go to be alone, be a place of reflection or help change the cycle of where their brain is at," Eric Kline, Adobe's head of global workplace experience, told the *Wall Street Journal*.

Why it's interesting

Making time for moments of boredom and downtime is being reinvigorated as a healthy necessity in life, with the potential to allow for more meaningful connection to the self and others. "In a world where overwork and busyness are the status quo, taking time to sleep, to embrace slowness, and be present in the now are acts of defiance," says Credidio.

VML

84

Well ambition

Wellbeing is no longer sacrificed on the altar of ambition.

A generation of workers is prioritizing wellbeing, hoping to trade striving for serenity. In our survey, 73% of respondents say that work comes second to the rest of their life and 76% claim they would not accept a job that was highly stressful.

January 2023 saw the resignation of New Zealand premier Jacinda Ardern, who acknowledged she no longer had "enough in the tank" to do her role justice. Since then, an array of public figures have hit pause on their high-flying careers, including Canadian musician Drake, actor Tom Holland, and Scotland's former first minister Nicola Sturgeon.

Businesses will need strategies to tackle this issue. More than half of respondents (56%) say they often feel burned out by their work, suggesting there will be an uptick in those seeking a temporary hiatus.

One solution sees companies offering early sabbaticals, dubbed "burnout breaks." While more commonly offered to employees with long service, PayPal, Meta, and Adobe are among those seeing the benefits of extending the perk earlier, after just five years' service. Sapro, a US consulting firm, saw its employee turnover rate drop below 5% after instituting a policy offering staff breaks of one to three months on half pay and full benefits, no questions asked.

Timeouts don't tackle the root of the problem, however. In an editorial for *Fast Company*, Samu Hallförs, CEO of Finnish company Framery, proposed the idea of burnout reporting,

where companies publicly report wellness markers, elevating wellbeing to the same status as their financial metrics and deepening their accountability in the process.

Brands are also stepping up as advocates. In Singapore and Malaysia, Heineken has continued its "Work Responsibly" campaign against toxic productivity with "The Ghosted Bar," a campaign encouraging workers not to neglect their social relationships by overworking. A teaser film depicted chairs and glasses moving by themselves in a bar to illustrate how those who overwork "ghost" their friends.

Why it's interesting

Hustle and grind is no longer aspirational as people seek a healthier balance. Brands can offer support by promoting permission to rest, underlining the value of proper downtime, while employers should embed meaningful support for mental health into the employee experience.

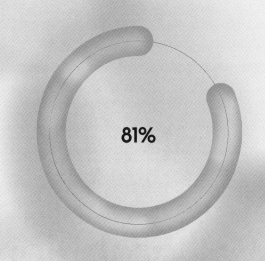

81%

81% think brands should be making an effort to help improve people's mental health.

85

Hypoxic therapy

Altitude training grows in popularity as intermittent hypoxia-hyperoxia training (IHHT) takes off in fitness centers.

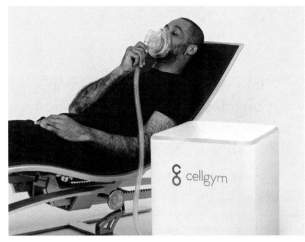

↑ Cellgym

Athlete-grade hypoxic training masks that reduce oxygen flow are increasingly being found in health and fitness clubs. Sales of hypoxic training equipment are expected to reach $230 million by 2026, according to a 2020 report by Wintergreen Research, indicating the strength of this sector.

German wellness company Cellgym has specialized in IHHT since 2010, aiming to make cell therapy accessible to as many people as possible. The benefits of regular IHHT include feeling more energized, a strengthened immune system, and improved quality of sleep. "Scientific research in hypoxia has increased in the past decade," Rainer Goytia, founder and CEO of Cellgym, tells VML Intelligence. "The thousands of studies on this topic

VML

> ❝
> ## Intermittent hypoxic training is an integral part of prevention and therapy.
> **Rainer Goytia, founder and CEO, Cellgym**

↑ Lanserhof Sylt

have shown positive results, indicating that intermittent hypoxic training is an integral part of prevention and therapy." Goytia points out one major hypoxia discovery, which won the 2019 Nobel Prize in Physiology or Medicine for the discovery of "how cells sense and adapt to oxygen availability," as being crucial to adding credibility to IHHT.

Cellgym's locations include Repose in London. The boutique fitness and wellness destination notes the benefits of regular weekly 25-minute hypoxic therapy sessions, including improved skin health, better cardiovascular function, increased energy levels, improved stress levels, and improved physical and mental strength.

Lanserhof Sylt in Germany offers 45-minute IHHT sessions and recommends taking up to three per week. Its treatment menu describes the training as "non-invasive cell stimulation without side effects" and has been long used by professional athletes to boost their performance.

Hotels are also leveling up their fitness centers with IHHT facilities. Aman hotel in New York City, various Six Senses locations, Gstaad Palace in Switzerland and Ham's Yard Hotel in London all have their own hypoxic studios for visitors to work on their high-altitude training.

Why it's interesting

Gyms and wellness spaces are setting themselves apart by offering IHHT facilities that are no longer exclusively for the benefit of athletes.

86

Fertility futures

Emerging technologies are revolutionizing human reproduction.

The Apple Watch can now be used as a contraceptive device. In September 2023, the FDA cleared Natural Cycles' use of Apple Watch temperature data as a viable form of birth control. This gives users of Natural Cycles—a digital birth-control app that uses body temperature to determine fertility windows—the option to import their temperature data from the watch instead of manually taking their basal body temperature each morning.

New York-based startup Gameto is working to redefine reproductive health. One way it hopes to do this is by making egg freezing and in vitro fertilization (IVF) more seamless, less painful, and less intrusive. Physician and Gameto cofounder Dr Dina Radenkovic envisions that the future of IVF will take place in "egg-freezing kiosks," she told the *New Yorker*. "I see it almost like an extension of the beauty studio, where being proactive about your reproduction and longevity just seems like an act of self-care." The startup was named a 2023 Technology Pioneer by the World Economic Forum.

A nascent area of biomedical research is working to turn stem cells into embryos—a process called in vitro gametogenesis (IVG). Biotech startup Conception is one group leading the charge. IVG would enable women to have their own genetically related babies at any age, or after surviving diseases like cancer that can prevent conception. It would also allow same-sex couples to have biological children together. "I personally think what we're doing will probably change many aspects of society as we know it," Pablo Hurtado, the company's chief scientific officer, told *NPR*.

Why it's interesting
Emerging technologies will give prospective parents more control over when, how, and with whom they have children—and have the power to change the very fabric of future families.

8   6

← Natural Cycles powered by Apple Watch
↓ Gameto

↑ Vagus nerve exercise videos on TikTok

87

Vagus nerve care

Wellness experts are tapping into the vagus nerve for its healing effects.

Scientific interest in the potential of vagus nerve stimulation is growing, with research exploring potential applications in conditions from obesity to depression. In tandem, multiple wellness treatments—and TikTok hacks—are popping up and claiming to tap into its healing and anti-anxiety effects.

As of January 2024, there were over 180 million views for the hashtag #vagusnerve on TikTok, and over 185 million views for "vagus nerve exercise." The practices shared include flicking the earlobes, placing ice on the chest or face, or deep breathing, with the aim being to slow down the heart rate and encourage the body to relax.

The trend is now finding its way into spa treatments and beauty products. Osea, a US skin care brand that draws on the power of marine ingredients, has created a Vagus Nerve collection. The range includes Vagus Nerve Oil, designed to be lightly massaged into the sides of the neck and rubbed

VML

behind the earlobes. Ingredients include olive oil, meadowfoam seed oil, and rosemary, lavender, and juniper oils.

At London's Mandarin Oriental Hyde Park hotel, the Oskia Cryo Wellness Facial experience, introduced in 2023, includes the 90-minute Oskia-30°C Vagus Re-Programming Facial, which incorporates "a sense-heightening experience on the back, neck, face, and scalp." The spa says that "cryo-blasts" stimulate the vagus nerve, with the cryotherapy incorporating "lymph manipulation and sculptural massage to further stimulate and support the body's natural detoxifying processes."

Alongside beauty therapies, stimulation devices are now hitting the market. At the Consumer Electronics Show (CES) in January 2024, Lithuanian health tech company Pulsetto showcased its vagus nerve stimulation device for relaxation and stress relief. Claiming to improve sleep quality and facilitate body recovery, it uses electric stimulation technology to "biohack the parasympathetic nervous system" in four minutes.

Also at CES, the ZenBud stimulator by US-based bio-engineering company NeurGear is powered by advanced ultrasound technology. Worn like conventional earbuds, it aims to supports mental balance and relaxation.

Why it's interesting
Consumers and brands are keen to embrace the benefits of stimulating the body's vagus nerve as part of their wellbeing practices, illustrating just how compelling a story the brain-body connection continues to be.

↑ Osea Vagus Nerve collection

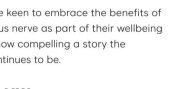

88

New diagnostics

New ventures are exploring ways to provide less invasive health diagnostics.

↑ Theblood cofounders Isabelle Guenou and Miriam Santer, courtesy of Theblood

British startup Daye launched a tampon that can test for sexually transmitted infections (STIs) in November 2023. The Vaginal Microbiome Screening Kit is an at-home STI diagnostic service that can also calculate the risk of vaginal infections and fertility complications. The company aims to "democratize access to comprehensive gynecological care for all."

Tapping into the insights that menstrual blood can provide, Berlin-based startup Theblood, cofounded in 2022 by Isabelle Guenou and Miriam Santer, is exploring exactly what health data it can reveal. In 2023, the company raised almost €1 million ($1.09 million) in pre-seed funding to further its research. Currently, Theblood offers a prototype test kit,

VML

↑ Theblood cycle test kit

available to consumers in Germany, to provide insights into the menstrual cycle and how to manage symptoms.

Guenou tells VML Intelligence that her own eight-year journey to a diagnosis of endometriosis was part of what prompted her to found the company. "We see that women kind of get gaslighted," she says, on women's journeys to diagnosis. "It's one of our goals to shorten the time to get a diagnosis... We don't have to be the first ones giving the diagnosis, but we are bringing more data to really find out what's going on." And, she adds, the doctors she speaks to are supportive of the insights their service could bring.

Guenou, who says the company eventually plans to offer its tests in other European countries, also notes mothers are ordering the cycle testing kit for their teen daughters. "I would say definitely we want to bring for the next generation a new approach to menstruation," she says. "That you can actually get data back from [menstruation], and that it's not just an annoying thing that pops up every month."

Another player in the field is Qvin, a US start-up that will began to offer its cycle testing kit within the United States in early 2024. It tests several biomarkers found in customers' menstrual blood, among them hemoglobin A1c, to measure blood sugar; TSH, for thyroid health and metabolism; and FSH, LH, and AMH, all reflective of fertility levels and perimenopause.

Why it's interesting

By testing menstrual blood, pioneering companies are signaling a new awareness of the unique factors that affect women's health, to help them glean valuable insights from a substance that's traditionally been viewed as an unmentionable waste product.

89

Emotional fixtures

People are designing their personal spaces to evoke positive emotions of safety, calmness, and acceptance.

Ikea unveiled a sculptural light and homeware collection with designer Sabine Marcelis in February 2023. Varmblixt is part of Ikea's "long-term goal to encourage a shift in the perception of lighting as simply functional to lighting as emotional," the company says. The range features a playful take on traditional lighting with colorful accents and unusual sculptures and shapes, and leverages direct and indirect light designed intentionally to evoke calmness, emotion, serenity, and curiosity in the home.

Mexican ceramic studio Menat is creating urns designed to comfort and address feelings of grief and loss. Photographer Marianna Jamadi collaborated with Menat to design the Kunokaiku urns for her parents. This turned into a wider collection of urns meant to be placed on display in the home and incorporated into a daily ritual as a way of coping and memorializing a lost loved one. Jamadi told *Wallpaper* that she felt "it's nice to have an object that you can interact with. That you can stay tethered to" in times of grief.

At the Consumer Electronics Show (CES) 2023, LG showcased the MoodUp fridge: an at-home appliance designed to reflect someone's emotional state. The refrigerator's LED door panels can be changed and customized with 23 individual color options, seasonal settings, emotional pre-set settings, and more.

Why it's interesting

Consumer appetite for emotional wellbeing is translating into everyday life. These brands are upgrading at-home appliances and furniture that enable people to surround themselves with comfort and serenity.

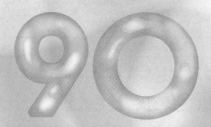

90
Future-proofed beings

Tech to safeguard future health is now a status symbol.

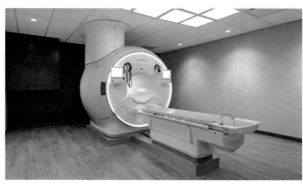

↑ Prenuvo

As medical technology evolves, several ventures are tapping into the human desire to preserve health and maximize longevity, with machines that promise to discover diseases at their earliest—and most treatable—stages.

In August 2023, Kim Kardashian helped to bring this trend into the spotlight when she posted a picture of herself beside a Prenuvo full-body scanner, calling it a "life-saving machine." Prenuvo, a US company led by founder Andrew Lacy and founding radiologist Dr Raj Attariwala, offers torso, full-body, and head-and-torso scans for the early detection of cancer and other diseases, in several US locations. In April 2023 the company opened a location in New York, and has opened eight more since, with plans to operate a further 11 in the near future.

Prenuvo says that its service "unlike conventional MRIs, which take hours and often involve contrast injections, scans for

VML

↑ Prenuvo founders Andrew Lacy and Dr Raj Attariwala

500+ conditions, including most solid tumors which can be detected as early as stage 1, in addition to aneurysms, cysts, and more—all without radiation, in under an hour." Prices span from $999 for a torso scan to $2,499 for a full-body scan.

At the Lanserhof at The Arts Club clinic in London, the medical services division says its focus is on "preventative medicine." Alongside Lanserhof's general medicine, cardiology, and nutrition services at its London location, clients can undergo the clinic's 3T MRI service, "designed to provide the most comprehensive and accurate diagnostic imaging available."

Why it's interesting

While some doctors caution the potential for false positives and unnecessary investigation with preventative services, for many people, health continues to be regarded as the ultimate wealth. Next-gen screening services reflect affluent consumers' desire to take control of the unpredictability of health and the human body.

VML

> # Next-gen screening services reflect affluent consumers' desire to take control of the unpredictability of health and the human body.

Innovation

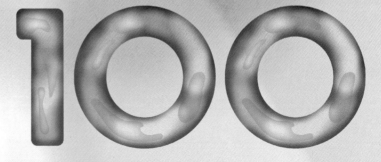

↑ Colossal Biosciences

Ultra-preservation

Can technology fend off extinction, or even reverse it?

"Humanity has become a weapon of mass extinction," according to UN secretary-general António Guterres, speaking at the opening talks of the COP15 global biodiversity conference. More than 40,000 species are said to be "threatened with extinction" according to the IUCN Red List, the world's most comprehensive source of data on extinction risks.

Biologists are now attempting a moonshot. The Earth Biogenome Project (EBP) is a 10-year project that will "sequence, catalog, and characterize the genomes of all of Earth's eukaryotic biodiversity." In other words, scientists will assess every plant, animal, and fungus on Earth, right down to single-celled organisms like algae, including those yet unidentified, in a bid to preserve the life on our planet. The scale of the project is mind-boggling: it has tasked itself with cataloging 1.8 million known species in just a decade.

VML

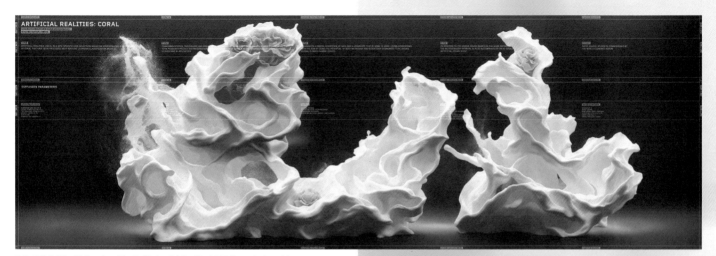

↑ Artificial Realities: Coral by Refik Anadol Studio, 2023. Commissioned by World Economic Forum

While the EBP attempts rescue on a grand scale, scientists are also working at the individual species level. A consortium of scientists and conservation experts under the banner of BioRescue aims to save the endangered Northern white rhinoceros. Just two female white rhinos remain in a conservancy in Kenya, but the project aims to use assisted reproduction and stem cell research to bring the species back from the brink.

Partnering with BioRescue on the Northern white rhino mission is genetics and biotechnology company Colossal Biosciences. The company specializes in disruptive technologies for the restoration of extinct species (or "de-extinction") and is engineering hybrids that share the traits of long-lost creatures like the woolly mammoth, the Tasmanian tiger, and the dodo. According to the *Financial Times*, the company is already in talks with US states on potential locations for rewilding sites to raise a herd of mammoths.

The company's mission is to "shed light on the biodiversity crisis while also building technologies to aid conservation," Ben Lamm, founder and CEO of Colossal Biosciences, tells VML Intelligence. They are working on rewilding once-extinct species with intentionality. "We want to ensure we can

VML

↑ **Artificial Realities: Coral by Refik Anadol Studio, 2023. Commissioned by World Economic Forum**

reintroduce animals in a way that actually helps the environment," says Lamm.

Impermanence in the form of memories is also being explored. Digital artist Refik Anadol delivered a talk at the TED 2023 conference entitled "How AI art could enhance humanity's collective memory," which poignantly imagined how we might train algorithms with images of natural species like flowers or corals, to retain the experience of them. "We as artists can utilize this potential not only to represent nature, but also to remember how it feels to be immersed in it in a digital age," said Anadol.

Why it's interesting

The growing urgency of the climate conversation is driving efforts to preserve what we can of the world's natural and cultural assets. While future generations face unimaginable challenges, these projects will form the bedrock of potential restoration and even de-extinction efforts.

92

Centenarian futures

Healthspans get a Medicine 3.0 treatment from longevity specialists and entrepreneurs seeking eternal life.

"My mission is for the human race to survive and thrive," tech entrepreneur Bryan Johnson tells Steven Bartlett in *The Diary of a CEO* podcast. Johnson, who was born in 1977, believes it is possible for all of us to live forever and the only objective we should have is "don't die." He has a clinic set up in his Venice Beach home and says he spends $3–$4 million a year on supplements, tests, and treatments to rejuvenate his biological age to 18.

Johnson has surrendered his life to data since 2021 and shares his routine and findings on Project Blueprint. In late 2023 Kate Tolo, then aged 27, was introduced publicly as the second person to opt in to the rigorous Blueprint protocol. By November that year, Tolo had already committed to three months of Blueprint and is said to have "concluded the health benefits outweighed the lifestyle costs" in a *Time* magazine interview. Those interested in joining the "don't die" pledge can sign up to the Blueprint Starter Kit from January 2024.

Another example of a company investing to improve biological age is venture capital firm Healthspan Capital, which supports a range of firms studying longevity biology (LongBio) since 2021. "Longevity biotech will revolutionize biomedicine by bringing aging under medical control," Sebastian Brunemeier, general partner and cofounder of Healthspan Capital, tells VML Intelligence. He predicts that "new tools like gene and cell therapy will enable more precise reprogramming of biology that will make our history of pills and plant extracts look medieval by comparison."

Longevity piqued the interest of media outlets in 2023, giving more muscle in this space and adding credibility to the topic.

VML

↑ Blueprint Project, courtesy of Bryan Johnson

National Geographic released an issue dedicated to the science of longevity; the *Economist's* fall publication was a dedicated special report on living to 120 that dove into ways to slow down aging, and in August, Netflix released a documentary series called *Live to 100: Secrets of the Blue Zones.*

Eric Verdin, chief executive of the Buck Institute for Research on Aging, predicts that most people could live to 95 in good health and says, "lifestyle is responsible for about 93% of your longevity—only about 7% is genetics." In spring 2023, Dr Peter Attia published *Outlive: The Science & Art of Longevity.* Attia believes leaders in medicine and tech should turn their attention to what he calls Medicine 3.0: proactive illness prevention and maintenance for late-life quality.

Why it's interesting

Seventy-three percent of global recipients say they eat to live longer and 74% like the idea of living a long and healthy life beyond the age of 100. Now technology and research in prolonging healthspans are paving the way to make healthy centenarians the norm.

VML

> New tools like gene and cell therapy will enable more precise reprogramming of biology that will make our history of pills and plant extracts look medieval by comparison.

Sebastian Brunemeier, general partner and cofounder, Healthspan Capital

93

Generation AI

AI's influence could be profound for the youngest of generations.

↑ TeddyGPT artwork, courtesy of Toymint

VML

↑ TeddyGPT artwork, courtesy of Toymint

AI will be hugely influential on the lives of generation alpha, born between 2010–2024, in much the same way that smartphones and social media have shaped the lives of gen Zers. They are already growing up with emotionally intelligent AI companions—like the child-friendly Miko 3 and Roybi AI robots—that aim to educate, form relationships, and grow with them.

In April 2023, Toymint introduced TeddyGPT, a toy that uses OpenAI and promises "to cater to each child's unique preferences and needs." The smart toy is expected to provide ultra-customized interactions when it is launched. In an interview with the *Financial Times*, Allan Wong, CEO of toy company VTech Holdings, said he believes that by 2028, AI teddy baears will be able to "generate stories customized for the kid rather than reading from a book."

Relationships will look different for a generation that has grown up with AI companions. "It's about creating human connection in different spaces," futurist Ian Beacraft said in a keynote speech at SXSW 2023 on the topic of AI, adding: "We're at a point where we have to understand how many of [gen alpha's] friends are real and how many are synthetic. And frankly, it may or may not matter."

AI is also poised to shape careers (for more, see trend #20 The AI workforce). "The future of work is here and now," Daniel Hulme, CEO of AI company Satalia, tells VML Intelligence. "We are already witnessing a Cambrian explosion of creative ways to use AI," he says, with organizations using AI to make the creation and distribution of goods more efficient.

If the trend of AI taking on mundane tasks continues, this will free up time for people to focus on creative, ethical, and social ventures. Hulme has high hopes for gen alpha. "The next generation will be equipped with an abundance of tools to bolster their creativity," he says. And, perhaps, have the potential to be economically freer to contribute to humanity.

Why it's interesting

As AI advances, it will bring more efficiency—and grant humans more time to be human. Generation AI, born into a digitally advanced world, could be the most emotionally engaged, creative, and purposeful generation to date.

94
Synthetic biology

In the future, could we program our biology like software?

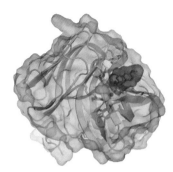

↑ Arzeda

Broadly speaking, synthetic biology is the practice of taking existing biological material and reprogramming or repurposing it to perform a new function. Basically, "you are coding and programming a cell to spit something out," Jennifer Lum, cofounder of Biospring Partners, a growth-equity firm that invests in life-sciences technology, told the *Wall Street Journal.*

The global synthetic biology market was estimated to be worth just over $11 billion in 2022, according to research firm Research and Markets, reaching nearly $36 billion by 2027—hitting an annual growth rate of almost 26%.

The latest innovations in synthetic biology see scientists growing whole models of human embryos, without sperm or egg, the BBC reported in September 2023. The Weizmann Institute team behind the research said their embryo model, which was made using stem cells, looks like a textbook example of a real 14-day-old embryo.

Artificial intelligence is accelerating the ability to program the body like software.

VML

Artificial intelligence (AI) is accelerating the ability to program the body like software. "It enables us to go beyond what nature has provided us," says Alexandre Zanghellini, cofounder of synthetic biology startup Arzeda. The company uses AI to design enzymes and protein sequences. To date, Arzeda has raised $51 million in funding and is working with Unilever to design detergent enzymes.

David Baker, a biochemist and computational biologist at the University of Washington, is applying AI to create new proteins not found in nature. Thanks to AI, Baker estimates that the pace of innovation in his field has increased by a factor of 10 during the past two years. "It is total science fiction. I still can't believe this works," he told the *Wall Street Journal*. "In 10 years, it is possible this will be the future of medicine."

Why it's interesting
Nature may only be the starting point for the future of healthcare. Advancements in technology—most notably AI—are bringing us one step closer to a future where we can recode our health from the cell up.

95

Virtual families

Could some of our closest relationships soon be with virtual beings?

Catriona Campbell, a UK-based artificial-intelligence expert, predicts that virtual children could be commonplace by 2070, saying the vision "may seem like a giant leap from where we are now, but within 50 years technology will have advanced to such an extent that babies which exist in the metaverse are indistinct from those in the real world." Campbell added that while this "fully digital demographic" might seem "strange," it "in fact represents what could be one of mankind's most important technological breakthroughs since the advent of the Bronze Age, given its potential impact on global populations and societal change."

As augmented reality and haptic technology advances, Campbell believes experiences of these virtual children will be more lifelike, to the point where we can feel and see the digital child in physical environment. In addition, via machine learning, these digital children could recognize and respond to their parents, in the same way real children do.

The concept of virtual children is currently being used to train adults in how to interview vulnerable children, BBC Science Focus reports. These AI children are programmed to "have 'memories' and answer questions like real children do." As the BBC points out, these virtual children fill a valuable need, as it's unethical to train real children to respond to these cues about past trauma.

When it comes to adult relationships, AI partners are becoming more realistic. Replika bills itself as "the AI

VML

↑ Replika

companion who cares," enabling users to create their own life-like companion. In February 2023, the US company introduced its Advanced AI mode, which is said to heighten the quality of conversation and memory capabilities. Replika's users variously praise the chatbot avatars for filling in "some too quiet corners in my everyday life in urban solitude," and for having "given me comfort and a sense of wellbeing that I've never seen in an AI before."

Why it's interesting

The future family is changing (see trend #10 Intentional communities). As our digital and physical worlds continue to converge, expect digital beings to become more prominent in everyone's lives.

> ❝
> # Virtual children could be commonplace by 2070.

96

Metamorphic cities

Self-morphing materials will shape the cities of the future.

↑ Creative Differences by the Automorph Network at the London Design Biennale 2023

↑ Creative Differences by the Automorph Network at the London Design Biennale 2023

Matter than can endlessly morph and reshape itself is found everywhere in nature. Now scientists are harnessing these properties to make buildings and cities adaptable and sustainable.

The Automorph Network brings together an interdisciplinary group of scientists, architects, and designers with the aim of fostering a new material culture; one based on matter that participates in its own design. Members are drawn from global academic institutions that span the Morphing Matter lab at the University of California, Berkeley, and the Hebrew University of Jerusalem.

At the London Design Biennale in 2023, the group presented Creative Differences, an exhibit that took inspiration from the natural world to propose new shapeshifting materials. As the group puts it: "triggered by air, humidity, or heat, two-dimensional materials come into life, becoming three-dimensional artifacts that construct urban, underwater, or field imaginary landscapes." Concepts include ceramic tiles that curve when fired; flat-pack material that can self-assemble into three-dimensional shapes in situ without the

need for energy; natural fiber composite that folds when exposed to humidity; and seeds that burrow themselves into the ground when activated by moisture.

Nature is also inspiring researchers at Cornell University. They are leading a project that imagines the convergence of architecture and biology, taking cues from morphogenesis—the way organisms form their structure—to plan "living" buildings that can react to their environment. The result might be building skins that can change color, or form windows on demand to cool themselves down.

At the University of Chicago, researchers at the Pritzker School of Molecular Engineering have devised a material that can autoregulate its environment by changing color and shifting from solid to liquid state, potentially paving the way for façade coatings that reduce the need for energy-intensive heating, ventilation, and air-conditioning systems in buildings.

This shapeshifting also extends to textiles. In November 2023, the Massachusetts Institute of Technology released details of FibeRobo, a new fiber concept, based on liquid crystal elastomers, which morphs in line with temperature. This could allow for more flexible textiles in applications from construction to fashion: imagine a curtain that retracts in response to heat, or a jacket that becomes thicker and more insulated as the weather gets colder.

Why it's interesting
Automorph Network suggests that "self-morphing systems could be the paradigm shift we all need to create a brighter, more adaptive, and more sustainable future."

97

AIdentities

Artificial intelligence is shaping who we are.

"Technology does not just reflect our identity, it shapes it," says Stefano Puntoni, Sebastian S Kresge professor of marketing at the Wharton School at the University of Pennsylvania, and codirector of the university's AI at Wharton center. Puntoni's background is in behavioral science and his work centers on consumer identities and how they are evolving in line with technology, a topic that is especially key now that high-order thinking is no longer exclusive to humans.

"It's very important for us, our mental wellbeing, our ability to function, that we feel good about ourselves," says Puntoni. "And one way in which we do so is by monitoring the progress that we make towards these identities that are important to us." This, he says, is hardwired and will not change. What will evolve is "the way that identities are expressed and constructed," meaning that automation will change the very nature of the things we identify with, such as being a photographer or a baker, for example.

On a positive note, automation may help bring us closer, he says, encouraging us to focus less on our differences. "Maybe racial, gender, or religious difference will become less important, where we see this new wave of intelligent agents entering the workplace," he suggests.

We're also likely to see a premium placed on human creativity and labor. In a 2023 piece for the *Wall Street Journal*, Puntoni cited studies by his team that uncovered "a stronger preference for human labor when consumption has

VML

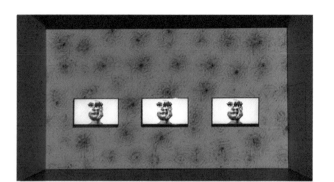

↑ Zach Blas and Jemima Wyman, im here to learn so:)))))), 2017. Exhibited at Proof of Personhood: Identity and Authenticity in the Face of Artificial Intelligence, 2023. Courtesy Singapore Art Museum

"

Technology does not just reflect our identity, it shapes it.
Stefano Puntoni, professor, Wharton School

symbolic qualities." One such study found that consumers preferred the frames of reading glasses to be made by hand, whereas for the more functional lenses, machine-made was preferred. Items that are "symbolic" (meaning that they say something about their owner and about their owner's identity) are more likely to enjoy this human premium.

Looking further ahead, Puntoni says, it's likely that we'll see "some kind of blend of technology and human," and in a sense this is already happening with the smartphone, which is "almost like part of your body. You hold it very close to your body; you touch it hundreds of times a day." We're also forming protorelationships with AI (for more, see trend #93 Generation AI). In the future, it seems AI will help to define us.

Why it's interesting

AI is changing the way human identity is constructed and expressed, and what makes us different now is rooted less in our cognitive abilities and more in "our socio-emotional processes and awareness," says Puntoni.

Resurrected palates

Woolly mammoths and dodos are making their way to our plates.

↑ Mammoth meatball by Vow

VML

Australian-based cultured meat company Vow unveiled the world's first meatball created from mammoth DNA in spring 2023. While the meatball is not yet ready for human consumption, the project is designed to showcase the advances in cell-cultured meat and its potential to revolutionize the food industry.

"We are on a mission to break the status quo of food using unexpected, delicious flavors and unforgettable experiences," Vow cofounder Tim Noakesmith says. "The future of food favors the brave."

Originally Vow intended to produce dodo meat, but the required DNA sequencing didn't exist. The mammoth meatball initiates a wealth of new possibilities for cultured meat. "Rather than simply replicating existing products, this technology offers us the opportunity to create something truly unique and better," says James Ryall, Vow's chief scientific officer.

Meat that is considered rare or even off-limits may soon be sampled in restaurants and on supermarket shelves. London-based Primeval Foods launched in 2022 with plans to bring cultivated exotic meats to diners. The startup is

currently working on cultivating lab-grown tiger, zebra, and lion meat to determine the optimal taste, texture, and nutritional value for people.

Cell-cultured food creations are on the rise and now span across meat, dairy, and coffee. Thirty-eight percent of gen Zers are prepared to try lab-grown food and 27% are interested in trying cell-cultured extinct species. Poised as a sustainable alternative to the current supply chain, this industry is expected to see healthy growth. According to a study by Grand View Research, the global cultured-meat market has a revenue forecast of $6.9 billion by 2030, up from $373.1 million in 2023.

Why it's interesting
While several companies are focusing on upscaling cultured meats such as traditional chicken, pork, and beef, selected startups are experimenting with opportunities that can diversify our palates and rethink the future of cultured meat. Tiger steak, anyone?

99

Mimetic AI

Mapping out the next five years in artificial intelligence.

Artificial intelligence (AI) is delivering transformational benefits for businesses. According to Daniel Hulme, CEO of Satalia and chief AI officer at WPP, the business is at work developing the next wave of large language models (LLMs) that can create brand-specific content—and AI tools that replicate how audiences perceive content. Yet in the long term, Hulme says, the generative AI we have now is just "a graduate in your pocket." It is "very smart and has learned quickly," but there is much more to come.

It's also just one branch of a complex collection of technologies. In fact, WPP considers AI through the lens of six categories: task automation, content generation, human representation, extracting complex insights, complex decision-making, and extending the abilities of humans.

Over the next couple of years Hulme believes AI will grow in sophistication and be armed with more specialization. "They're going to become much more multimodal—so not just imagery and text, but also sound and video."

Right now, most systems use LLMs, a type of artificial neural network. LLMs are great at processing tasks, but they can also be inefficient and energy intensive, and struggle with continuity. Hulme expects a paradigm shift based on the rise of spiking neural networks. These transmit information in a biological way that more closely mimics the way our own brains work.

Looking further ahead, our graduate will progress rapidly, says Hulme. "In two years' time you might achieve master's level

VML

ability, where it's able to achieve a more complex goal by sequencing a chain of questions." This chimes with the views of Inflection AI's Mustafa Suleyman, who tipped interactive AI as the next phase of AI in an interview with *MIT Technology Review* in September 2023. Stanford professor Andrew Ng told a Consumer Electronics Show (CES) audience in January 2024: "Autonomous agents that can plan and execute sequences of actions are just barely working, but I feel like there's a lot of traction to the research and commercialization side."

From there, AI might jump to "PhD level, where you're able to give it a very complex hypothesis," says Hulme. "It's never been solved before and it's able to go out there and test and experiment and try to solve it. And then a few years later we might end up having a professor in our pocket."

"A professor in our pocket" is another way of referencing artificial general intelligence (AGI), which imagines technology capable of any cognitive task that humans can perform. "I think real true AGI is probably seven or eight years away," says Hulme, although, he adds, perhaps we should not always consider the pinnacle of intelligence to be human.

Why it's interesting

The future of AI is promising, but it's time to think of it differently, as a "new energy source that allows us to grow and remove inefficiencies," suggests Hulme. If it can be leveraged to "help organizations achieve their purpose," he adds, "the collective purpose of enterprise will actually make the future amazing for all of us."

> The future of AI is promising, but it's time to think of it differently, as a "new energy source that allows us to grow and remove inefficiencies."

Daniel Hulme, CEO, Satalia, and chief AI officer, WPP

100

Post-human narratives

Artists are imagining the post-human future.

↑ Symbiosis, Polymorf

↑ Heterosis, The Greenhouse, Mat Collishaw, 2023 © Mat Collishaw

↑ Nature Always Wins, Universal Everything, 2020

Spurred on by ecological crisis, artists are offering narratives that decenter humanity, in a bid to nudge us toward a less humancentric perspective in the here and now.

Petrichor, a new show from British artist Mat Collishaw at Kew Gardens from October 2023 to April 2024, presents a series of works exploring humanity's turbulent and complex relationship with nature. *Even to the End*, a large-scale projected work, takes viewers on a poignant journey, immersing them in nature that transitions into a ravaged wasteland. Another Collishaw work, *The Greenhouse*, depicts London's National Gallery in an eerie state of abandonment, overtaken by nature. Walls are overgrown with foliage and trees reach for the roof.

This same vision of nature taking back control is echoed in *Nature Always Wins* by design collective Universal Everything,

which showed at London's 180 Studios in late 2022 as part of a showcase. The series depicts nature run rampant, with buildings, roads, and even a jumbo jet consumed by foliage.

At SXSW 2023, experience design studio Polymorf and Studio Biarritz presented *Symbiosis*, a multisensory extended-reality experience that transported viewers 200 years into the future. In this post-human biotope, humans, nature, and technology have co-evolved into hybrid, symbiotic life forms comprising genetically altered beings, (chemical) robots, hybrid technologies, and autonomous intelligent systems.

Other artists are turning their attention to what might come after us. At the 2023 Ars Technica animation festival, a session entitled *Data, Bodies, Space* showcased short films that muse on the posthuman future. Adopting the style of a nature

> ## Our humancentric position—only thinking from a human perspective—is toxic and we can't sustain that in the current crisis with nature.
>
> Marcel van Brakel, founder
> and lead designer, Polymorf

documentary, *Rehousing Technosphere* by Copenhagen-based design duo Wang & Söderström presents a colorful post-Anthropocene vision, in which new digital life forms are building new habitats, digging, foraging, and thriving.

Why it's interesting

Imaginary future life forms may seem far-fetched, but artists have a deeper purpose: to encourage respect for the needs of other species. Marcel van Brakel, founder and lead designer at Polymorf and codirector of *Symbiosis*, tells VML Intelligence that "our humancentric position—only thinking from a human perspective—is toxic and we can't sustain that in the current crisis with nature."

↑ Rehousing Technosphere by Wang & Söderstrom. Part of the Ars Electronica Animation Festival: Data, Bodies, Space

Expert predictions and reflections

To mark 10 years of "The Future 100" we asked experts to predict and reflect on the following questions within their sectors.

What one thing are you looking forward to in 2024?
What has been the single biggest change over the past 10 years?

BRANDS	
	Mark Read, CEO, WPP
2024	**PAST 10 YEARS**
"Looking ahead to 2024, we're excited about the potential for AI and machine learning to transform the marketing landscape, allowing our clients to better understand their customers, predict behavior, and tailor campaigns at an unprecedented scale."	"The rise of digital platforms and technologies over the past decade has fundamentally revolutionized how brands connect with consumers. The proliferation of social media, mobile technology, and data analytics has enabled more targeted, personalized, and effective marketing strategies to reach and engage the right audiences at the right time."

LUXURY	
	Jing Zhang, global editor-in-chief, *Jing Daily*
2024	**PAST 10 YEARS**
"A search for meaning, craft, slowness, and authenticity—I see this as a reaction to our analysis of the past 10 years. Luxury brands will search to distinguish luxury's unique attributes, culture, and history from others in the fray. I think this fits into a more considered sense of consumption we will all experience in 2024."	"Digitalization and the democratization of access to the world of luxury. The past 10 years have seen the domain of luxury increasingly revealed to the public, and luxury is engaging with fans in transformative new ways through the digital and social media worlds. The industry no longer feels like a 'walled garden' but has developed into a culture that sits within broader culture, even if it is the traditional playground of society's wealthy."

VML

TRAVEL	

Tom Marchant, owner and cofounder, Black Tomato

2024	PAST 10 YEARS
"One trip I think we're going to see more of in 2024 is the pursuit of finding silence. If you look at travel as the antidote or the opposite to your day to day, we're increasingly living in a world of noise, so we're looking to find moments of quiet and calm, both from a natural and an environmental perspective. I don't necessarily mean silent retreats. It's more about being able to open a door, step out into a landscape, and not hear anything but the earth itself."	"There's been an evolution in the recognition that creating sustainable and regenerative travel experiences is crucially important, not only for clients, but also for communities around the world."

CULTURE	

Kirsty Sedgman, doctor of audiences and cultural studies expert, University of Bristol

2024	PAST 10 YEARS
"I'm excited to see a new social contract with kinder modes of coexistence at its core. In an age where bad behavior is everywhere and the social contract seems to be collapsing, many of the things we consider reasonable are relics of a bygone age, fraught with selfishness, discrimination, and unfairness. Embracing 'unreasonable' behavior in the name of justice—well, is that such a bad thing?"	"One welcome change over the past 10 years has been the rise of relaxed performances, parent-and-baby events, and the 'extra live' movement in theatre more broadly. This change has been spearheaded by disability activists in order to provide a more welcoming space for autistic and other neurodivergent audiences, as well as for parents with young children, who often need a more relaxed atmosphere than sitting still and silent in the dark."

RETAIL

Leticia Credidio, founder, Leticia Credidio

2024	PAST 10 YEARS
"It'll be an exciting year for independent and small brands as consumers are demanding more transparency and craft. Self-care and slower-paced choices are also now on people's priority lists—this is something that we as a brand have been looking forward to seeing in retail."	"The fashion industry and the retail landscape have gone through drastic changes with the fall of mass garment production and rise of conscious shopping. Over the past 10 years most of us have been learning how to spot greenwashing, and started to choose sustainable brands and quality over trends."

FOOD

Alix Cherowbrier, strategy director, Bompas & Parr

2024	PAST 10 YEARS
"We'll be seeing more cross-pollination between unexpected categories and food and beverage, as worlds collide to generate genuine innovation, from archeological spritzers to deepfaked desserts. I'm excited to see ingredients of yesteryear resurrected and consumed through enchanted rituals, and mood-optimizing tonics disperse into the mainstream."	"Food and drink have shifted from being steadfast to being holistic. Over the past 10 years, we have seen a higher sense of the self echo through how diners consume food and beverages, with social media trends shifting us from being voyeurs to being interactors in restaurant settings. Menus are now polysensory, allowing the food and drink we consume to permeate the self."

VML

BEAUTY	
	Kimberley Ho, founder and CEO, Evereden
2024	**PAST 10 YEARS**
"A return to science-backed claims and professional expertise behind products. With a deluge of new brands, there has also been so much marketing noise in beauty that consumers are fatigued and are now moving back to wanting real science when choosing products."	"The democratization of beauty brands in a way that has coincided with the rise of ecommerce and social media. Allowing growth in new and successful brands in the past 10 years more quickly than ever before, because the barrier to entry in reaching consumers has become lower."

TECHNOLOGY	
	Daniel Hulme, CEO, Satalia, and chief AI officer, WPP
2024	**PAST 10 YEARS**
"I'm excited to see how Large Language Models will use machine reasoning to become much smarter and safer. And I'm even more excited about seeing leadership start to educate themselves in AI so they can pragmatically and effectively start embracing these technologies to drive real value."	"How AI should be embraced by organizations has been well-meaning, but occasionally off the mark. A huge amount has been invested in data lakes and data science teams, which hasn't always generated ROI. It's important for organizations to now focus on AI tech that directly generates value. Examples would be AI for content creation, as well as using synthetic audiences to rapidly test and deliver incredible customer experiences."

10 years of "The Future 100"

Our annual forecast of 100 trends to watch celebrates its 10th edition this year. That's 10 reports and 1,000 micro trends shared over the past decade. "The Future 100" is here to inspire brands and individuals by connecting with cultural trends and consumer expectations for an innovative future.

VML

Acknowledgements

VML Intelligence would like to thank the following experts who gave their time and insights in interviews to inform our trends:

Andrea Ang, digital editor, Vogue Philippines

Sam Bompas, cofounder, Bompas & Parr

Leticia Credidio, founder, Leticia Credidio

Chris Duffey, strategic development manager, Adobe Creative Cloud

Marcus Engman, creative director, Ingka Group

Ranice Faustino, marketing communications head, Vogue Philippines

April Gargiulo, founder, Vintner's Daughter

Kimberley Ho, founder & CEO, Evereden

Daniel Hulme, CEO of Satalia and chief AI officer, WPP

Daniel Hettwer, founder, Hidden Worlds Entertainment

Tom Marchant, owner and cofounder, Black Tomato

Joyce Oreña, beauty editor, Vogue Philippines

Sebastian S Kresge professor of marketing, Wharton School, University of Pennsylvania and codirector, AI at Wharton

Mark Read, CEO, WPP

Kirsty Sedgman, doctor of audiences and cultural studies expert, University of Bristol

Rogier Vijverberg, founder and creative lead, Jimmy

Jing Zhang, global editor-in-chief, Jing Daily

We would also like to thank the following colleagues for their valued input:

Sasha Grover

Shaziya Khan

Joyce Ling

Sebastian Martinez

Jessica Nuñez Orozco

Maria Pavlopoulos

Ernest Riba

Felipe Ritis

Sophie Robinson

Lydia Tamarat

Darby Waligorski

ABOUT VML INTELLIGENCE

VML Intelligence is VML's futurism, research, and innovation unit. It charts emerging and future global trends, consumer change, and innovation patterns—translating these into insight for brands. VML Intelligence offers a suite of consultancy services, including bespoke trends presentations, futures reports, and workshops. It is also active in innovation, partnering with brands to activate future trends within their frameworks and execute new products and concepts. The division is led by Emma Chiu and Marie Stafford, Global Directors of VML Intelligence.

For more information visit:
vml.com/expertise/intelligence

About The Future 100

VML Intelligence's annual forecast presents a snapshot of the year ahead and identifies the most compelling trends to keep on the radar. The report charts 100 trends across 10 sectors, spanning culture, technology, travel and hospitality, brands and marketing, food and drink, beauty, retail, luxury, health, and innovation.

About the data in this report

Unless otherwise stated, all findings in this report were collected by VML with SONAR™ in September 2023. The study fielded September 13–October 16, 2023, when we surveyed 9,000 adults across nine markets (1,000 participants per market). The markets covered in this research are Argentina, Brazil, China, Colombia, France, India, Mexico, the United Kingdom, and the United States. Respondents are representative of their respective market in regard to age, gender, and income. Upon analysis, the global data was weighted so that five regions were equally represented: LATAM (Argentina, Brazil, Colombia, and Mexico), EMEA (France and the United Kingdom), the United States, China, and India.

CONTACT

Emma Chiu emma.chiu@vml.com
Marie Stafford marie.stafford@vml.com

REPORT AUTHORS

Emma Chiu, Marie Stafford

WRITERS

Emily Safian-Demers, John O'Sullivan, Nina Jones

SUB EDITORS

Hester Lacey, Katie Myers

CREATIVE DIRECTOR

Shazia Chaudhry

COVER

Peach Fuzz, Pantone Color of the Year 2024, courtesy of The Development x Almost Studios

FONTS USED

Clone Rounded Latin; Dystopian; Snowflake Sans